Minor Prophecies

Minor Prophecies

The Literary Essay in the Culture Wars

GEOFFREY H. HARTMAN

HARVARD UNIVERSITY PRESS

Cambridge, Massachusetts, and London, England   1991

This book is printed on acid-free paper, and its binding
materials have been chosen for strength and durability.

Library of Congress Cataloging-in-Publication Data

Hartman, Geoffrey H.
     Minor prophecies : the literary essay in the culture wars /
Geoffrey H. Hartman.
          p.   cm.
     Includes bibliographical references and index.
     ISBN 0-674-57636-5
     1. Criticism—History—20th century.   I. Title
PN94.H35   1991
801′.95′0904—dc20   90-49880
                                                               CIP

For Renée

Preface

A major theme of this book is the tension between two kinds of critical style: that of the learned specialist and that of the public critic (a.k.a. man of letters). There is the writer who develops literary studies as a discipline requiring method or an immense dose of historical knowledge, perhaps both; and the writer who has a public in mind that looks at the arts as its common and intelligible heritage, often made less rather than more accessible by the interventions of the critic. In contemporary polemics this contrast of styles has often been overstated, as if critical writing, when pursued with a certain intensity and a technical or innovative vocabulary, were a dehumanizing threat to public-minded intellectuals, and even a reflex of nihilism.

Linked to the issue of critical style are substantive problems of communication, authority, and consensus. The work of the critic necessarily touches on political philosophy as well as hermeneutics. But the lightness or incompleteness implied by "touches on" stands in contrast with both formal philosophy and didacticism. My essays are meant to address the very status of the essay as a reflective and clarifying genre. They would like to give the issue of style some historical room, to show how interesting and productive it has been, and how close to the development of the medium of expository prose.

I may be accused of defending my own style, of engaging in special pleading. My style is what it is, and does not resolve a tension I continue to value. In mingling specialized material with general observations on culture I may provoke feelings of discomfort in both Common and Professional Reader. Chapter 1, in particular, makes a certain demand; those who do not need a crash-course in the evolution of literary theory could skip that chapter, while noting that its theme, the *culture* of criticism, rehearses the tension I have described.

This book, then, is about critical prose. But it does not draw a strong ideological distinction between prose and poetry in the manner of Sartre or Marcuse. Those who agree that the style to be pursued should aim at an audience of equals rarely agree as to what literary features display that aim. While I suggest (following Erich Auerbach) that the modern prose emerging in the seventeenth century points to a more inclusive and democratic public, Marcuse argues that after Shakespeare, "Verse makes possible what has already become impossible in prosaic reality. In poetry, humanity can transcend all social isolation and distance and speak of the first and last things . . . Criminal and saint, prince and servant, sage and fool, rich and poor join in discussion whose free flow is supposed to give rise to truth" ("On the Affirmative Character of Culture"). The bourgeois era, according to Marcuse, fosters only a sham or abstract equality, though even this is not without value. "The critical and revolutionary force of the ideal, which in its very unreality keeps alive the best desires of individuals amidst a bad reality, becomes clearest in those times when the satisfied social strata have accomplished the betrayal of their own ideals." The quarrel I have with such generalizations bears less on the expressiveness of prose or poetry than on how to interpret the relation of a medium to social reality: in what way are cultural forms its reflection, and how is this to be established? I recognize the contradiction between reality and idea evoked by Marcuse, but remain agnostic concerning the truth of his politically inspired hermeneutic or the system that might produce true equality.

I am sure this book is full of unconscious debts. In the more documentary essays there is much that is attributed, yet I have sought to avoid tracking everything down and have kept the formal acknowledgments sparse. I may not omit, however, Lindsay Waters, who encouraged the line of speculation in these essays, once it emerged from its mazy life into something like consistency. I also thank Bill Abelson, Hilary Jewett, Kevis Goodman, and Ann Louise Coffin McLaughlin for help in preparing the manuscript for publication. This book is dedicated to my wife in abiding love and affection, and because she has tolerated my scribbles for thirty-five years.

New Haven, Connecticut   *G.H.H.*

Contents

. . . however high we position ourselves in order to judge our time, the future historian will judge it from a still higher point; the mountain on which we think we have made our eagle's nest will be only a mole hill for him; the judgment we have delivered regarding our epoch will figure in the dossier of our own trial. —*J. P. Sartre*

"Eat radishes and write denunciations!"
—*Dostoevsky, on the ideal of the Slavophiles as interpreted by fearful liberals*

A terrible danger: that American-political frenzy [*Getreibe*] and the irrepressible knowledge industry [*Gelehrtenkultur*] will merge.

—*Friedrich Nietzsche*

The breakup of essence is ethics. —*Emmanuel Levinas*

Minds would leave each other in contrary directions, traverse each other in numberless points, and at last greet each other at the journey's end. An old Man and a child would talk together and the old Man be led on his path and the child left thinking. Man should not dispute or assert but whisper results to his neighbour and thus by every germ of spirit sucking the sap from mould ethereal every human might become great, and Humanity instead of being a wide heath of Furze and Briars with here and there a remote Oak or Pine, would become a grand democracy of Forest Trees! —*John Keats*

Introduction: Pastoral Vestiges

The first law was a dietary law. Because of its mythic context and startling consequences, we don't recognize it as such. Knowledge rather than eating was to be regulated by the prohibition against the fruit of the paradisal tree. Regulations about food appear later, yet eating and knowing get mixed up, as though equally basic.[1] In our time, whether we think back over fifty or more than a hundred years, the question of a destructive rather than nourishing and immortalizing knowledge has come to the fore again.

The benefits of science and technology, in the shadow of two World Wars, a Holocaust, and the threat of nuclear apocalypse, force us to reconsider certain ancient myths like that of the expulsion from paradise or Prometheus' gift of fire (also, like knowledge, something stolen from the gods). Eating is a sign that we are mortal, but knowledge was put on the side of the immortal. Yet knowledge has proved to be mortal in at least three ways: one generation doubts the findings of another; the applications to which knowledge has been put often prove to be catastrophic as well as beneficial; and, most recently, a conviction has grown that the mind itself has suffered a wound. "Something deeper has been worn away than the renewable parts of the machine," Valéry wrote after the Great War. The balance of hope and dread is affected; "our fears are infinitely more precise than our hopes"; it is no longer possible to dominate our anxiety about what may come. "Among all these injured things is the mind. The mind has . . . been cruelly wounded; its complaint is heard in the hearts of intellectual men; it passes a mournful judgment on itself."[2]

To say that this book is about the disturbed balance of hope and dread in relation to what knowledge may achieve would be deceptive. *Minor*

Prophecies remains a reflection on literary studies. But it concludes that what at first seemed like a domestic quarrel about the style of the critical essay has a larger context and implications. The quarrel involves several related issues. The first is the public or communicative aspect of criticism—how open, how unspecialized the critical essay should be. The second is a discomfort with the aesthetic element in art or anywhere else, and often a drive to expose it as a mystification, an "aesthetic ideology" that hides its self-interest or does not want it made explicit. (This endeavor, paradoxically, can become highly technical, almost a specialized subdiscipline.) The third is the growth, in quantity but also in doubtful prestige, of literary criticism. Does that kind of writing have a specificity of its own? Can we honor the claim that criticism is more than inflated book-reviewing? Shouldn't we abandon literary studies for cultural studies, which have done a better job—using the very techniques developed by the literary avant-garde—in exposing the mediated or even occulted status of quasi-objective, quasi-authoritative texts?

I say what can be said, *in a historical context,* about a criticism that is specifically literary or art-centered, and so raises the question of style, both vis-à-vis art and itself. More crucially, I come to the conclusion, but only gradually in this sequence of essays, that literary criticism has responded to, and has in part been formed by, the disturbed balance of hope and dread diagnosed by Valéry. I argue in the final essay that the tendency to cultural prophecy increases in the period between the Wars, that uncertainty about the future, now that our civilization too has shown itself mortal, provokes visionary schemes that mingle despair and remedy in prophetic predictions about the West. To this tendency, I believe, literary criticism, insofar as it can be seen as a whole, opposes a contrary knowledge—if knowledge is the right word for an insight pervaded not only by irony but by the overdetermined medium of language. The dense, equivocal or polyvocal, nature of language interposes; the medium itself seems to speak as an admonitory countermagic to seductive cultural generalization. This language spell cannot itself escape all suspicion. But about literary criticism there is nothing magical, even if it points to elements in art that mock—in both senses of the word—a lost power of representation and clarification. Criticism shows that to read the future is as hard as to read those works of art; the time in which we live remains, in Keats's words, a "purgatory blind."

2

The issue I do not explore in depth is whether it is good for literary studies to shoulder the task of justification, of developing a discourse on social justice that would contribute to social justice. I put as a question what many would see as overdue. Yet it has not been shown why literary studies should be converted into cultural studies and take up a burden that belongs to political philosophy, the social sciences, and law schools. Even when we wave the question of field boundary by invoking claims of conscience or our special expertise as readers, other concerns arise.

They include the tendency of culture-critique to become an incrimination of culture—at least of Western society, accused of seeking knowledge in order to gain power. Power over nature, and power over anything "other." No more happy knowledge then: the pastoral mask has fallen. Indeed, there is often a rush to self-incrimination. No one seems ready to plead the Fifth Amendment, and the self-criticism mandated by totalitarian societies we impose on each other, voluntarily. Such demystification tightens the net in which we are caught. If there is no innocent *rerum cognoscere causas,* if all knowledge is guilty, then we must also be suspicious of the demystification that taught us this lesson—of its relation to empowerment.

Shelley talks with sublime indistinctness of a shadow cast up from the soul. A shadow like that lies heavy on the idea of culture today. Valéry tried to give it a clearer form, a diagnosis. Many of these essays wish to do the same. In summary there is, on the one hand, the view that has prevailed since the Enlightenment, and in literary studies since Matthew Arnold's vision of a disinterested play of ideas, that culture does away with ideological politics and even the class structure. There is, on the other hand, the record: persistent inequality, two World Wars, the Holocaust, more wars, continuing racial, religious, and national strife. History does not seem to be univocally the story of an emancipation, of humanity's exodus from its self-imposed bondage. Rousseau's famous opening shot, "Man is born free, and everywhere he is in chains," resonates today as it did two centuries ago. So the idea of culture (not, necessarily, Western culture alone) darkens. Rousseau, Freud, and Foucault—as well as the reviving appeal of religion—suggest a limit to secular hopes. But can we clearly set forth the charges against culture? A global inculpation runs the risk of becoming totalitarian: everyone and everything could be implicated. At some point human life itself must be

3

guilty because it kills to eat and lives off other species. As Emerson wrote in his essay on Fate: "However scrupulously the slaughter-house is concealed in the graceful distance of miles, there is complicity, expensive races—race living at the expense of race."

We are back to the relation of eating, guilt, and knowledge. The issue is hardly a modern one, raised as it is in the Hebrew Bible's dietary laws, in sacrificial practices, and such primary stories as Cain and Abel. Yet what was distinctively religious may no longer be so, except by an intensity that makes us wonder how alert we are when we neglect its presence in the ancient texts. We are blessed with two kinds of fundamentalism today: a religious fundamentalism, which distorts the ancient texts by simplifying them; and a political counterfundamentalism, which elaborates a doctrine of natural rights against allegedly corrupted or corrupting codes.

Both fundamentalisms are unfriendly to those of us who refuse to side against texts, however wary we are as readers trained in the hermeneutics of suspicion. Literary studies in fact are exercises to increase that wariness while refusing to throw the text away, or to exalt something called the spirit, which the letter supposedly kills. For should reading go the way knowledge seems to be going, then the bridgehead of secular thought we have secured over hundreds of years will disappear into one fundamentalism or the other, the religious or the political, perhaps a potent brew of both together. That does not seem to me a prophecy so much as a description of what we are already experiencing; and I have no remedy except to urge that literary studies do not abandon the teaching of reading as a historical and ongoing discipline, that technical and hermeneutic criticism is kept up, and that literary critics remain unashamed of their concern for art.

It is not a commitment to social justice that is being questioned here. It is the confusion of that commitment with the chivalric behavior of literary scholars who hasten to displace themselves and their discipline. Until we are certain that history and literature, anthropology and literature, social concern and literature, are not reconcilable, until an either/or confronts us, historians might try to become better readers and literary critics better historians. The new historicism is, therefore, on the right path, except for the ideology that makes it seem new. The new historicism points to the barbarous xenophobia and the shameful exploitation of conquered populations that characterized a militant culture of colonialism—yet we meet them almost everywhere in history. It is a bitter story and has not ended. It is also an old story, not a new and startling one. Yet there *is* something remarkable in the new historicism: not its disclosure of some perfidious Western link between knowledge and power, but the movement's subversion of the claim that knowledge breeds sympathy, and so a tolerance of difference.

It is knowledge more than power that stands accused of not leading to sympathy, or else perverting it subtly. Power after all is a fact that we live with; but that knowledge might transform the brute fact of power, that justice, as a reflection of sympathetic inquiry, might modify the reliance on force, is a premise few are willing to abandon. If the knowledge historians bring has nothing redemptive about it in content or effect, and if, generally, empathic modes of thought have done little to alter the course of history—even when, as in Christianity, love and charity are promulgated—if, as in Voltaire's *Candide,* the narrative of oppression, though diverted here and there, never turns into an epic of liberation, then reading history will not change the world any more than reading literature will. In fact, to find betrayal and bloody-mindedness everywhere validates Voltaire's mockery of history as a chronicle of human idiocy and folly. The so-called Philosophy of History merely orders that idiocy and folly, mixing method and madness. Though the new historicists are new moralists on the side of social justice, their symptomatic parables only madden sensitive consciences further. Voltaire's laughter in *Candide,* sparked by a curious and supercilious knowledge of non-European cultures, is not extinguished (any more than its prototype, the laughter of the gods) by Foucaultian demystifications of the artful way power extends itself—even in "enlightened" Europe—through the ordering of discourses and other cultural institutions.

We justify the contemplative in terms of the active life. Yet it is possible to argue for the contemplative life even if knowledge is uncoupled from startling practical results, and interpreting the world has little bearing on changing it. One would have to stress a negative virtue: that thought is often pleasurable in itself and does not add to the world's harms even when it discovers more of them. Not a lofty argument, to be sure, but not unconstructive either, since ordinary life might benefit, and a Thoreau can make his beanfield a blessing (a "bene"). *Walden*'s unpretentious nature-consciousness becomes the token of a human independence and freedom too often spoiled—as is nature—by more coercive and prophetic types of speculation.

In Thoreau we touch of course the persistence of the pastoral convention in literature. The prophet, especially the American visionary in the puritan tradition, becomes a shepherd again. Yet can pastoral survive, once we identify its contemplative attitude with the bystander—with the marginal poet, for example? Pastoral presupposes a natural or necessitated life of leisure, song crafted from the position of either apprenticeship or exile. The greater world is there, its pressure is felt, a more potent voice beckons. But pastoral glances at that world through the art of minimalized reference, through a piping that takes pleasure in evoking what a more heroic existence rejects. In "Soonest Mended" John Ashbery welcomes an unheroic generation, convalescing from the burden of the past, and released into the ordinary:

> To reduce all this to a small variant,
> To step free at last, minuscule on the gigantic plateau—
> This was our ambition: to be small and clear and free.[3]

Today the figure of the bystander is deeply problematic. It has been damaged by the European Holocaust, whose memory revives with every devastating book or testimony. Given the passivity of so many who knew or could have known, is it possible *now* to "stand and wait"? Recall Milton's *Lycidas,* where the poet turns to Nature as if its agency could have intervened. I mention Milton *because* of the enormous difference between the tragedies, and so to recall Adorno's haunting question: Can there be poetry after Auschwitz?

The damage seems to spread from pastoral to poetry, and so to art in general. To single out the Holocaust does not mean that all other suffering, all other injustice, is depreciated. On the contrary, now the issue of intervention poses itself all the time. "We cannot not know," Terrence des Pres has written. A major cultural figure like Havel did not become a bystander.

The attempt to examine an injustice as extreme and unforgivable as genocide needs a certain coldness, a barrier to rage; and it is possible that pastoral could provide it, if only as an alienation-effect. But the thought that penetrates every defense is that the bystanders remained inert, or even exploited the expulsions and the killings. The civilized world rather than Nature (as in *Lycidas*) was in complicity or stood by. Milton was able to save the pastoral axiom of a sympathetic cosmos by giving it an ornamental farewell—mourning, as it were, over the conceit as well as over his poet-friend, exhibiting a style that had been discredited but not entirely disenchanted. Can one, after a tragedy of such different scope, recover the courage for art?

The pastoral mask has fallen, I said at the beginning. If the fate of art is linked to the fate of pastoral—a large claim, not to be substantiated here, and in which "pastoral" stands over against total demystification—then it is important to seek vestiges of pastoral. All the more so if pastoral restrains, even while it acknowledges, the "dread voice" of prophetism. Should pastoral fail as a style, as a significant element in perception, what will prevent poetic fury from becoming apocalyptic and turning—as at times in Milton—against the imaginative pluralism of art itself? I want to suggest some vestiges or hiding places of pastoral at the present time.

My main speculation concerns a body of literature almost lost after the fall of Rome, yet largely defining what was meant by culture till the eve of World War II. Though "culture" is an impossible word to pin down, let me call it the sum of those institutions that persuade us that knowledge is a good; and better than good when disentangled from the suffering and subjection of others. The revival of the Classics, a movement that helped shape the vernacular literatures of Europe and took centuries to complete, was a determining moment in that conception of culture. Not because the view of life conveyed by Greek and Roman was gentler or more human—it is hard to say which was crueler, Christianity or Paganism. But the *study* of the Classics begins to occupy a special place in the life of the mind. Despite residual Christian scruples, knowledge of the Classics in the Renaissance is not, or no longer, guilty knowledge. An enlarged space is created for secular grace, and culture moves closer to play. While it had no necessary bearing on justification—on grace as the play of God in man—it yielded a foretaste of that harmony.

Between Christian society and the Classical Revival the relations were various and complex. From today's vantage point, however, one feature stands out. Essential for the "play" of culture, is that the Classics were enjoyed, despite moral objections, for their stylistic and representational vigor. The guilt that besets us whenever we recover traces of a suppressed way of life did not spoil *this* renaissance. For the relation of the triumphant (Christian) to the defeated (Hellenic) order had not been that of brute repression. Christians were the sufferers originally, and the imperial Romans conquered much of Europe before their victims absorbed and conquered them. Once the taboo was removed from the Classics, therefore, a pastoral glow invested them, whether their content conformed to Christian morality or not. They are not *tristes tropiques* and they are not the "other" destroyed by a superior (that is, imperialist) faith. Sad or happy, Classical culture becomes the object of a happy contemplation. A lost ethos reappears, miraculously preserved, and all the more liberating because it seems to have escaped from a preoccupation with guilt, despite the taint of slavery. It is a "yea-saying," as Nietzsche describes it, that embraces both a stark vision, "the flux and destruction of all things, the decisive element in any Dionysian philosophy" *(Ecce Homo),* and the artistic values shaping that flux, making it bearable.

Yet Nietzsche also marks the end of such "pastoral" study of Classicism. He intuits the theological politics of Greek tragedy and associates art and agon so intimately that this link carries over to philosophy as well, and to a scholarship that can no longer claim immunity from the battle. The connection between knowledge and will to power is not incriminated, however, because it is conceived at a level other than opportunistic national policy. For Nietzsche imperialism and ascetic morality are two sides of the same metaphysical force that defines the power-hungry actor: there is either a triumph of the will or a triumph of the will over itself.

Forms of knowledge, as they front that will, are as unstable as a ship in a storm, and the storm is always blowing. Greek tragic art amazes Nietzsche because, despite its radically pessimistic vision, the beauty of its form was strong enough to found our own sense of form. He concludes that aesthetic illusion has a reality-function of its own. In a remarkable image he combines the figure of an amoral will that destabilizes all forms, and the innocence of aesthetic play: "As children and artists play, so plays the ever-living fire. It constructs and destroys all in inno-cence. Such is the game that the Aeon plays with itself."[4]

A picture like this is antithetical to the humanist's vision of a cultural heritage that progressively moralizes us. Child/Artist/Aeon are at once anarchic and aesthetic as they play with fire. Mastery and immunity blend as one ideal: the goal of mature growth *and* something untouched by growth that remains eternally, willfully immature. What is especially intriguing is that the Aeon is not unlike a bystander, magnified.

For the bystander is not necessarily a figure of indifference like Joyce's god paring his fingernails. He could be a figure of whatever in child or artist has escaped trauma, the salamander in the fire. Wordsworth muses in *The Prelude* on poetry and geometric truth, "And their high privilege of lasting life / From all internal injury exempt." But were I to choose one poet in whom a tragic and sceptical vision consorts with the pastoral convention—in the way Nietzsche sees an interaction in Greek tragic art of aesthetic illusion (Apollinian) and abysmal truth (Dionysian)—it would be Shelley. Shelley's Aeon is the Witch of Atlas, the most remark-able nymphal consciousness in literature, playing with passions "beyond the rage / Of death or life," and as final a revival of the spirit of Classical pastoral as we are likely to get.

A tension between bystander and activist will always be with us. One can think in formal terms of the Greek chorus: not a figure above the conflict but a spokesman with a normative point of view, buffeted by events in which he cannot intervene, at least he cannot change the outcome. Or think of a direction the mystery story has taken, with the "innocent bystander" drawn involuntarily into the action. Finally, imagine a repre-sentational change, comparable in scope to the omniscient narrator van-ishing from the literary scene. Say that this change goes in the direction of proscribing all except two basic types of characters: activist and para-site. No bystanders would be allowed; everyone must testify or be made to testify. Given so coercive a morality, detachment or neutrality might seem preferable.

After the second World War there was an attempt by Jean Paulhan to "give back all her voices" to France, including that of neutral bystander caught in the crossfire of Occupation politics. There was also an attempt by Heidegger to detach his philosophy from the ruins around him. The way he ends his *Letter on Humanism* (1947) shows the temptation and difficulty of resorting to pastoral imagery at this time. "Language [*Sprache*]," Heidegger writes, "is so the language of Being as clouds are the clouds of heaven. Thought places with its speech [*Sagen*] unapparent furrows in language. They are even more unapparent than the furrows made in the field by the slowly pacing peasant."[5]

Those final similes evoke a thinker's pastoral care for language and a sense of the labor involved in analogizing, without confusing, words and the phenomenal world. Each sentence could not be better expressed, for the coda as a whole seems to renounce temporal haste and rhetorical pathos, while concentrating on the simplest, most impersonal modes of speech. Yet the exercise comes too late for those who know what was done to language and thought in the Nazi era. Endless waves of coordinated propaganda had exalted peasant, soil, or patrimony *(Boden)*, embodiment *(Blut und Boden, Wirklichkeit)*. Denounced as the antitype of this ideal were the intellectual *Luftmensch,* and the deracinated, wandering Jew. Heidegger himself was free of these stereotypes but he did join the attack on *bodenloses Denken:* on a thinking, often labeled metaphysical, that had alienated authentic modes of being-in-the-world.

The paragraph may disclose a continuity in Heidegger's work and restore an intention that had strayed; it may have this power of rectification and beyond that a power of reclamation. This is Heidegger after a calamitous brush with prophetic politics, the bystander-thinker or "middle-voice" he always truly was. But the enormity of the destruction, unmentioned here or anywhere in the *Letter on Humanism,* has created a change we are still trying to assess.

After a period of recuperation, in which aesthetic and formal values returned and the politicization of art and scholarship faded like a bad dream, today some intelligent players insist again on omnipolitics. The best result, in this direction, can only be a rethinking of the debate between aesthetics and Marxism in the American 1930s, a debate that produced Kenneth Burke's expansion of the vocabulary of motives to both literary and social thought. Kantian or Arnoldian theories of a disinterested play of ideas were not debunked or ideologized by him but regrounded in a purposiveness based on anthropological insight. (So mysticism is viewed as a form of the hunt: "In the quest one is naturally silent, be it as the animal stalking its quarry or as the thinker meditating upon an idea.") To understand the danger of politicizing culture or aestheticizing political issues, we can also profit from the work of the Frankfurt School. The worst result would be a generation whose trust in the mind comes from the mind's capacity for mistrust, and who intervene, therefore, only on the basis of a demystification.

The culture wars that have recently flared up show that the need to justify art continues to be felt. At the same time most of the battles take for granted the importance of the arts. Literary works in particular have become an educational staple, necessary to the production of literacy—a very basic literacy often, and certainly not that of the finishing school. The teaching of English or any other written language would be impossible today without the enticement of popular novels and poems. We realize at last how basic literature is to knowledge and aspiration; it has no truck with luxury. But now the idea of what culture is has changed. We stress intimacy and identity rather than a "second culture," like the Classics, from whose vantage point descent or native endowment might be viewed dispassionately. Hence there is loss as well as gain. Commitment to a particular community, defined in ethnic, religious, or gender terms, tends to be not only primary but near-total, since it is felt that the culture of that community must still be created, or if already developed should be preserved against the competing and invasive options that characterize modern life. The proponents of "difference" and "otherness" often foster, paradoxically, a new isolationism, affecting the relation between communities.

The return of this didactic and political activity could be welcomed, nevertheless, as a sign of intensified ethical and social awareness. But it should be remembered that the relation of art to the didactic has always been ambivalent. Art is the sweetener, Horace declared; it succeeds by a skillful blend of sweet and bitter, *dulce* and *utile*. Medicine is best administered in that form. So the use we make of art should also be distinguished from pure and simple preachment. If art succeeds because of the mixture, you cannot insist on the bitters alone. What we find in the universities is a rising demand for a didactic approach, for advocacy teaching that uses art in a cause. Criticism renounces its freedom and returns to the missionary position.

This is the danger, at least. But why exactly is the insistence on an explicit objective a danger? It does not feel dangerous. In any movement there is movement, the joy, the energy of participation and action. The didactic itself becomes for a while a source of fervor and enthusiasm, and sweetens the dull or coercive element. Yet through the totalitarian experience we have learned that the *demand* for brotherhood and sisterhood can be an ideological tyranny: that it is a sentimental, not a realistic demand. It leads to a preference of coerced consent over discord. "Though we have done beautifully in becoming—and with what heat!—antinazi democrats, antitotalitarians, antifascists, antiracists, and anti-apartheid, we have not learnt to distrust the beatific smile of fraternity."[6]

In literature as in law the quality of consent matters. Reasoning on literature may not have the same prestige as reasoning in such socially sensitive or decisive areas as law and government, yet from childhood on the use and abuse of words is linked with the training of consent. We learn to accept yet also to examine the words we receive, just as we learn to accept and contemplate the activity of reasoning. In literary criticism too, as long as art is not simplified into propaganda or corrected into ideology, the complexity of any justifying frame will come into view. We become aware of the history of interpretation, of its reversals of judgment and dramatic revisions. The essays in this book concentrate, therefore, on that frame, which is given as close a reading as anything within it. The work of art and the work of reading go together; neither art nor the criticism of art are seen as completely independent.

Literary criticism provides justification, explanation, or advertisement —often all three. An awareness grows in the imaginative reader at the same time that while art requires commentary (at least extended captions), its resistance to critical frames is part of its integrity. Whether we call this resistance "pastoral" or "aesthetic" is less important than to understand it. "Aesthetic" points to a value present beyond any appropriation of it by current utilitarian ideas; "pastoral" associates this value with a quality endangered by an industrialized and centralized modern society. In visual or musical works the resistance we allude to coincides with a dislike of a "foreign" syntax—of purely verbal meanings. Both music and the visual arts, moreover, have acquired a public space (theater, museum, concert hall), in which their value can be exhibited. This mode of being published (exhibited, performed) can lead to a confusion between public value and display value, and so increase the chances of commodification. The verbal icon also may not be immune to this process; many novelists consider a critic's words as merely a necessary publicity, a marketing device like bubblegum in packs of baseball cards. However that may be, in the case of literature the critical essay has made a bid for independence, and its subordination to works of art is deceptive. It is this bid for independence I examine in *Minor Prophecies*.

The subordination of criticism to the work of art can be genuine if the possibility of genius is acknowledged. An older term, "genial criticism," reminds us of that. But precisely because criticism publishes art a second time, because it gives it a sort of baptism or confirmation, moving it into a sphere dominated by collective norms, the relation of critical essay to the public domain remains wary. This wariness of criticism, not only vis-à-vis art but also its own explanatory role, amounts to a *reprivatization* that counteracts art's exposure to public and economic exploitation. If there is one tendency that inspires critical writing and sets it apart from cultural prophecy it is the avoidance of false consensus. Good critical writing does not judge or explain art in a coercive way; it evokes what Emerson called *the alienated majesty of our own thoughts,* thoughts neglected or rejected by us, and found again, here, in the restitutive work of the artist. We recognize in the artist, but also beyond him, our own potential genius. Criticism stages a recognition scene that speaks "of nothing more than what we are."

The tension between aesthetic reticence and public pedagogy (the contrast can be stated in other ways too) moves the issue of critical style to the fore. How public should the language of criticism be? Should what is important in art be translatable into terms of colloquial prose, or does that effort coopt the work of genius, repressing its asocial or antisocial component? And, again, does the insistence that criticism imitate the seeming clarity of public speech neglect the creativeness of critical prose itself, both as a technique of discovery and a style developed over time?

Coleridge, responding to an attack on technical vocabulary in moral and religious thinking, makes three strong points against the imposition of a colloquial style. The first is historical: terms and phrases that originate in specialized schools become colloquial: "The science of one age becomes the common sense of a succeeding." His second argument is sociological: "From the intensity of commercial life in this country, and from some other less creditable causes, there is found even among better educated men, a vagueness in the use of words, which presents, indeed, no obstacle to the intercourse of the market, but is absolutely incompatible with the attainment or communication of distinct and precise conceptions. Hence in every department of exact knowledge, a peculiar nomenclature is indispensable." This argument shades into a third, which points to an independent consciousness of the processes of language in both critic and creative writer. "Every new term expressing a fact, or a difference, not precisely and adequately expressed by any other word in the same language, is a new organ of thought for the mind that has learnt it."[7]

Jacques Derrida also rehearses this question of style, but in a form that joins the history of philosophy to the history of rhetoric. From his commentary of 1962 on Husserl's *Origin of Geometry* to "Psyche: Inventions of the Other" of 1984 he explores how an original or inaugural invention in the fields of science, philosophy, and art gains "recognition by a public community not only for the general truth value of what it is advancing on the subject of invention (the truth of invention and the invention of truth) but at the same time *for the operative value of a technical apparatus henceforth available to all*" (my italics).[8] Derrida does not see the question of acceptance and institutionalization as entirely empirical. All inventions, he argues, to be transmittable and persuasive, require the imaginative projection of a public: of a "countersignature" that doubles or splits the original inventive act and has always already inscribed itself in the author's own "signature." Such othering ("outering," Coleridge might have said) is a formal condition for authority to be bestowed on the author, for his invention to be confirmed by an empirical shift from private realm to public, from personal origin to tradition.

After a chapter that seeks to chart the course of literary criticism over the last hundred years, I take up more directly this issue of style, adjudicating between inventive specialization and the claims of public or at least sociable (conversational) speech. My sympathies are largely with the Uncommon rather than Common Reader, or with the productiveness of the conflict between them. Even though my emphasis (as I will explain) has shifted since writing those chapters, I see no reason why a single kind of style should prevail. My emphasis has shifted because I understand belatedly a lesson that can be drawn from the turmoil of 1918–1940. It seemed to me at first that politics in that period were so overwhelming that literary and cultural reflections became a mere appendage to them, and "theory" was needed to reinforce art's nonideological dimension. But in Chapter 10, "Literary Criticism and the Future," I revise my point of view and suggest that in this period the literary essay made a pitch for independence and succeeded in establishing itself more firmly: not as a superstructural reflex or a weapon in the ideological wars but as a critique of cultural prophecy.

My shift since *Criticism in the Wilderness* (1980) and the first essays of this book to be completed (Chapters 2 and 3) involves me in a certain amount of repetition. In "Literary Criticism and the Future" the same facts are considered at a somewhat different angle; but even a small perspectival difference can be revealing. I argue that the secularism of critical prose, its unservile journalistic punch, was directed less against religion or its "escapist" byproducts than against the mere substitution of politics for religion.[9] "Religion has lost its power; the social ideals have not yet achieved theirs," Ludwig Lewisohn wrote in 1919. Fascism and communism entered that vacuum and became political religions. Speculative schemes created a region "where passions had the privilege to work, / And never hear the sound of their own names" (Wordsworth on the intellectual atmosphere following the French Revolution).

The displacement of religion meant the advent of new mystiques claiming religion's high ground: its bonding function, its ability to transmit an impersonal heritage or interpersonal mediation, and an authoritative public discourse at once assertive and selfless. This last aspect is the one most directly related to the project of *literary* criticism, which examines every pretension to prophetic speech, yet supports whatever may counteract the cheapening of words. Because so much during that period was animated by prophecy and propaganda, critical reading grows in importance. It is during these years, especially in England but with remarkable examples from Continental Europe, that the critical essay moves toward "close reading" yet tries to maintain the Common Reader ideal. "The limit itself became a new dimension," as Yeats said in *A Vision*, though not of the essay as such.

As we look back today on Common Reader and Public Critic, they beckon to us with visionary intensity. They are clouded, however, by an internal contradiction. Critics help to establish the terms of discourse: about art, but also about cultural matters generally. They educate taste or

15

intuition and seek a judgment (I put this in a Kantian way) that speaks in a universal rather than parochial voice. We are made aware of creative genius as something all could share rather than as the mysterious birthright of a few. Yet can this awareness, clarified and disseminated by criticism, escape being commodified, becoming *common* in the pejorative sense? It is not more honest to acknowledge the envy of *uncommon* greatness that critics may hide in the form of dismissive judgments?

The Common Reader ideal, though a modest and useful construct, has evaded a contradiction in the genius idea, present from its eighteenth-century beginnings. To deny genius, Northrop Frye has said, is the death-wish in society; but to affirm that all have it, or all in a specified biological or ethnic grouping (the turn that Nazi "democracy" took) leads to terrible delusions, to a coercive and ultimately destructive demand for collective fulfillment. At best, then, Common Reader and Public Critic are split personalities, shuttling uneasily between the utopian hope that works of genius can transform society, until all share that genius, and a severe doubt that genius can be accommodated in society except as a sublime sort of common sense.

Concerning the need, beyond such contradictions, for cultural criticism, let Frye, whose project bears the mark of Blake's struggle with the genius idea, have the final and sensible word. I quote from Frye's *Anatomy of Criticism:* "A public that tries to do without criticism, and asserts that it knows what it wants or likes, brutalizes the arts and loses its cultural memory . . . The only way to forestall the work of criticism is through censorship, which has the same relation to criticism that lynching has to justice."

The Culture of Criticism

In an era of the sound bite, the preemptive critical strike, and the short-range collective memory, a centennial overview may seem outmoded. One's judgment of such a venture might be all the more severe if the language of theory is applied: I could be found guilty of "false narrativization" or seeking to impose a "master narrative." Northrop Frye's *Anatomy of Criticism,* written "before the Flood," remains the last systematic and acceptable account of criticism as a totality.[1] Frye took off from a sentence in T. S. Eliot but no one was deceived: he wished to terminate donnish or impressionistic criticism, to establish literary study as a teachable discipline located in a humane and soul-enlarging sphere between mathematics and music, or linguistically between grammar and the theology of the poets. Frye created an overarching structure that was itself a work of wit, without entirely giving up local brightness of detail—wit at the level of the discriminating sentence. The sort of anxiety I will eventually describe as a characteristic of our culture from the waning years of the nineteenth century, and peaking in the period between the World Wars, is nowhere to be found in him: his relation to Spengler, for instance, or Toynbee, or Jung and Eliade, is unperturbed by cultural politics. In this he follows Aristotle, whose *Poetics* acknowledge the genetic link between art and religion, but who finds terms of analysis that appear to be formal rather than culture-bound. Frye's achievement reminds us that descriptive (not to be confused with prescriptive) Poetics are not dead, despite proliferating and promiscuous representations that have no interest in those formal categories except as fodder for parody.

But the Flood did come; and when it ebbs Frye's *Anatomy* and perhaps his *Great Code* will rank as monumental relics of an exceptional moment of Freemasonry in our discipline.[2] Which goes to prove Blake's point about Genius arising and dying without a predictable succession. Indeed, our general ambivalence about institutionalization may relegate Frye to a place he often sought out: education at the primary and secondary level, which is the stubborn basement of language and literacy upon which one must build. He heightened, nevertheless, both the intellectual and the imaginative stakes of advanced literary study; and if what followed after seemed to diverge radically and to abandon a magnanimous formalism for a deconstructive formalism, or ethnopoetic, micropoetic, and ideological case studies, his example bestrides the Flood. My centennial overview, and the other (chronologically less ambitious) essays in this book, do not aim to encompass the past or to disburden the future by a system, but to keep solvent a segment of our institutional history jeopardized by the contemporary rate of oblivious change.

For those who approach literary studies with literary sensitivity, an immediate problem arises. They cannot overlook *style,* their own or that of others. Through their concern with literature they have become aware that understanding is a mediated activity and that style is an index of how the writer deals with the consciousness of mediation. Style is not only cognitive; it is also recognitive, a signal betraying the writer's relation, or sometimes the relation of a type of discourse, to a historical and social world. To say that *of course* words are a form of life is not enough: words at this level of style intend a statement about life itself in relation to words, and in particular to literature as a value-laden act. Thus, even without fully understanding it, one is alerted by a similarity in the opening of these two essays, the first by T.S. Eliot, the second by Terry Eagleton.

> The Right Reverend Father in God, Lancelot Bishop of Winchester, died on September 26th, 1626. During his lifetime he enjoyed a distinguished reputation for the excellence of his sermons, for the conduct of his diocese, for his ability in controversy displayed against Cardinal Bellarmine, and for the decorum and devotion of his private life.[3]

One afternoon, Walter Benjamin was sitting inside the Café des Deux Magots in Saint Germain des Prés when he was struck with compelling force by the idea of drawing a diagram of his life, and knew at the same moment exactly how it was to be done. He drew the diagram, and with utterly typical ill-luck lost it again a year or two later. The diagram, not surprisingly, was a labyrinth.[4]

Each of these paragraphs, written more than fifty years apart, suggests a desired intimacy with the now distant *Lebenswelt* of its hero. Both evoke a lost concreteness, the fullness of a life in history, even though that life might have been a mortal failure. Eliot writes about it from the edge of mimicry, Eagleton with a directness approaching parody.

Thinking about the similarity, one is tempted to ask whether the Marxist critic does not share with the critic struggling for a postreligious faith a wishful sense of parousia. Was there, or will there be, an era in which mind and act, knowledge and reality, are not dissociated? What emerges in any case is expressed in terms of the historical imagination; and it hovers about the issue of appropriation: whether a past or estranged mode of existence (also of discourse) is recoverable.

At the risk of making too much of a presentational device, let me follow up this hunch. We remain today in the era of historicism brought about by so many eighteenth- and nineteenth-century scholars and by speculative philosophies of history associated with Vico, Herder, and Michelet. Moreover, we have gradually become interested not only in the great turning points of individual or collective existence (birth, career choice, marriage, death; kings, priests, diplomatic history, inventions, revolutions) but also in everyday life: *its* diplomacy, ideology, accidents, junctures. Eagleton is quite sparing of such details, except when he polemicizes against academic projects that always take place indoors and know little about the collective world:

Meyerhold . . . occupying a whole town to produce a play to celebrate the third anniversary of the Bolshevik revolution, with a cast of 15,000, real guns and a real battleship. Or . . . Erwin Piscator in the 1920s at the SPD theatre in Berlin; where you might find him directing a play in which Brecht had a hand, with music by Eisler or Weill, film-effects by Grosz, stage designs by Moholy-Nagy, Otto Dix or John Heartfield.[5]

19

Such "moments," Eagleton claims, are paradigmatic; typical of what academic "narratives" forget when they fail to reinsert literary works into cultural and political life. Yet Eagleton's historical vignettes sound like voice-overs in a propaganda documentary.

Precisely because historicism was so successful, and gave us all those proper names and dates, the contemporary mind staggers under the detail. For other reasons, too, a New Literary History begins to organize itself and tries for a less positive narrative form. Eagleton has not found it, despite the throwaway quality, sometimes rising to caricature pitch, of his prose. But he does expand Benjamin's resonant idea of the energy (especially the repressed vulgar energy) of a moment or an epoch breaking out of reified time to redeem itself from manipulation—to make itself present in a form that discomfits progressive schemes. Benjamin paradoxically places hope in that rising up of the historical memory rather than an abstractly happy future. My purpose is not to describe his thought exactly; instead I want to suggest that we too remain within historicism, reacting to the expanded horizon of fact it has brought about, now integrating by an impossible embrace and now violently throwing off the burden of multiplying and fragmenting perspectives.

Reading back on this centenary some hundred years, we would come upon Wilhelm Dilthey's *Einleitung in die Geisteswissenschaften* (Introduction to the Humanities). Here too we are made aware of a certain style. In his 1883 preface Dilthey announces his intention to link up "a historical with a systematic procedure, in order to solve the question of the philosophical foundation of the humanities with the highest degree of certainty."[6] That is quite a mouthful and indicates an acknowledged quest for wholeness amid the profusion of data and schemes that historicism has generated. The historical portion of his book, Dilthey says, would determine the place *(geschichtliche Ort)* of particular theories, preparing in this way the systematic task of laying down *(Grundlegung, Begründung)* an epistemological foundation. Dilthey's connectivism joins ideas and metaphors that those ruminants Heidegger and Derrida will chew on; we are in the presence of a grand style, made grander still by German syntax and compound words. Today it all seems like an elegant variation of clichés from the history of ideas, intending to teach us that the concept of uniformity postulated by the Enlightenment is inadequate to the manifold energies, the historical and psychological specificity, or our vital (willing, feeling, representing) nature. "In the veins of the knowing subject, constructed by Locke, Hume and Kant, there flows not real blood but the diluted essence of Reason as pure mentation."[7]

Yet Dilthey is not to be dismissed, as his later influence on German intellectual history and on thinkers like Ortega y Gasset suggests. We may question his style, but the dilemma he expresses, and struggles to resolve, remains ours. If we are to value the will to knowledge that has uncovered these many different forms of life, we must find for them some coherence, even a unitary aspect. Dilthey believed that not only a typological ordering (in particular, of worldviews) but a more foundational analysis could occur. It would reveal the totality and interrelatedness (his terms) of life, and explain how we can intuit the world of others: the historical world.[8]

In this very period Nietzsche was developing untimely thoughts on knowledge. He felt it had run out of control and was jeopardizing the ideal of a balance of faculties. "The philosopher shows the highest dignity, when he concentrates—tames—into unity the limitless will to knowledge."[9] "Humanity," he also wrote, "has knowledge as a beautiful way to do itself in." Written between 1872 and 1875, immediately after *The Birth of Tragedy,* these observations give the other side of the knowledge explosion Dilthey tried to organize into innocence.

The question is what role knowledge plays, and whether it will throw light on itself—on its own place in human history. If scholarship and specialization continue to reign, can a culture grow from them? Nietzsche doubted it; he thought learning was a substitute for religion, and that it would go the way of religion. Yet for Dilthey a *Lebensphilosophie* drawn from the moral sciences (the early term for human sciences, or *Geisteswissenschaften*) was an imperative. That is why hermeneutics became a central concern. If historical knowledge was to become personal knowledge, then hermeneutics would have to show that understanding others, and the historical past, was possible.

The problematic place of "history" as a higher, because unifying, form of knowledge is suggested by a comparison that takes us from the 1880s to the present. In a preface to *Allegories of Reading* (1979) Paul de Man tells us he wanted to write history but ended up with "reading" as his subject: "I had to shift from historical definition to the problematics of reading."[10] What does this shift mean? Dilthey too defers something. At the end of his preface he mentions that he has postponed completing his biography of Schleiermacher because "ultimate questions of philosophy" had to be resolved before he could continue his exposition and critique.

What is the equivalent for de Man of this "ultimate question"? Dilthey's move upward to a philosophical hermeneutics *(Aufbau)* is replaced in de Man by "reading" *(Abbau)*. Dilthey's idealism invests history with a hopeful unity that keeps breaking down. De Man's interest in rhetoric undoes standard principles of canonicity, or of period definition, and suggests that a foundation for humanistic studies cannot now be found.

De Man too had to clarify a philosophical question, but for him it was the question of philosophy itself, its presumption vis-à-vis literature. Philosophy, whether of history or of language, is itself a form of rhetoric. Reading tests the claim that a language of knowledge exists that is more rigorous than literary language—more aware at least of rhetorical figures in their duplicity, their intertwined cognitive and persuasive aspects. The very separation of philosophy and literature into self-contained disciplines is challenged by de Man's kind of reading. Literature (a term that includes literary studies) is said to be as preoccupied as philosophy is with the "fallacy of unmediated expression." Yet because literature is less pretentious in claiming to overcome this obstacle, it is also less deceiving.

Dilthey appears certain of the ultimate intelligibility of world and text. De Man's cautious title, *Allegories of Reading,* not only implies that all interpretation has some divination in it—that even in its modern and secular form it has an unacknowledged, though negative, affinity to figural allegory[11]—but also suggests, more radically, that our very desire for intelligibility discloses something that continues to resist it, a stubborn, gratuitous remainder that cannot be resolved but only described as "literary," "linguistic," "figural." In Kant and Hegel too there is a moment when the conceptualizing reason meets that check. Though reading wants to make the text readable, it never produces more than an "allegory" of this desire.

Ultimately de Man's title is a kenning for literature itself as a body of works that cannot be systematized by scientific types of analysis (logic, grammar, structural metagrammar, holistic schemes). Any type of reading that tries to do away with itself or, obversely, to substitute itself for the work is in error, for either way it seeks an intuitive or unmediated relation. Yet reading must seek that relation if it aims to *understand*. Reading is and is not understanding, therefore. In this sense literary works are always already "readings"—the forestructure of criticism, to use a term from Heidegger. Literature would not exist if there were a purer sort of understanding—of the soul in words or of words in the soul (absolute words, inscribed on the "tablets of the heart").

De Man's emphasis on reading rather than on understanding helps us to see the change that has occurred since Dilthey. The change takes place within hermeneutics, defined by Schleiermacher as a "philological discipline." Dilthey, Schleiermacher's most influential interpreter, emphasizes philosophy over philology. He describes mainly his precursor's attempts to free hermeneutics from its regional base in theology and law. Interpretation theory had to find a valid foundation, one that would be independent of such regional or applied contexts. As a general hermeneutics it becomes philosophical and produces an understanding of understanding, a disclosure of "the facts of consciousness" *(Tatsachen des Bewusstseins)*. An emancipated philosophical hermeneutics also allows all oral and written expression to fall under one rule of explication, so that the distinction between sacred and secular, literary and nonliterary, classic and nonclassic would disappear as an a priori frame, though not as an empirical datum with generic and social features. Only a general science of understanding will unify the humanities and provide them with a philosophically valid foundation.

As can happen in intellectual history, the recovery of earlier manuscripts reverses a direction of inquiry. Dilthey knew only a late version (1838) of Schleiermacher's *Hermeneutik*.[12] It was not till 1959 that all the relevant versions were assembled, under the sponsorship of Hans-Georg Gadamer. The expanded corpus allows us to see an oscillation in Schleiermacher's thinking. He seeks to honor the "technical" (psychological) and the "grammatical" sides of interpretation. Alternatively, he distinguishes the part that "divination" plays in understanding an author from the part played by the words themselves, whose grammar and context must be studied objectively. Divination is complete when we have forgotten the words; grammatical study is complete when we have forgotten the writer of the words. Schleiermacher tries to see hermeneutics as a combinatory art of the two modes. They should work reciprocally *(Wechselwirkung)*. But he cannot make up his mind which

23

mode is higher and which lower. Sometimes hermeneutics proper is identified with divination, but then statements are made that give primacy to understanding a "whole" that is said to be language itself. "Language," an early manuscript declares, "is all that may be presupposed in hermeneutics, or all that can be found."

How can hermeneutics unify the humanities when it cannot unify itself? No wonder Dilthey has to take time off to clarify ultimate philosophical problems. By choosing the word "reading," de Man moves away from the effort to found the humanities on interpretation theory. He reconstitutes the subject of literary studies as language—language, not as an abstracted or objectified entity, but as it produces reading. Reading constructs models of intelligibility that it can also deconstruct. All such "allegories of reading" are shadow functions that sustain a mind seeking to control mutability. There is no absolute knowledge to be separated out and systematized: concepts always present themselves, if at all, in linguistic form. The claim "I understand language" is the largest a thinker can make, as is also clear from Wittgenstein's *Investigations* or from Valéry's praise of Mallarmé, that he used language as he had invented it.

Schleiermacher provides only one of the frames for recent literary studies. Saussure and Freud have been more influential, precisely because philology (in the case of Saussure) and the culture of philology (in the case of Freud) were converted to nonantiquarian and intensely practical uses. In both there is uncertainty about the historical or material basis of signification, but this only stimulates a new description of the way meaning comes about: Saussure explains how sound-shapes become signifying words, Freud how dream thoughts become conscious, and thus interpretable.

Saussure's work is so important, for literary studies also, because it suspends the two favorite areas of Dilthey; it does not touch psychology, and it circumvents, though it acknowledges, history. Already in the notebooks Saussure suggests that when we deal with what is "in" words, we are still dealing with words, rather than with a preverbal intention. What stands behind the esoteric verses he analyzes is not a *sujet créateur* but a *mot inducteur*.[13] He lays the basis for a text-production theory, which must advance from phonemes to the word, the phrase, the sentence, and then the whole we call a text.

Yet his greatest contribution is his definition of the conceptual factor that links signifier (the acoustical word) to signified (the referential word). He found that the linkage, though conceptual, was also conventional or arbitrary: no intrinsic reason or genetic-historical ("diachronic") process could be held to motivate it. The linkage took effect within a "diacritical" framework of differences between words, regulated at every level by language itself in its synchronic or systematic aspect.

The idea of a linguistic system obviously leads to the idea of a literary system.[14] I want to emphasize, however, a comparison with Freud, since a great deal of theory in the last thirty years has come out of an alliance of semiotics and psychoanalysis. This should be a surprise, since Freud's interest is in psychology, or "divination," while Saussure's is in "grammar," or the system of language. Though Freud advances in the same direction as Saussure when he rejects essentialist conceptions of meaning, which explain dream symbols according to a fixed (archetypal) number of "keys," he also holds that a dream cannot be understood without further access to the mind of the dreamer, that is, to the dreamer's associations; and this situation is mobile. Meanings can be assigned to a particular symbol or dream, yet each sequence remains indeterminate, as if the "dream language" were a sentence without closure that keeps us in the grip of the penultimate.

Yet is the relation between dreams and meaning more fluid than that between words and meaning, if we start at the acoustic, micropoetic level rather than at the level of standard language? Like Saussure in his notebooks, we often see, or hear, words within words and become fascinated with ghostly "matrices" and "mannequins" that live anagrammatically within hermetic kinds of language. Saussure abandoned this area because it was too chancy. The relation between verses and their inner word (usually a "sacred name") was not subject to strong verification: two words or names might suggest themselves, and the whole issue became a game whose rules were difficult to set. We glimpse here a problem strictly analogous to dream interpretation: how to relate indeterminacy and overdetermination. This will be a crucial task for most theories of linguistic meaning, as for theories of poetic meaning.

Freud, moreover, though he professes ignorance concerning the material in the unconscious (images seem more primal than words, yet images are often a rebus translatable into words), brings that material into the domain of "word presentation" by an associative method ("free association") that is basically verbal. The difference between unconscious and conscious thought is precisely word presentation (see, for example, *The Ego and the Id*).[15] Where consciousness is, there is language; the obverse is not so clear. It seems that language allows dream thoughts to enter a preconscious and so retrievable stage, even if the structure of language (its syntax or rhetoric) cannot be proved to subsist in the unconscious. Jacques Lacan, however, applying Saussure, seeks a semiotic, verbally active view of the unconscious. Both Freud and Saussure, in any case, contribute to a renewal of scientific interest in linguistic process as it affects every aspect of human life, from slips of the tongue to complex literary works, from psychobabble to mythology.

The historian Marc Bloch once said what many have felt about times such as antiquity for which there are relatively few sources: "One could profit from the fact that the documents were lacking." In the contemporary period, after the philological discoveries of two centuries, there are so many documents that, as in my own essay, the problem of choice, of representative sampling, becomes oppressive. The history of poetry overwhelms the poetry of history. Whereas during the lean years of historical research a single text, even line, might be used significantly, it is not so today, as Péguy remarks in *Clio*. "That a line, that a word should illuminate a world," Clio is made to say, "that, allow me to tell you, is a technique of art, and such artistic techniques in the modern world are, precisely, what I am forbidden to use."[16]

Yet without them how can this wealth of materials be mastered, even provisionally? History-writing today is a form of criticism, of reasoned, artistic choice. Every history of criticism has to include itself as an act of criticism. However scrupulously comprehensive a Wellek is, his exclusions may prove as telling as his inclusions.[17] We admire a history like his for being more than a chronological repertory or catalogue raisonné. Yet Foucault has delineated the arbitrary though very real divisions in the history of discourse, on such cleavage lines as true and false, mad and sane; and Hayden White has studied the "metahistorical," that is, the rhetorically or tropically determined, order of such grand historical syntheses as Jacob Burckhardt's, which already shows the burgeoning impact of historicism and philology.[18]

I have mentioned that Nietzsche, at this time, was aware of the cultural and political aspects of this immense broadening of the horizon of knowledge. There are adumbrations in him of a will to power over *texts*. It is by no means a power exercised, as in contemporary regimes, through falsification. A text becomes, rather, a dangerous field of forces that struggle *in* the author *for* the work. Readers too have to recognize in themselves a will to power, or at least to knowledge, and must either achieve an empirical equilibrium or establish themselves on terra firma by means of theory. We are surprisingly close to an aristocratic type of reader-response (better: reader-responsibility) doctrine. Péguy's Clio—although one has to be on guard with her, since she represents the pagan soul—cannot see history as more than a random accumulation. The scandal for her is that no history exists, only temporality in its unachieved form. Everything is done and undone in time, and the act of reading reveals that scandal most articulately. For each reader is an author in the sense of auctor, an augmentor who helps to "achieve" the work but who may also spoil or disestablish it. Reading, she repeats often, is "l'acte commun, l'opération commune du lisant et du lu"; it is "literally a co-operation, an intimate, inward collaboration . . . thus a disconcerting responsibility."

Are we all becoming pagan again, this time as a reaction to excessive learning? It would be interesting to view Walter Pater in this light, as well as the wave of impressionist critics who flourished in France and England from the end of the last century to World War I. They deal with the rise of science and scientific philology in their own way. For them reading is a mode of forgetting as well as remembering: a cleansing of perceptual powers that were blocked by needless learning, and a renewal of that learning through particular passing moments, which only the crystalline magic of art might fix in all their texture. Wellek's *History of Modern Criticism*—magisterial, hygienic, encyclopedic—represents a swing back. Combating the sustained dilettantism of Saintsbury, whose career began exactly a century ago and whose flood of books, including *A History of Criticism and Literary Taste*,[19] shows a settled English tendency to mingle aesthetic appreciation and connoisseurship, Wellek conceives of criticism as a unified subject, at least since around 1750.

Yet in a review of Wellek, Erich Auerbach, while praising the extraordinary fullness and usefulness of the work, objects that it leaves out too much and is not genuinely unified.[20] Criticism, he points out, is bound up not only with aesthetics and remarks on the other arts (which Wellek often respects) but also with modes of historical research and philology (which Wellek treats only occasionally). The history of criticism, in short, should include the history of scholarship. Moreover, literary criticism is crisscrossed by too many themes and vectors. Any "history," therefore, becomes a multifaceted reference work, unless the author can find one dominant event or motif. This perspectival fullness, which is both a cause and a result of historicism, Auerbach identifies subversively as the very problem defeating Wellek's *History*. Perspectivism is held back ("tamed," Nietzsche might say) by the retentive authority of classical paradigms and the concept of the fundamental unity of human nature. But it breaks through in the second half of the eighteenth century (just where Wellek's account begins) as a Copernican revolution gradually pervading our entire consciousness.

Auerbach helps us to realize that by the time the Modern Language Association was founded in 1884, historical perspectivism had triumphed, despite the emergence of new forms of classicism or pseudoclassicism, especially in the guise of "national universals"—racially oriented ideologies that argued the purity and universality of a particular national tradition. Auerbach retains, like Curtius and Spitzer, a clear sense of Europe as a potentially unified area study; after the Second World War this faded, and his late essay "Philology of World Literature" goes beyond Goethe to announce that "Our philological homeland is the earth; it cannot be the nation any longer."[21]

Yet Romance philology had given Auerbach a sense of criticism's holistic shape, for a time at least. "The field I represent, Romance Philology," he writes, "is one of the smaller branches on the tree of romantic historicism, which experienced, if only in passing, Romania as a meaningful totality [*Sinnganzes*]."[22] That small branch proved to be a golden bough. Scholars of German or English rarely saw their province as a *Sinnganzes*. In Germany during the Nazi era a virulent nationalism tried to impose a false unity on the culture by purging its debt to all but the Nordic heritage. Curtius' *European Literature and the Latin Middle Ages* was an act of spiritual resistance, repossessing Goethe as a European and affirming Germania's kinship with Romania.[23]

In England the literary tradition was, at the beginning, more discontinuous. Philology had fewer materials to study and soon became "criticism"—a word generally reserved on the Continent for belletristic reviews and essays. Even when, with F. R. Leavis' championing of the Cambridge "School of English," a unified sense of modern canon developed, the notion of "living English" was concrete only in spirit. It did not benefit from that massive, ramified research into all aspects of literary and colloquial language that characterized such masters of Romance philology as Meyer-Lübke, Menéndez Pidal, Ferdinand Brunot, Karl Vossler, and others.[24] Their work, cresting in the more focused literary studies of Curtius, Spitzer, and Auerbach, covered all aspects of linguistic reality, from court to city, from learned jargon to the *lingua del pane,* from nursery to stock exchange, from the foyer to the demimonde of café society and theater.

German scholarship, intense and self-protective, was a "culture of learning" that proved unable to resist a political takeover in the 1930s. After Hitler seized power many important scholars left, or were forced to leave, and they benefited higher education in both England and the United States. Yet after the First World War, French and English universities had already begun to turn against the Germanic tradition in philology. (The German universities together with the Sorbonne, were famous—or infamous—for their Ph.D. requirements.)[25] Cambridge founded a school of English that separated off "antiquarian" philological scholarship, and this became the model for modern English studies once the New Criticism took hold. In the United States a gradual reform movement modified "philology for philology's sake," experimented with a core curriculum in the liberal arts, accepted Croce's emphasis on the expressive unity of all artifacts, and gravitated toward French academics like Cazamian, who saw historical studies as merely auxiliary to a criticism that welded data into a "central intuition" about the *idée génératrice* of the work.[26] In the late 1930s both graduate and undergraduate studies began to be affected by the influx of refugee scholars, polyhistors who carried with them a broad and sophisticated knowledge of European culture.

The American academy had been deeply split from early on between an extreme medievalism and an extreme antiprofessionalism. It retained an archaic system of lectures and ritualized examinations at the same time as it continued the genteel tradition. In the 1930s the college remained a world apart, as if real thought or professed learning would unbalance undergraduates instead of fitting them for extramural careers. It imitated Oxbridge and fended off the graduate school's philological curriculum. French culture played its part as a guide to urbane conversation. And especially *entre deux guerres* it was not the universities at all but the journals and magazines that spread what literary culture there was.

Randolph Bourne's comments on the undergraduate, drawn partly from experiences at Columbia around 1910,[27] and Malcolm Cowley's on Harvard around 1916[28] converge in an important way. Bourne said that American students lacked philosophy or that they never got beyond "a sporting philosophy, the good old Anglo-Saxon conviction that life is essentially a game whose significance lies in terms of winning or losing." This left the undergraduate in "a sort of Peter Pan condition . . . instead of anticipating his graduate or professional study or his active life."[29] Cowley saw a costume drama being acted out, in which students were taught to "regard culture as a veneer, a badge of class distinction—as something assumed like a suit of clothes or an Oxford accent."[30] In literary studies two main currents, humanist and aesthete, though opposed to each other, suggested an unreal milieu "in which the productive forces of society were regarded as something alien to poetry and learning."[31] This dissociation from native grounds was completed by the students' experience on the European front in World War I. Cowley's description of the "Lost Generation" and its "spectatorial attitude" remains powerful. "School and college had uprooted us in spirit; now we were physically uprooted, hundreds of us, millions, plucked from our own soil as if by a clamshell bucket and dumped, scattered among strange people. All our roots were dead now, even the Anglo-Saxon tradition of our literary ancestors."[32]

A famous page in Henry James's book on Hawthorne had remarked the presence in England and the absence in America of public institutions to support a writer's needy imagination. Though there were more "items of high civilization" in 1916 than in Hawthorne's time, it is clear that Cowley's generation felt a lack of "texture in American life," to repeat James. A renewed search for cultural emplacement and native roots began. Mencken's *The American Language*,[33] Van Wyck Brooks's concept of a "usable past," Cowley's "exile's return" and idea of a worker's culture, and, above all, Bourne's clear-eyed understanding that "ideas and knowledge about social relations and human institutions are to count as urgently in our struggle with the future as any mathematical or mechanical formulas did in the development of our present"[34]—these amounted to more than nationalism. The very idea of a culture of criticism was involved, a revision of Arnold's views as effective in the United States as Leavis would be in England. Cultural studies, Bourne thought, would revive a line of national classics (Thoreau, Whitman, Mark Twain) not "tainted by sweetness and light," and this would help to inaugurate a criticism of American institutional life. The "texture" of that life was too thin; it had no real philosophy behind it, and very little community.

Arnold's idea of culture, Bourne charged, had become a quantitative matter, an excuse for the acquisition of more foreign art. That was all wrong, for the important thing was to "shut ourselves in with our own genius" and to end "that old division which 'culture' made between the chosen people and the gentiles." Bourne's program for achieving this remained very general. The little magazines were to play a role, becoming "voices for these new communities of sentiment."[35] It was indeed a culture of journalism, not yet a culture of criticism, that arose in the 1920s and 1930s. For the best essays were not directly social or America-centered if we think of such critiques of European literature as Edmund Wilson's *Axel's Castle*[36] and its antiphon, *To the Finland Station*.[37] These books are much weightier than Wilson's mingling of memoir and criticism when it comes to American subjects. The critical memoir, however, so finely practiced by Bourne in the small magazines or the *New Republic,* would become a tradition in America, from Waldo Frank to Alfred Kazin and Irving Howe.

Why did a Marxist or sociological criticism not develop after World War I in the United States? Charles Beard had published his economic interpretation of the Constitution in 1913. Veblen's related work had produced four significant books by 1918. Nor was the period between the World Wars unproductive: Van Wyck Brooks, in his earlier phase, saw and denounced the cleavage between the business world and the world of culture that drove American writers and intellectuals into a state of alienation; Waldo Frank wrote three books on America that gained much esteem and which still seem remarkably strong analyses, based in part on his knowledge of Europe, in part on Spanish-American sympa-

31

thies; Granville's Hicks's bitingly clear *The Great Tradition*[38] ordered writers since the Civil War according to their engagement with the class struggle and capitalist America; and Kenneth Burke mixed his own philosophical and anthropological brew as if he were defying Prohibition. Thinkers like Lewis Mumford tackled the problem of galloping urbanization from more than an architectural point of view, as did the Southern Agrarians.

One can look at the matter the other way around: how did a strong Marxist-inspired school of thought evolve in Europe, especially in Germany? It is clear that the situation of the German intellectual differed considerably from that of the American intellectual. Until the demise of the Weimar Republic the issue of socialism (of the Right or the Left) was rife; one could hardly avoid it. Moreover, after the founding of the Frankfurt Institute for Social Research, some intellectuals gained financial as well as moral support. All this ended of course shortly after Hitler's seizure of power. But enough time had been given to develop common themes and disputes that went on even after Adorno, Horkheimer, and others were forced into exile.

In the United States there was no such effective umbrella organization. There were intense intellectual friendships, but institutional support came mainly from journals like the *New Republic* and precarious party affiliations. The tendency to journalism, moreover, diffused as well as energized: the Frankfurt School, though it had better university connections, was not subordinate to academic policy and produced unaccommodated studies both scholarly and contemporary. It would be naive, moreover, to underestimate the anti-intellectual and jingoistic currents once the United States entered the war in 1916. After Beard resigned his Columbia University post in protest against the dismissal of two professors, the *New York Times* published an editorial with the following blatant sentiments: "Columbia . . . is better for Professor Beard's resignation. Some years ago Professor Beard published a book . . . no professor should have written, since it was grossly unscientific. . . . It was the fruit of that school of thought and teaching . . . borrowed from Germany, which denies to man . . . the capacity of noble striving."[39] Marxist thinking would be caught in the net of anti-German feelings; it had no firm base in or outside the university; it relied on the hit-and-run methods of weekly journalism.

Above all there was a danger of substituting propaganda for thought. No doubt this was equally true in Europe; but on the Continent Marxism gradually acquired a strong philosophical base. Max Weber lectured on historical materialism at the University of Vienna in 1918; and by 1930 French thinkers, whatever their patriotic feelings, were once more seriously engaged with German philosophy. But American thought, if I may generalize, had still to come to its philosophy, through Veblen, Beard, Dewey, Peirce, and others. It was precariously introspective; and with the rise of propaganda there was no institutional counterpoise. "When politics fill the sky," Bourne wrote in a letter, "the lid is most serenely clamped down on philosophical introspection . . . In this country I can think of no intellectual effort outside Veblen's that has not been propaganda."[40]

The rejection of the "new orthodoxy" of propaganda, as Bourne also calls it, went together with a desire to find—by introspection—what culture, what classicism, there was. When Bourne writes that "culture is not an acquired familiarity with things outside, but an inner and constantly operating taste, a fresh and responsive power of discrimination, and the insistent judging of everything that comes to our minds and senses,"[41] we understand that there are not too many things outside. The American situation, in a way, was the opposite of the European, where historical study had increased the burden of the past. Perhaps a *native* Marxism, or sociology of knowledge, was too much to hope for.[42] But the greatest problem was to find a center from which diffusion would occur; this center could only be the university. It was not until it made an alliance with the university that the New Criticism was influential in America. Yet to "incorporate" criticism, to make it a university subject, seems to move it away from Bourne's ideal of a broad "community of sentiment"—unless the university has indeed become the nearest thing extant to a democratic institution, a republic of letters. Even so the sense that the university is middle class and that formal higher education cannot produce a culture of criticism leads us back to the question whether such a culture can ever be, or whether academic criticism is not at one and the same time auxiliary to culture and corrosive of it. "The revolutionary world is coming out into the classic" was the hope Bourne expressed, as he looked beyond Arnold. Trilling, also looking beyond Arnold—through Freud, and after yet another World War—seemed more

33

pessimistic. He wondered about a drive so destructive or disestablishing that revolutionary turmoil was only its symptom. Was the end freedom from the middle class or freedom from society itself?

Arnold associated culture with diffusion: "a passion for diffusing, for making prevail, for carrying from one end of society to the other the best knowledge, the best ideas." The "great men of culture," he said, would "divest knowledge of all that was harsh, uncouth, difficult, abstract, professional, exclusive." We are to humanize knowledge, "to make it efficient outside the clique of the cultivated and the learned."[43] No better definition has been given of what a modern education might achieve. Yet the passion Arnold attributed to the bearers of culture could as easily be characteristic of great missionaries. They too (in principle) spread sweetness and light. By transfusing the one passion into the other, Arnold becomes the saint of secularization.

The limits of such cultural evangelism are clear. It is eleemosynary rather than radical: the utopian energies in religion or political thought are filtered out. They are made to gravitate to the side of anarchy rather than culture. This may seem ironic by 1984, the centennial of the MLA, the year George Orwell chose for his antiutopia, and today, when our concern has turned to the totalitarian rather than anarchic consequences of utopian thinking. When culture is threatened more by violent schemes of order than by disorder (although the two may be joined by a vicious dialectic), then cultural theory becomes "critical" in the sense of being methodically suspicious of the limits imposed on imaginative activity by officially sanctioned modes of speaking and writing.

Arnold simplified both the Bible and the secular canon for the sake of a humanized knowledge. What will remain of religion, he declared famously, is its poetry; and he meant by poetry a muse that was the opposite of harsh. Yet both poetry and the Bible contain difficult elements that the enlightened mind tries to explain away. In its supernatural or historical strangeness, and our attempts to come to terms with that, the Bible may even be the preeminent *literary* case. For the study of literature has to accomplish two things at once: it must acknowledge the otherness of a text, and it must accommodate that otherness. This double process of familiarization and defamiliarization depends for its particulars on the situation of the interpreter: which side of the process one feels compelled to emphasize.

Many texts are only too obviously stumbling blocks for the intellect, or have been made such by a priestly appropriation. As Arnold's inheritor, Northrop Frye considers it his life's work to bring the Bible back into the possession of all. To demythologize a Bible-inspired writer like Blake, without denying either the force or the intelligibility of myth, is the cultural task.[44] Another equally strong inheritor of Arnold, Lionel Trilling was also devoted to using literature as a guide to the liberal imagination. Yet he became uneasy about the tendency toward accommodation, especially in the academy. He therefore pondered the wish in the artist, but also in seminal thinkers like Freud, to get "beyond culture."[45]

That wish is paradoxical enough, since we cannot slough off culture any more than we can the body. One clear result, however, is that the notion of subculture transforms itself into that of an adversary culture.[46] Another clear result is a new focus on Rousseau, not as a supposed primitivist but as a sophisticated modernist who deprives us of the solace of equating freedom with either nature or culture. The wish to go beyond culture is, in any case, not only modern. There have always been real or imaginary journeys in search of the Other. Claude Lévi-Strauss's *Tristes Tropiques*[47] continues both More's *Utopia* and Diderot's *Voyage de Bougainville*, while Todorov's *Conquête de l'Amérique*[48] rehearses a sad and significant "American" history not unlike the "Eastern" history, deformed by mythic desires, that Said's *Orientalism* takes to task.[49]

For Hegel the expulsion from Eden was already a self-inspired alienation, even if the Bible represented it as imposed and distanced it into myth. It was the necessary consequence of our desire for a more intimate knowledge of whatever exists or can be made to exist. Yet if the societal bond has tightened its grip, a modern and acute stage of rebellion may have been reached. Going "beyond culture" becomes more than resisting a dominant ideology. It suggests the abandonment of all mediations, the radicalism of "liberty or death," an opposition (almost mechanical) in the name of renewal or revolution.

We stand here on treacherous ground. How many sins have been committed in the name of revitalizing culture through repristination? Arthur Koestler writes:

From the psychologist's point of view, there is little difference between a revolutionary and a traditionalist faith . . . All true faith involves a revolt against the believer's social environment, and the projection into the future of an ideal derived from the remote past. All Utopias are fed from the sources of mythology; the social engineer's blueprints are merely revised editions of the ancient text.[50]

On a more innocent level, the appeal of the word "Renaissance" continues to schematize literary histories as a succession of convention and revolt, decadence and revival, unity and fall from unity ("dissociation").[51] It does not matter what the decadent stage of a culture is called: Spengler (well known to Frye) chose "civilization." F. R. Leavis' earliest pamphlet bears the title *Mass Civilization and Minority Culture*.[52] What does matter is seeing the connection between political and literary theory, while keeping the two apart. When "minority" recurs in *Kafka: Pour une littérature mineure,* by Deleuze and Guattari,[53] it has exchanged its elitist connotation for an eloquent fan of antielitist meanings, but it continues to express the writer's war against the dominant tongue of his culture—in which he cannot, yet must, perform. "A gypsy literature which ha[s] stolen the German child out of its cradle and in great haste put it through some kind of training, for someone has to dance on the tightrope" is how Kafka, in a letter to Max Brod, describes his discontent arising from within a civilized or—as Deleuze and Guattari prefer—"territorialized" language.[54]

The kind of thing that worries these writers did not concern Arnold. Culture for him was high culture; and the idea that it might oppress rather than enlighten the uncultured classes—that it might prevent the unfolding of popular or vernacular energies—was not an issue. One could not go beyond culture except toward anarchy. If anything threatened culture from within, it was philistinism, parochialism, and, most insidiously, the critical spirit itself. The function of criticism was in a sense to make that spirit "organic" again (though the term comes from Saint-Simon) by taking us beyond the negative or transitional stage of "Wandering between two worlds, one dead, / The other powerless to be born" *(Stanzas from the Grande Chartreuse)*. As in Saint-Simon's "productive" philosophy, a new society should emerge from the "critical," that is, postrevolutionary phase of history, which had dissolved received opinion and established structures.

Yet even in Arnold the issue of revolutionary change has begun to shift toward assessing what is involved in diffusing culture and educating all classes. There is a sense of energies to be released, and a countersense of mediations and forms of knowledge that might block rather than facilitate that aim. Education and culture are benefits that move into a more ambivalent position vis-à-vis both social reform and revolutionary politics. On the whole this ambivalence is subjective. It takes the form of a compensatory desire for an original or unmediated relation—a relation jeopardized by the very progress of civilized society. In America and on the Continent this desire is more overt than in England. We glimpse it in various American Adams: in Thoreau's and Emerson's wish to break through to an autonomous individuality or an authochthonous culture; in Whitman's "barbaric yawp." We glimpse it in Nietzsche's antiphilosophy and in such Yoda figures as Zarathustra. Veils, figures, mediations, and illusions are crucial to Nietzsche, but they only expose the groundless ground, the abyss, that is bridged through art. Our own time's breakthrough mentality finds its strongest image in Thomas Mann's *Doctor Faustus,* based on Goethe's Magian myth also inspiring Spengler's *Decline of the West.*[55]

We cannot look back a hundred years without looking back further. Then it becomes clear that a new class marker adds itself to the old. Learning now alienates the learned classes (whatever their social status) from the illiterate classes but also, to a degree, from themselves. "Overcivilization" becomes an issue. Faust's complaint at the beginning of Goethe's play, about the life-inhibiting effects of book knowledge, is enlarged and made socially significant by Nietzsche's attack on *Gelehrtenkultur.*[56]

How does a growing consciousness of *this* alienation feed back into the tradition of scholarship that helped to produce it?

We find, first of all, anti-self-consciousness theories that suggest that learning can make itself organic again—through becoming, for example, poetry ("the breath and finer spirit of all knowledge," says Wordsworth). Art is felt to be more, not less, important now that science and scholarship grow exponentially. What Arnold names culture is, similarly, life-integrated rather than life-disturbing; it leads to a necessary "criticism of life." Scholarship, at the same time, becomes more archaeological, or genetic, seeking not only (as it had always done) origins but the point in history where logos and arche coincide to yield "Knowledge not purchased by the loss of power" (Wordsworth). Something like a recovered Adamic language, in fact.

This secular fundamentalism arises in place of (yet not always displacing) religious fundamentalisms. According to Derrida, all perspectives derived from it involve a blindness toward language. Language never was and never can be foundational: where language is, foundations have moved. The shift into words, into that temporal spacing, is radical and ongoing. Words have no center at which they become logos, The Word. Derrida therefore says that his critique is directed at "logocentricity."

Now very few philosophies of life set out to make words into a fundamentalist tool. We are not talking about propaganda or religious proclamation. We are talking about a more general and pervasive reaction to divisive multiple options as our knowledge of mediation grows, nourished by historicism and increased hermeneutic skills.

Some years ago I wrote a book called *The Unmediated Vision*, which traced the attempt of poets since Wordsworth to gain a more direct view of life than was allowed by culture.[57] "The modern poet has committed himself to the task of understanding experience in its immediacy. He has neglected the armature of the priest—the precautionary wisdom of tradition—and often, the inculcated respect for literary models."[58] The result of this heroic and impossible task was a paradox. The poet came to know the need for mediation all the more strongly. He saw himself, in fact, as a mediator of a special kind. He would "live the lack of mediation."

My double emphasis, on embodiment (the direct, sensuous intuition of reality) and on the lack of authentic mediation, exhibits that blindness to language of which Derrida speaks. Yet in both respects I was more a phenomenologist than a fundamentalist. The "concrete aesthetics" of Gaston Bachelard, except for his use of selected beauties rather than whole poems, might have seduced me. For Bachelard focused on basic sensory orientations and elemental images. He subtly decomposed, by a method learned from science (and cinematography), the prey into the shadow—*Abschattungen,* nuances.

To preserve an image (such as "the flame of a candle") despite its changeable, nymphlike essence, Bachelard pursued a *happy* kind of psychoanalysis.[59] Freud thought that the function (distinct from the meaning) of dreams was to allow us to continue sleeping; and images, or the evocative names Bachelard utters on their behalf, applying his immense verbal culture, support a state he identifies with reverie. This is a contemplative yet productive state of mind, which recalls things in their *durée* rather than in abstract or administered time.

Phenomenology is not of one kind of course. Bachelard stands closer to Husserl than to Hegel. The main thrust of both, however, is understood to be a return to things—to a therapeutic immediacy that is drawn out of the very process of mediation and no longer reifies consciousness.

The theory of intertexuality seems to have doomed phenomenological criticism by viewing all mediations as irreducible and essentially verbal. They are the shadow thrown by man's own intellect. For literature this means there is no *hors texte* but a rhetorical debt that cannot be canceled and must be borne as patiently as capitalist bankers tolerate what the Third World owes. The return to things is always really a return to a text. We relive—that is, rewrite—words always already uttered, texts always already written.

It is difficult, however, to gauge the *intrinsic* value of a text when the *originative* value, associated with an individual author (a "subject") fades into a play of pretexts. The shift from source study (genetic-historical) to intertextual study (structural-synchronic), which I comment on later, gives us both more and less control over the burden of mediations: more, because there is the promise of a method of analysis good for all cultures; less, because we are taken out of the *one* culture without being inserted into *one* other. Every other culture is not only equally "near to God" (historicism) but equally far from interpreter or observer. A homogenizing or flattening out occurs that signals to Erich Auerbach the end (in the real world too) of national diversity and cultural heterogeneity. In *Mimesis* Auerbach sees the common and the elemental emerging once more.[60] They seem to augur the dissolution of the dynamic, colorful past of the Western nations whose changing sense of reality he has just delineated. The theory of archetypes, certainly, whether applied to literature from a Jungian perspective, in which they are elemental psychic determinants, or from the perspective of Northrop Frye, in which they are principles of structure revealing the "total form" of human cultural achievement or desire, supports Auerbach's perception from within the history of scholarship.[61] There *is* a return to elementals (in Bachelard as well), but there remains the problem of how to prevent this from becoming anti-intellectual and destructive, from turning in the name of truth against the method that disclosed it.

Such a turn is present, at least potentially, even in Benjamin, who glimpsed the struggle Auerbach so vividly depicts. The taking into consciousness and the representation of what it means to be historical are falsified, in Benjamin's eyes, by the repressive weight of the official story, whatever European nation we deal with. A gulf opens, therefore, between culture and social reality, as Benjamin too tries to go beyond culture to recover, by a sort of delayed archaeological explosion, the story of the victim, the barbarism on which every cultural movement is built, the *unacknowledged* suffering and labor of the lower classes.[62] That is the one mediation always omitted. Benjamin seems to argue that the French Revolution failed to transform either life or letters—or that what it achieved has to be done again, perhaps again and again. Moved, like so many contemporary thinkers, by a "hermeneutics of suspicion" (Ricoeur), he ranges intelligibility on the side of plausibility, as if even intelligibility were suspect; this approach thickens Benjamin's style and impedes standard communication. A complex prose tries to point to significances hidden by force majeure or linked to a base of repressed passions.

Though the intertextual method is as pedagogic as explication de texte, and more consistent in its specific literary emphasis, it does not make clear why a certain signifying practice has force as well as significance. The issue involves the reception of language: as we speak it in an immediate context, and as a written code extended in time like a work's interpretive history. It is an issue that motivates speech-act theory and also reader-response criticism—from the reception aesthetics of the School of Konstanz to the psychological version developed from the "community" of the American classroom, to Stanley Fish's work on interpretive communities generally, and to Frank Kermode's on the inevitability of paradigms and institutions that help fix meaning.[63] Here I want to follow briefly two academic critics who accept intertextuality but use it very differently.

Theorists interested in the alliance of significance and force often understand the latter as power (following Nietzsche or Foucault) and give the whole issue a political or psychopolitical twist.[64] Harold Bloom maps the echoing presence of poet in poet and transforms textual space into an agon, an internalized power play.[65] That space is wrested by the living from the dead; more precisely, a special oedipal theory of conflict, between father (precursor poet) and son (ephebe), helps Bloom to delineate six modes of resolution called "revisionary ratios"—where ratio is a figure of failed adequation. The later poet, according to Bloom, can never live up to the precursor, and Blake is doomed to be less than Milton. Yet a poet's only chance to be among the great is to engage with prior and overshadowing greatness. This idea parallels the "embarrassment of tradition" thesis of W. J. Bate. Both points of view are concerned with the making of the modern artist and reflect an era in which art could succumb to learning, to that increased burden of mediations.

Bloom's version of intertextuality joins force to significance through a special theory of the poetic personality. Yet for an intertextualist like Michael Riffaterre, the poem is purely a medium, the superconductor of a collective discourse. Where Bloom's uncanny ear finds precursor echoes everywhere, Riffaterre analyzes every striking expression as the transformation of a cliché. Creativity is measured as the deviation *(écart stylistique)* from a norm, which Riffaterre calls a "matrix" and which his unusual learning (at times he is the *Grand Larousse* himself) finds in the environing sociolect of topoi and tropisms. A double determinism characterizes art and impresses us with its inexorable logic. The artifact is systemic, every negative (deviant) term becoming positive (normative) by the end; that positive, moreover, is a social cliché the poet has elaborated, not canceled. Force joins signification through this fatality of meaning; in an unforeseen and strangely sterile sense the common language is "illustrated." Yet Bloom too has his—less banal—fatality. He sees English verse as a diminishing thing because of the burden of textual mediation, but also because the presence of greatness drives young imaginations to a self-deceiving denial of mediatedness. Artistic autonomy is as much an illusion in Bloom as it is in Riffaterre. Bloom admires,

41

however, the personal wager sustaining that denial. Though he out-rightly labels the denial a lie (there is no unmediated creativity), it is the generative or founding lie of fiction.

Riffaterre's theory and Bloom's are connected through their strong disclosure of the intertextual situation of the writer. Riffaterre stresses it as the prerequisite for intelligibility, Bloom as the prerequisite for an originality that must survive within and against it. Riffaterre in context (which includes Jacques Lacan, Roland Barthes, Michel Foucault, and Paul de Man) reacts, like T. S. Eliot, to naive versions of Romantic originality. Bloom could reply that such impersonality theories are sim-ply the old classicism writ large. Yet both theories comment on the artist's drive "beyond culture." Riffaterre is nothing if not methodical in show-ing that the artist always deviates into sense. For Bloom, the deviation is the meaning. A text is basically devious because the artist's will to orig-inality deceives the consciousness of indebtedness; that will triumphs only at the cost of self-deception, or forgetfulness of the Other. We are back to Nietzsche's concept of culture guilt and the catastrophic need for disburdenment arising from it.[66]

Now scholarship is an especially heavy part of culture, so that the question of how to handle it must surface. It is here that Derrida's view of language is noteworthy. His close analysis of both literary and philo-sophical texts shows that language is a "deconstructive" medium that serves to disseminate whatever is heavy by substituting itself. It dispels what Hegel called "the pathos of substance," as if to say, My yoke is light. Such "lightness" (also evoked by Roland Barthes's "pleasure of the text") technically derives from the self-referentiality of language. To understand how language works has ethical implications. Such divisive or deadly polarities as fundamentalism and nihilism (the one a panic reaction to the other) become less terrifying, though they do not disappear. Not a par-ticular philosophy but linguistic action itself will sublimate them. In this respect, deconstruction is a happy discipline, a *fröhliche Wissenschaft*, and remains close to phenomenology.

My attempt to translate from one tradition (Continental) to the other (Anglo-American) may produce a misunderstanding. To transpose Der-rida's thought (as it extends Nietzsche, Husserl, and Heidegger) into an English text-milieu raises a question of style—of critical style. My para-graphs are perforce a mixture of technical phrases and impressionistic metaphors. They do little justice to the rigorous play of terms in Derrida. Moreover, English criticism since I. A. Richards has made great efforts to free itself of impressionism, so that it would be unfair to resurrect that discredited mode. It is therefore best to affirm at this point that Derrida's philosophical criticism is exact and learned. It is a form of scholarship, but it is also reflective about the relation of scholarship to culture, about the problem of field specialization ("philosophy," "criticism," "political science") and the division into faculties that seemed to Schiller a cultural wounding quite comparable to the Fall (see especially the sixth of his *Letters on Aesthetic Education* [1795]).

This review of scholarship has turned into remarks on the relation of *criticism* to culture. No wonder! Is not criticism the place where the conflict between culture and scholarship is worked out? How scholarly should cultured persons be? And how technical their styles of writing, or even their life-styles?

Such questions overflow the boundary of the history of taste, although they are important to courtesy books and figure largely in discussions of social ideals from courtier to Common Reader or gentleman-scholar. We are only just emerging from a period when the amateur tradition prevailed in literary studies—even while considerable scholarship was taking place. Criticism may use scholarship against culture, but it may also use cultural ideals against scholarship. I want to refocus the issue to emphasize the relation of culture to what may offend it—in particular, to learning, mainly science and scholarship, but also the deliberate recourse to "terms of art."[67]

Culture and learning are matters that surface together in Nietzsche. This contemporary of Arnold's turns from philology to philosophy in order to oppose the *Gelehrtenkultur* (pedant culture) around him; it is interesting of course that he was also Dilthey's contemporary at Basel. Nietzsche particularly fears that a pedant culture will combine with an "American" type of democratic leveling (shades of Leavis!) and produce thoughtless displays of erudition instead of concentrated and sublime works of philosophy or art. It is less the populace that is the target of Nietzsche's elitism than the class he knows best: learned professors whose unbridled drive for knowledge *(Erkenntnistrieb)* is truly a barbarism. Culture controls major human drives, and philosophy's specific task is breaking in the intellect. For this it has to mobilize art, which Nietzsche describes by a word that means untapped as well as immense *(unerhörte Kunstkräfte)*. The philosopher tames the monstrous pathos of truth: without him the drive toward absolute knowledge would become frenzied and anarchic.

While Arnold's culture consists of "ideas" that can be "diffused," Nietzsche's culture is linked to a heroic concept of philosophy as well as to art, to works of intellect like Hegel's and Schopenhauer's. Classical balance or proportion—cultural sanity—is a sublime achievement, not a social compromise.

This brief comparison can be moralized. Recent emphatic efforts to reconnect literary studies to history and politics may be drawing their animus from ignorance of the theory of culture, which is (as in Raymond Williams) the best way into the subject. Literary criticism should not be divorced from the history of scholarship or from theories of culture, which are often indebted to scholarship.

More particularly, we see that "philosophy" plays different roles—and may indeed be different things—in Germany and in England. In Germany, and to an extent in French circles, philosophy is philology raised to a higher power. It remains a depository of the classicist ideal, which maintains a sense of the unity of knowledge and the universality of culture, despite the pressures of nationalism and the influx of a truly enormous freight of historical and linguistic scholarship. So Dilthey, in his ambitious attempt to unify the humanities, is drawn back to the union, or at least the cross-pollination, of all sorts of learning in the German Romantics. The aim of Romantic philosophy fully corresponds to that of classical unity, but "unity" now moves closer to "totality": what Lovejoy describes as the Chain of Being in its temporalized plenitude. Philosophy is, in the main, "identity philosophy," and it proceeds by a "spiritual chemistry" that resynthesizes learning into culture—a culture Arnold takes for granted (though it must escape "the clique of the learned and cultivated") but that Nietzsche, like Goethe, considers a prize to be struggled for and, at times, a grand and necessary illusion.

English philosophy, like everything English, champions common sense and remains stubbornly untechnical. Except for Coleridge's lively and unconsummated efforts, it does not try to make a disparate and expanding knowledge cohere by a monumental synthesis. English culture is strangely self-assured, as if Shakespeare and Co. had finished that work. In their wake the English language has magic in its web. "The colour and richness of the European Renaissance," Raymond Williams writes, "interacted with the vigour and realism of the popular tradition to create wholly new national forms."[68] Herder, sensitive to the impoverishing ravages on German culture exerted by French neoclassicism, praises Shakespeare for having created a vernacular literature that kept learned and popular traditions in touch with each other—through what Eric Auerbach, in his fine Shakespeare chapter in *Mimesis,* calls the mixture of styles *(Stilmischung)*. Philosophy is made superfluous by English and may even be harmful to the achieved organic texture of the language.

So closely is the language identified with the culture that we can talk today of "the rise of English" and know it refers to English studies. The battle, moreover, concerning the place of theory in contemporary criticism makes sense because of the bifurcation I have described, which assigns philosophy a different role in each culture. The change of terms—from philosophy to theory—reflects mainly the move away from "identity philosophy" toward its obverse: "critical theory," or a philosophy of difference, which accepts dialectics when supported by historical fact but rejects the possibility of a Hegelian synthesis. Instead of a progressive and reconciling logic, we have Theodor Adorno's "negative dialectics."[69] Instead of a theory of meaning depending on primitive roots (origins) and their derivations, we have semiotics and structuralism, with their "diacritical" understanding of the workings of language.

The relations among culture, scholarship, and criticism—how they strengthen or oppose one another—is a problem that engages the best minds in literary studies, today as well as a hundred years ago, and even as far back as the Romantics. The problem is posed in various terms, and it would be premature to claim that these terms do not matter. But when we read F. R. Leavis' observation that whoever takes education seriously today "will inevitably find himself thinking of the problem as one of resisting the bent of civilization in our time—of trying to move against the stream,"[70] we realize that Trilling's "beyond culture" has affinities with Leavis' "beyond civilization" and that both connect with the overt "critical theory" of Adorno and the Frankfurt School. Yet English style *is* marked by a distrust of speculative systems or abstract thought, which often manifests its peculiar energy by creating technical terms. To use a

45

concept from the very discourse English tradition rejects, these terms may "reify" a thinking they intend to liberate.

There are many ways in which such reification may block literary studies. For E. P. Thompson it indicates the "poverty of theory" that has never caught up with an extraordinary social achievement, the making or self-making of the English working class. Theory is still superstructure thinking, with "enormous condescension" toward the English artisan. I. A. Richards had to overcome impressionism without falling into a professionalism that would again interpose a set of special terms. He tried to get literary studies back to the texts and away from any vicarious substitute for the *experience* of those texts. For him the enemy was not philosophy (the commonsensically written *Philosophy of Rhetoric*[71] is one of his most interesting works) but a tradition—if one may call it such—of high-class gossip. The genteel though informed conversation of don and amateur is exemplified by the endless volumes of George Saintsbury— though Saintsbury, it should be added, was delightfully unpedantic, and so important to his own era. Richards changed academic criticism into "discourse"—Blackmur will nicely say "the discourse of the amateur"— by increasing the voltage of principled thought and resolutely directing it toward primary sources. Leavis went further. Wary of science, or what it does to our language, wary of learning too for the same reason, he rejected all technical philosophical thought. He did not deny that the more tacit manner he adopted had its own rationale, but he held that its extroversion would be harmful. The right tradition was already there, if complexly so; a critic simply allowed it to continue, to flow on in its own path, despite a growing corps of social engineers.

It is admirable with what consistency Leavis represents English culture as the nature we should follow. The idea of what Coleridge called the "clerisy" is full-blown in him, but now it is totally the university, not the church, that quickens and concentrates "the cultural sensibility in which tradition has its effective continuance." We cannot tell from such a sentence where central authority lies, whether in the individual sensibility or in tradition or in both; indeed, that generous indeterminacy is for Leavis the best guide to a criticism of life at the present.

But a shift has occurred that obliges us to look at nontacit "philosophical criticism." This shift is overdue, for even if we discount the prestige of philosophy in Continental Europe, we no longer can neglect (1) the emergence of the Frankfurt School in the 1930s (and its émigré presence in America in the 1940s); (2) the impact of German philosophy on French thought, from Kant and Hegel through Husserl and Heidegger; (3) the growth of a Marxist-inspired criticism among eminent academic philosophers, but also among literary personalities like Lukács, Benjamin, and Bakhtin; (4) the influence of psychoanalysis and semiotics; and (5) our own native mutterings, especially in Blackmur, Ransom, and Kenneth Burke. It is often remarkable how they anticipate burdens that are returning from abroad with exotic appeal.

The shift threatens the decorum of the conversational style, with its avoidance of explicit learning or technical terms, and which goes back to the ideal of the "honest man" *(honnête homme)* in France and to the Common Reader tradition in England. It may be that this style can be restored, that the new philosophy, which puts all in doubt, will be absorbed into a prose as remarkably free of jargon as before. But for the moment I want to emphasize what the shift involves.

Before it took place the main task of scholarship was to reconstruct a work or a period in its own terms, so that there would be no prejudgment, or we would become aware by this process of our own basic presuppositions. In this way, sensibility and judgment might be trained, and historical study would not be antiquarian.[72] Literary scholarship could and did include the question of the relevance of a recovered past to contemporary culture. Historicism and hermeneutics cooperated in this venture of reconstruction, which assumed a unity in the object of study that was findable because it had been expressed in the original tongue and could be expressed once more in a later tongue.

The shift has to do with a sense that reconstruction is not only harder than we thought but based on insufficiently analyzed preconceptions. They concern the fit or correspondence between language and meaning. Croce's identification of expression and intuition—which seemed to emphasize the presence of meaning—now seems to say the obverse: we have indeed the expression, but where is the meaning? Language is so much part of what is meant that we cannot turn it inside out to reveal some core truth. It may even make that kind of "essentialist" search for embodied meanings harder, as if only the linguistic veils existed and did not lead to an Isis-like presence behind them. This perception can also be

47

stated quasi-technically: it is often said that literary language displays a polysemy, or an excess of the signifier over the signified. The unity of the work, in any case, often described as "organic"—as if words grew naturally from some clear and prior intent—is questioned.

A brief example can make this issue less abstract. The thesis that Satan is the hero of *Paradise Lost* (Milton, Blake averred, was of the Devil's party without knowing it) suggests that even the most structured work may contain imperfectly reconciled elements. Unity lovers can argue that Satan's sympathetic prominence is a flaw or dramatic ploy that does not last beyond book 2. But those who tolerate contradiction or breaks in the code will respond quite differently. Satan or whatever he represents (and wherever *that* comes from) grabs the poet, in the way characters are said to take over the author and run the novel. This makes the author not only a manager but a medium; and what comes through, perhaps despite the author, is suprapersonal: here, an involuntary sympathy with the opposition and perhaps with the oppositional as such.

Our questioning of the unity of the work of art is not so modern as it seems. It imports an older mode of study into a new context. Throughout the nineteenth century the prestige area for philology was ballad, folk song, and other forms of vernacular oral literature. When philological research extended to the Bible, Higher Criticism was born, and instead of a unity of inspiration or composition, a multiplicity of "sources" emerged, held together by an anonymous process of compilation.

The sense that authors are compilers rather than creators is strong at present. It has brought about a sophisticated renewal of interest in medieval literature. Literary theory marries philology![73] Not quite; yet there is a sort of courtship motivated by the wish (never quite dead) to create on "objective" or "impersonal" art, the vernacular substitute for a lost classicism—with the added advantage that this art is not patrician but a "poetry of the people."

The ideological factor is not unimportant. Max Ernst claims that surrealism helped to destroy "the fairy-tale of the artist's creativity . . . western culture's last superstition." Deleuze and Guattari, defining Kafka's oppositional language as an instance of minority literature, sound strangely like the brothers Grimm when they extol the communal origin of a poetry (ballad and epos) that "sings itself." Literature, we hear, is not a "literature of masters" but "the affair of the people . . . There is no subject: there are only collective arrangements of utterance."[74] Between Grimm and Guattari the crucial scholarly event was Propp's analysis of folktales: it came out of an older philological tradition and recognized theories of folk or communal origin, "emphatic," as Gummere says, "against all poetic individuality."[75] Yet by eschewing the question of origins, Propp institutes narratology, today the most flourishing field in literary studies. It is hard to think of the structural approach without Propp and ironic that his study of popular materials founded a poetics of narrative broad enough to include the sophistication of a Proust.[76]

By questioning the unity of the work of art we are not "battering the object" (Wimsatt)[77] but questioning that object's ultimate origin in a subject—in the well-defended or enclosed individual. "Points have we all of us within our souls / Where all stand single," Wordsworth wrote of early and near traumatic experiences; yet the single point through which we try to define a work, a personality, or an epoch keeps decentering itself. This reference point, a sort of impossible *nunc stans* may always have to be posited, even if its status is called into question or described as purely theoretical. We can gain a glimpse of it insofar as it is ideological (see Paul de Man's study of Husserl and Lévi-Strauss).[78] Yet it does seem to be a constructive necessity (a point zero) rather than an immanent or ontological proprium. As such, it leads us to acknowledge the fictive or figurative element in all areas of human thought, not in art alone.

It should be clear how far we are—in theory—from Leo Spitzer's attempt to discover through an author's style his or her spiritual "etymon"[79] or from Georges Poulet's "cogito," another point from which, as from an unmediated origin, the imagined world of a writer projects.[80] Let me honor in passing these strong humanistic thinkers, at the edge of the shift being described, who did so much to show what we lose by it.

Deconstruction has made us cautious about postulating a *topos noetos* (mind place), or logocentric vantage point, from which everything would appear whole and clarified.[81] Some principle of holistic analysis may be unavoidable. Georg Lukács, after contrasting Greek harmony expressed by the epic, with modern fragmentation expressed by the novel, displaced the holistic emphasis toward a utopian sphere in *History and Class Consciousness,* where he uses it to criticize the reified, alienated character of capitalistic societies.[82] Lukács later agreed that his postulate was "idealistic"; yet it is interesting that this Winckelmannian and Hegelian notion of the balance of spirit and body or part and whole in Greek culture still finds a subtle extension in Erich Auerbach's famous essay on Odysseus' scar.[83] Not till Derrida do we see a sustained dehellenizing critique of the holistic attitude in contemporary thought.[84]

In Derrida language as concept, but also as a signifying practice, is mobilized against the logos—not only because the logos was often reduced to a neoclassical principle of *mésure,* or merely rational proportion, so that literature is called on to save imagination from abstraction, but chiefly because the logos was misrepresented in the opposite direction as the Incarnate Word, whose virtue communicates itself to the literary icon. Yet literature is not a fuller language, one in which figures begin to come true. To deconstruct is to disclose, in philosophical as well as literary writing, that "fallacy of unmediated expression" (de Man). There is no resting or reference point inside or outside language on which to set the Archimedean lever that would control the system.

Poulet and Spitzer both taught at Johns Hopkins in the 1950s (with J. Hillis Miller and Jean Starobinski as younger colleagues); and it was Johns Hopkins in addition to Yale that, by a reaction not uncommon in these matters, spear-headed the critique of logocentric literary thought. (The collections edited by Ehrmann and by Macksey and Donato situate that reaction.)[85] The 1960s, before they became politically adventurous, were a period of accelerating intellectual ferment; and though American scholars were not attuned to *theory,* they struggled in their *practice* to modify the dominance of incarnationist views of symbol and metaphor and Anglican versions of literary history. These histories accepted Eliot's view of a seventeenth-century dissociation of sensibility and described with awe and relish eighteenth-century battles against dullness, coarseness, and the rise of Romanticism.

From the perspective of the 1980s, such infighting is more than a revaluing of Romanticism. It shows how difficult it is to give up foundationalist aspirations. The compromises that guard against relativism in literature are numerous and creative. Casuistic studies appear centering on the problem of "belief" in art, just as at a later stage "intention" replaces belief as the sticking point. But even in the midst of the New

Critical idolatry of the metaphysicals and of the poetry of wit (which was said to "test" belief), Frederick Pottle insisted on historical "shifts of sensibility" that made the absolute privileging of a period or a style unscholarly.[86] Northrop Frye also wished to rise above value judgments that combated relativism and the feared encroachment of mass culture. He calls most such judgments leisure-class gossip, "the literary chit-chat which makes the reputation of poets boom and crash on an imaginary stock exchange." Acknowledging that "value-judgments are founded on the study of literature," he adds that "the study of literature can never be founded on value-judgments" and evolves "a systematic criticism as distinct from the history of taste."[87]

A hard look at Frye (abstracting him from other contexts in which his wit and generosity place him) suggests that he is influenced equally by two ideals. One is Arnold's cultural evangelism; the other is the intelligibility and teachability of science. It is the latter that interests us at this juncture. G. M. Hopkins calls rhetoric the teachable part of literature, and Frye's effort to stretch Aristotelian poetics until it covers "the verbal universe" extends not only the work of the Cambridge anthropologists but also that of the new rhetorical studies associated with such different scholarly personalities as William Empson, Kenneth Burke, Edgar Stoll, Ruth Wallerstein, Rosamund Tuve, and Walter Ong. The work of European scholars from Eduard Norden to E. R. Curtius and Heinrich Lausberg should also be mentioned. The list could easily swell out of proportion. Together with the rise of Czech and Russian Formalism,[88] this wave of rhetorical scholars contributed in their way to a "science of literature" created by the synchronic method of semiotics and the general field theory of Jakobson and Lévi-Strauss, who unified the *sciences humaines* under the banner of a radiant linguistics and stimulated some of the most influential primers of applied rhetorical criticism today, by Tzvetan Todorov and Gérard Genette.

With his taxonomic genius, Frye—unafraid of terms of art and rejoicing (like Kenneth Burke) in their inventiveness—helped to establish an English "science of literature" without the onus of the name. Pottle too promulgated a scientific ideal as part of a *methodological* relativism enabling the unpartisan description of shifts of taste. Frye's concept of science is more difficult to extract, but it seems to involve a *methodological antirelativism*. If value judgments are indeed founded on the study of literature, and the *Anatomy* is a study of literature, then the *Anatomy* is also a study of what founds value judgments. But here a shift occurs from the subject of study (literature) to the system of study (criticism). This is basically the shift we have already described, and it elides the problem posed by historicism: the pressure that historicism's multiple perspective, its relativism, exerts on value judgments. Value is quietly invested in the system of study itself. Criticism, according to Frye, seeks "a unified structure of knowledge, as other sciences do."[89]

Scholarship has done its work only too well. We know that civilizations are mortal, that they have bibles or divine charters, that non-Western thought is linguistically and taxonomically fascinating, that the West has an imperialistic intellect that can appropriate anything. Perhaps we deserve the dilemma of affluence that makes us more restless than Ahasuerus. We wander from territory to territory seeking new sacred books, new classics, new revelations of the vernacular, in feminist criticism, in Afro-American scholarship, among the Bororo or the American Indians. Whatever is unknown must be discovered and represented. An absence of authorized mediations is compensated by a multiplicity of virtual mediations.

Yet how similar this situation is to that of radical thinkers a hundred or even two hundred years ago! The return to origins, a reversal of the *translatio studii* or Western gradient of culture, remains the same. It is not as fixed on the East; it tends to be nativist. Yet both types of return are found from Vico on. Vico uncovered the vernacular roots, as it were, of Roman law. His "dark italics" influenced not only a new philosophy of history (and, with Auerbach, of humanistic studies) but an ambitious epic of humanity culminating in Hugo's *Légende des siècles*. Closer to our time, the Cambridge anthropologists (Frazer, Harrison, Murry, Weston) broadened the base of classical studies and recovered the outlines of a primal sacred romance or drama. Eliot's *Waste Land* and Frye's *Anatomy* are indebted to their scholarly visions. And is not feminist criticism seeking to modify high culture by a reversal of patriarchy and the discovery of a more authentic East (as in Bachofen) or native origin? Commenting on the Romantic ballad revival, Herder says that poetry is the mother tongue of mankind. Feminist writers extend this search for a mother tongue, a true vernacular.[90]

There are differences too. Hölderlin's passage east, his quest for originality or "fire from heaven," is still expressed in terms of an imitation of the ancients *(Bildung* through *Nachbildung)*. The character of their greatness—or how a modern poet might appropriate it—was the only issue.[91] Yet as our literary universe becomes centrifugal and decanonized, as our awareness of intertextuality grows, we find ourselves dealing not with the classic work of art but with the classic case, with norms that emerge from a bewildering mass of historical variants only through a skillfully applied criticism. The classic case, then, is very much a construct displaying intelligibility rather than verity.

Criticism, says Barthes, the dialogue between author and commentator, is not homage to a fixed, recoverable truth but "a construction of the intelligibility of our time."[92] From an Enlightenment point of view, such intelligibility is not only necessary but good: it dispels mystification but allows us to reason together. Continental thinkers, who have experienced close up the effects of systematic lying in the form of propaganda, hold a double view on this matter: Barthes's definition of criticism is not entirely happy with itself. It wards off fundamentalism and the political or fanatic return to origins. But it acknowledges that intelligibility is a culture-bound standard. Art as a signifying practice remains free as well as bound. Under certain circumstances it may even become a "discours de la folie" revealing that the *aliénés,* including Freud's Schreber, are unorthodox critics. They go beyond culture but not beyond language: what they do remains "discourse." Thus, in ways that cannot be predicted, though they can be studied, art exhibits human freedom even when it discloses human unfreedom. Sartre analyzes and denounces authors like Mauriac who manipulate their characters, just as he insists in *What Is Literature?* on the mutual generosity that should prevail between writer and reader.[93]

When Bakhtin demonstrates the polyphonic character of the novel, which makes it impossible to reduce Dostoevsky's writings to a single authorial point of view[94] (one might compare Wayne Booth's demand for intelligibility based on just such a reduction),[95] we again sense an identification of art with freedom against a background of unfreedom—the disunity of life, its fragmented perspectives. Bakhtin exposes a constitutive unintelligibility in the modern novel, corresponding to a "dialogic principle" in human relations. But can we tolerate such ambiguity, such unresolved diversity, without structures of domination or dialectic? Kenneth Burke's analysis of Hitler's *Mein Kampf* is a model study of propagandistic rhetoric as it imposes its "sinister unifying."[96]

Philosophical criticism, Continental style, is agreed that the attempt to link art with freedom—or to see it as an antidote to propaganda and, in more common situations, to "practical language"—cannot fall back without modification on the idea of creative genius or the autonomous subject. Here Saussure's concept of *langue*,[97] Lacan's modification of American ego psychology,[98] and Marxist critiques of the subject as an interiorized fetish join the theory of cultural mediation, or what is often known as "intertextuality." The term is useful—and I have used it—but it is not inevitable. Even "cultural mediation" has problems: it suggests only that we cannot go beyond culture, not that the idea of culture should be contrasted with social reality. Culture in the narrow sense could be the ideology of an elite, as culture in the broad sense (mass culture: the spectacle of everyday life, sport, stars, life-style) could be the anonymous ideology of the bourgeoisie, also highly encoded, though seeking to appear natural and spontaneous, the opposite of art. The assumption in this kind of analysis—strongly associated with Barthes (first in *Mythologies*)—is that there is another way of facing reality, a truly natural way not distorted by the downwardly mobile myths (*gesunkenes Kulturgut*) of high culture. Marxist theorists invest that natural energy in the proletariat, which should produce its own culture; Barthes is content to remain hygienically antibourgeois.

I have said that we should not neglect philosophical criticism. To do so is to deny a verbal zodiac our time has entered. Another terminology, sometimes textuality, is being evolved; a testing takes place that only gradually exhausts or transforms itself. (In Barthes's *Lover's Discourse*,[99] the metalanguages of scholarship and theory are already being resynthesized into art. The prose of this pleasurable text is drawn from the special dictions that wished to succeed it.)[100] We should know the new terms; we do not have to think in them. But if we think them through, at some point the difference between Continental and Anglo-American criticism evaporates. Writing about Blake, Eliot states the problem of cultural mediation as trenchantly as anyone after him.

> It is important that the artist should be highly educated in his own art; but his education is one that is hindered rather than helped by the ordinary

processes of society which constitute education for the ordinary man. For these processes consist largely in the acquisition of impersonal ideas which obscure what we really are and feel, what we really want, and what really excites our interest. It is of course not the actual information acquired, but the conformity which the accumulation of knowledge is apt to impose, that is harmful.[101]

Blake was a nonconformist all right. "He was naked, and saw man naked, and from the center of his own crystal."[102] Yet Eliot also recognizes the disadvantage of that nakedness, which made Blake fashion his own system, so as not to be enslaved by another man's. "Blake did not have that more Mediterranean gift of form which knows how to borrow as Dante borrowed his theory of the soul; he must needs create a philosophy as well as a poetry."[103] The defect is not Blake's alone but also Milton's, because of the relative discontinuity of religious history in Britain.

The local divinities of Italy were not wholly exterminated by Christianity, and they were not reduced to the dwarfish fate which fell upon our trolls and pixies. The latter, with the major Saxon deities, were perhaps no great loss in themselves, but they left an empty place; and perhaps our mythology was further impoverished by the divorce from Rome. Milton's celestial and infernal regions are large but insufficiently furnished apartments filled by heavy conversation; and one remarks about the Puritan mythology an historical thinness. And about Blake's supernatural territories, as about the supposed ideas that dwell there, we cannot help commenting on a certain meanness of culture.[104]

This passage is remarkable because it links literary form and texture to a national culture seen as a reflection of religious history. Its emphasis, however, on the superiority of Roman religion and Mediterranean culture is condescending. Eliot's view, moreover, on Blake's relation to popular imagery needs the correction of E. P. Thompson. Frye too corrects Eliot by showing that Blake is much more than a *bricoleur;* he terrifies not only because of his honesty but also because of the "fearful symmetry" or "total form" that articulates his poetry as minutely as does any borrowed medieval system.

What Eliot stigmatizes as Milton's *heavy conversation* is really a last line of resistance—from within a poetry conscious of its sublimity—to the coming dominance of the prosaic. An urbane prose will supervene, eschewing terms of art and heavy rhetoric, and which Eliot himself continues. I will explore this prose in Chapter 2. Yet Eliot defines the issues with accuracy and with more economy than most kinds of philosophical criticism. His economy has another side, however. Despite an early interest in philosophy, Eliot will not or cannot make use of it as a method or a frame. What he finds missing in Blake he himself lacks almost as much. The culture of criticism in England has a philosophical thinness that essays by Sartre, Ortega, Benjamin, Adorno, and Burke never display. The fact is that Eliot, like Leavis after him, and most English critics to this day continue to "erect their impressions into laws" (Rémy de Gourmont), and in so doing allow the impressions to resist those laws. It is the most complicated game in town: seeking authority, impersonality, and intelligibility, while monitoring the cost.

Tea and Totality

In almost every order of discourse there has been a call at one time or another for a higher seriousness. We are asked to pursue "some graver subject" or a more exacting style. The call may come, as in Milton or Keats, from within the poet's sense of a vocation spurred on by exemplary forebears: the reputed career of Virgil, for example, who left the oaten pipe of pastoral and playful song for the pursuit of didactic verse in his farmer's manual *The Georgics,* which is climaxed in turn by the trumpets stern of his epic *Aeneid,* which deals with a warrior become culture-bearer. This call for a higher style or a graver subject has also burdened philosophy. However diverse their mode, in Husserl, Heidegger, and Wittgenstein the ideal of rigor besets what with a phrase from Spenser's proem to the *Faerie Queene* we may term their "afflicted style."

It is not otherwise in literary criticism. Grave it certainly is, and didactic, so that the formalist or playful thinker who does not justify his enterprise by appealing to theory or science is not considered worthwhile. The real terror we have experienced, and are still experiencing, produces a pressure on our purposes that is itself not unterroristic. "A theory of culture," George Steiner writes in *Bluebeard's Castle,* "an analysis of our present circumstances, which do not have at their pivot a consideration of the modes of terror that brought on the death, through war, starvation, and deliberate massacre, of some seventy million human beings in Europe and Russia, between the start of the first World War and the end of the second, seems to me irresponsible."[1]

Steiner is right in refusing to neglect a haunting and intractable catastrophe. But as we read his appeal from a book that asks with anguish why

European high culture could not stem Nazi barbarism, we wonder how far even a relevant "theory" would take us. It would remain an interpretation; it would raise the further question of how interpretations acquire the force to change anything. The sincere thinker, moreover, need not be the effective one: men and women of conscience may unwittingly trivialize a subject by becoming obsessed with it. At a time when the air is as full of strident sounds as it was once of fairy folk, the question of what kind of seriousness our discipline may claim, or what sort of style might best convey it, is more troublesome than ever. The purpose of literary commentary cannot be simply amplifying the clichés of our predicament.

Some question of style has always existed. Literature, we are told, should please or move as well as teach. Rhetoric has forensic and religious roots, however cognitively developed. Our culture depends on formalized arts of verbal exchange, which have their rules and limits, as in an adversarial court system and a parliamentary mode of debate; and they determine what is evidence rather than what is truth. They may even put obstacles in the way of those who think they know the truth, for we do not live with each other in an unmediated relation but in a strongly rhetoricized world where verbal and stylistic choices must constantly be made.

Yet just as logic tries to escape or purify rhetoric, so literary criticism too has tried to control words or else recall them to their direct, most referential function. It may seem strange to admit that the literary critic is often no friendlier to imaginative literature than the logician. In this self-deputized censor, the critic, there is love-hate rather than friendship; and recently this passionate engagement has tended to sort itself out in a schizoid way. The drift toward the extreme in modern art is so strong that it is not, on the whole, resisted. The resistance comes when a critic breaches the ramparts of decorum and modifies the language of literary criticism itself.

For that language has remained as unpretentious as possible. Critics, after all, should be critical, and fend off inflated rhetoric, faked authority, and indigest foreignness. Suspicious of their love for literature, they are even more suspicious of the literary element in themselves. They are sober people who shield themselves from contamination by the hygiene of their practice. Their tone is nicely aggressive and their nasty conservatism is great fun after the fact—however pernicious and parochial it may have been in its own time.

How many know of Stuart Sherman's attack on H. L. Mencken in a book called *Americans*? His essay is entitled "Mr. Mencken, the *Jeune Fille* and the New Spirit in Letters"; and the *jeune fille* clearly plays the same role for Sherman as the young corruptible student does for Denis Donoghue, who worries about creative critics inciting their disciples to dithyrambs instead of dissertations. Here is one of Sherman's sallies:

> The *jeune fille* . . . feels within herself . . . an exhilarating chaos, a fluent welter . . . She revels in the English paradoxes and mountebanks, the Scandinavian misanthropes, the German egomaniacs, and, above all, in the later Russian novelists, crazy with war, taxes, anarchy, vodka, and German philosophy . . . Lured by a primitive instinct to the sound of animals roving, she ventures a curious foot in the fringes of the Dreiserian wilderness vast and drear; and barbaric impulses in her blood answer the wail of the forest . . . Imagine a thousand *jeunes filles* thus wistful, and you have the conditions ready for the advent of a new critic. At this point enters at a hard gallop, spattered with mud, H. L. Mencken high in oath . . . He leaps from the saddle with sabre flashing, stables his horse in the church, shoots the priest, hangs the professors, exiles the Academy, burns the library and the university, and, amid the smoking ashes, erects a new school of criticism on modern German principles.[2]

Sherman has some reason to be apprehensive of the Germanizing spirit in literary studies: unfortunately even his name sounded as if a German were pronouncing "German." He wanted to save America from the Saxon in Anglo-Saxon.[3] What a paradox that the *jeune fille* would not prefer the delicacy of the French tradition which has named her type to the Carlylese coarseness of Mencken. Sherman intends the *jeune fille* to read Sainte-Beuve rather than Nietzsche, though he concludes that Mencken's style, "hard, pointed, forcible, cocksure," might substitute for a stiff freshman course in rhetoric and remove the softer forms of "slush" and "pishposh" from her mind.

It is clearly not only Mencken's macho manners (Sherman's are nothing to boast of) which cause the offense. As today, there is a struggle going on to define the American spirit in its true independence. There is, further, a struggle over what democracy means in education. Finally, there is a near-physical disgust at German philosophizing as an idiom that could infect our entire verbal constitution. How would Sherman react, now that even philosophers in the Romance languages have succumbed to the Germanizing style? Sartre, Lévi-Strauss, Lacan, Foucault, Derrida, Kristeva, Althusser—where may delicacy and true aesthetic feeling be found?

I have been dealing with prejudices about style rather than with particular philosophical issues. Critics in the Anglo-American tradition are arbiters of taste, not developers of ideas. Their type of judiciousness is almost always linked to a strong sense for the vernacular, more precisely, to the idealization of the vernacular as an organic medium, a language of nature that communicates ideas without the noise or elaboration of extraverted theory. To argue too much about what is deeply English or American means one has to acknowledge the outside; and being inside— an insider—is what counts. Perhaps this assumption of inwardness can be laid to every nationalism. Acculturated, one secretes one's culture. Yet unself-consciousness or antiself-consciousness, however attractive it may be, is surely a limitation rather than expansion of the critical spirit. In the Anglophile tradition, the critical spirit, as it approaches Mencken's gallop, is suspected of being a modern form of enthusiasm as dangerous as the dogmatic spirit it displaced.

This suspicion of the critical spirit reaches an English high in the most influential of modern arbiters: T. S. Eliot. Such pronouncements, especially, as "From Poe to Valéry" and *Notes towards the Definition of Culture* are urbane exercises to limit criticism in the name of culture. It is symptomatic that the epigraph on the title page of *Notes* is taken from the *OED* and reads: "DEFINITION: 1. The setting of bounds; limitation (rare)— 1483." This conservative scrutiny of words, which communicates itself even to strong epigones like Trilling (just as Heidegger's etymological virtuosity turns up in Derrida), causes Eliot to say that rescuing the word *culture* is "the extreme of my ambition."

I come then to the extreme of *my* ambition. It is to understand what happened to English criticism in the period of roughly 1920 to 1950, when a "teatotaling" style developed in academic circles despite so many marvelous and often idiosyncratic talents, from Eliot himself to Richards, Empson, Leavis, and (in America) Trilling.

Now what happened is that, in a sense, nothing happened. An order of discourse strove hard to remain a discourse of order. The happening was all on the side of art and literature; and the courage of the critic lay in acknowledging the newness or forwardness of modernist experiments. Compared to his own *Waste Land*, Eliot's essays are prissy. Compared to the novels of Lawrence, Leavis' revaluations are cultic gestures, precise elliptical movements charged with significance for the one who has truly read. Criticism is asked to exhibit an ideal decorum, to show that despite the stress of class antagonism, national disunity, and fragmentation, concepts of order are still possible.

In adopting this demeanor English commentators followed an ingrained tradition. They took no solace from the notion of a science or a theory of literature: that was the Continental way, leading from Dilthey to Lukács, and then increasingly to reflections inspired by Marxism and structuralism. The English classical writer, even when the stakes were high, wished to please rather than teach, and to remind rather than instruct. This critical tradition, keeping its distance from sacred but also from learned commentary, sought to purify the reader's taste and the national language, and so addressed itself to peers or friends—in short, to a class of equally cultured people.

The highest recommendation of such criticism was the artfulness of its accommodation. Richards' *The Philosophy of Rhetoric* is as careful of its audience as Ruskin's *Sesame and Lilies*. It is not philosophy as Lukács, Adorno, Heidegger, or Benjamin practiced it, who can leave ordinary language behind or beat it into surprising shapes. I emphasize these writers in German not because they had no choice but precisely because they did have a choice: namely, German classical prose as it culminated in Goethe, and still provided Freud with a style that made his science accessible.

The "friendship style" (as I tend to name this accommodated and classical prose) has political as well as sentimental ramifications. Writers in the later eighteenth century can talk of a "republic of letters," and Keats of a "freemasonry of spirits." Indeed, in Matthew Arnold the idea of culture moves to oppose the idea of class: culture, he said, exists to do away with classes. Even if the audience addressed in the friendship style may be as provisional and uncertain as Addison's and Steele's was when they published *The Spectator*, the guiding fiction is that all the members of this society correspond on equal footing. They are "lettered"; and in terms of style there is an attempt to erase from their demeanor the "patronage style," that is, a vacillation between exaggerated modesty and extreme gravity, between presenting oneself as "all too mean" and all too manic. The friendship style cancels the disparity between the social class of the writer and his transcendent subject matter or ambition.[4]

Criticism, then treads lightly: its prose can be savage, but only when affronted by pedantry or the self-inflated nonsense of other writers. From the time of the neoclassical movement in seventeenth-century France, it was a form of good conversation, a discourse among equals. This speakeasy quality still joins *The Spectator* to *The New York Review of Books*, which is notorious for using Anglos. Only in Germany, and then after Hegel—when an attempt is made to separate the *Geisteswissenschaften* ("moral" or "human" sciences) from the natural sciences—is literary criticism burdened by ideas of *Bildung* and *Aufbau*, as if it had at once to anticipate and survive "absolute spirit." (So Dilthey's Berlin Academy lectures of 1905–1910, coinciding with Lukács' literary prentice years, were entitled "Der Aufbau der geschichtlichen Welt in den Geisteswissenschaften" [The construction of the historical world in the human sciences]. Yet even after the First World War, when Lukács published his *Theory of the Novel* (1920), then *History and Class Consciousness* (1923)—works whose emphasis on "totality" may be said to have inaugurated the philosophical type of criticism that was to dominate France as well as Germany—even in that postwar decade the radical editor A. R. Orage *(The New Age)* would caution Herbert Read in words that reflect the decorum of Anglo-French criticism, whose pattern-book was Sainte-Beuve's *Causeries*. "Not articles," Orage advises Read, "but causeries." "Beware of the valueless business that insists on *essay* in place of causerie. 'Everything divine runs on light feet.' "[5]

If we take the position, itself a literary one, that how we say it is as important as what we say, then the contrast that developed between English and Continental types of discourse should not be disregarded. There is no need to insist that one style must be used for every situation; and there may well be a mingling of tones, sometimes uneasy, in the best critics. But the contrast between "tea" and "totality" is too striking to be evaded by mere habits of tolerance.

Let me recapitulate my argument so far. The great virtue of the English, Basil de Selincourt said in the 1920s, is their unconsciousness. And Goethe remarked of Byron: "All Englishmen are as such devoid of inwardness [*eigentliche Reflexion*]; distraction and party spirit do not allow them to achieve a quiet development. But they are imposing as a practical people."[6] I do not quote these statements to malign a critical tradition but to point out a paradox in it that should make us wary of its practical emphasis. So deliberate an unconsciousness tends to quiet the real unconscious. It does so, Goethe suggests, by diverting the mind from spiritual to practical matters. And when we think of the contemporary situation in the United States, who will cast the first stone? Talent is taking refuge in business schools, law schools, and computer science; and *eigentliche Reflexion,* even when it appears, as in certain types of philosophic criticism, is denounced as navel-gazing or mandarinism.

The dominance of review essay and expository article reflects in a general way the self-delimitation of practical criticism in America and England. Though these forms of commentary serve primary texts, they now claim to teach rather than preach. And to teach as unself-consciously as possible. "Culture is the one thing that we cannot deliberately aim at," Eliot remarks in his *Notes* on culture. The intrusion of large questions involving religion or philosophy puts the exegete at risk; not because such questions are unimportant but because they are so very important. The practical is defined as the teachable rather than as "lived religion" (Eliot) or the *Umwelt* of "birth-death-existence-decision-communication with others." Paul Ricoeur, author of this rather Germanic sentence, associates "preaching" with such a "totality" as it informs every effort to articulate what we know. Preaching, he emphasizes, invades all good teaching; and teaching that claims to be method rather than discourse—that claims to be a purely objective mode of questioning or communication—has not understood anything about theory, or the domain of preunderstanding.[7]

My own purpose is more modest than to rethink the relation of teaching and preaching, although it seems obvious enough that great preaching did not reject ordinary language, but through the mode of parable, for example, or Swift's "attacking play" (C. J. Rawson) produced a strange intersection of ordinary and extraordinary conversation. My purpose is to reconstruct historically the provenance and character of the classical style in criticism, which has now become the teatotaling style. With a book like Denis Donoghue's *Ferocious Alphabets* we are, in terms of argument, not far from Maugham's summing up of the tradition he embodies. "To like good prose is an affair of good manners. It is, unlike verse, a civil art." To understand why alternate and challenging styles have developed in the last half-century one must first value an older prose that was at once classic and journalistic.

I begin by stating the obvious: a battle of styles as well as books broke out in the seventeenth century, from which came the clarified expository and journalistic medium we relish today. The Royal Society in England as well as the French Academy played an important role in the spread of this purified style. In America it gradually took hold against the "fantastic school" represented by such forceful theological writers as Cotton Mather. Mather intended to humble the understanding, to make it aware of its "imbecility" by a contagious parody of impotent speculative maneuvers adorned with puns and quibbles. In Mather it is sometimes hard to tell whether his display of learning and parascientific knowledge is a genuine attempt to "solve the phenomena" by elevating the mind toward the wonders and riddles of the universe (that "totality" which mere tea-drinkers can never taste) or whether it is not a subversive manifestation of fallible wit in even the most splendid of bookworms. Whatever the truth, Mather knew his style was questionable, and in his handbook for the ministry, the *Manuductio* published in 1726, he defends himself as follows:

> There has been a great deal of ado about a STYLE; So much that I must offer you my Sentiments upon it. There is a *Way of Writing* wherein the author endeavours, that the Reader may have *something to the Purpose* in every Paragraph. There is not only a *Vigour* sensible in every *Sentence* but the Paragraph is embellished with *Profitable References*, even to something beyond what is *directly spoken* . . . The Writer pretends not unto *Reading*, yet he could not have writ as he does if he had not *Read* very much in his Time; and his Composures are not only a *Cloth of Gold*, but also stuck with as many *Jewels*, as the Gown of a Russian Embassador. This *Way of Writing* has been decried by many, and is at this Day more than ever so . . . But, however

Fashion and *Humour* may prevail, they must not think that the Club at their *Coffee-House* is, *All the World* . . . After all, Every Man will have his own Style, which will distinguish him as much as his *Gate* [gait].

It was indeed the coffeehouses mentioned by Mather that played a certain role in producing the new, chastened prose; and except for the exigencies of alliteration, I might have entitled this essay "Coffee and Totality." In the sober yet convivial atmosphere of the coffeehouses news and gossip were exchanged, and the literati conversed on equal footing. As Socrates brought philosophy down from the heavens into the marketplace, so Addison and Steele insinuated it into these bourgeois places of leisure, less exclusive than clubs yet probably as effective in transacting business in a casual setting. I am no sociologist, however, and do not want to ascribe too much to either tea or coffee. In the pleasant spirit of generalization adapted from the English sphere one might say it was in these sociable places that "theories" were tested, that the conversational habit became the opium of the intellectual, and a lucid, unpedantic form of prose developed. It is in this era too that the English tradition modifies both the scientific and the French demand for a univocal and universal language by appealing to the mingled force of a middle or epistolary style. More exactly, by appealing to the symbiosis, rather than clash, of learned and vernacular traditions, a symbiosis that had previously characterized English poetry, even if the results were as different as Spenser and Shakespeare. The mingled style develops into the ideal of unaffected conversation, in which something is held in reserve and solicits reader or listener. It intends to provoke a reply rather than to dazzle, and it subordinates ingeniousness to the *ingenium* of natural wit. Such an ideal naturalizes rather than banishes Latinity, or seeks an equivalent in English to the philosophic ease of Plato's Greek. "It is straight from Plato's lips, as if in natural conversation," Pater will write, "that the language came in which the mind has ever since been discoursing with itself, in that inward dialogue which is the 'active principle' of the dialectic method" (*Plato and Platonism*, 1896).[8]

The triumph of modern English, though not quite yet of modern American, is anticipated by this ideal of criticism as an extended conversation, civilizing difficult ideas without falling back into gossip or opinionation. That criticism as a causerie may have had its origin in French circles of the seventeenth century, that it was formalized and even patented by Sainte-Beuve (so much so that Proust, closer to Pater, wrote an *Against Sainte-Beuve*), does not make it less attractive to the British. It is true that many intermediary developments should be taken into account, such as the nervy style of Hazlitt; and that even in recent times the grip of the causerie has not gone unchallenged. Many writers between 1920 and 1950 try to make criticism more professional. They feel its dandyish or donnish character, and they signal a return to the vernacularist movement in Puritan England, which intended to "ratifie and settle" English as the national language. "It is more facil," George Snell wrote in 1649, "by the eie of reason, to see through the *Medium*, and light of the English tongue; then by the more obscure light of anie forreign language . . . to learn unknown arts and terms."[9] Yet both in journalism and in the university the following basic features of genteel criticism kept their hold.

It should be neither utilitarian as in business, nor abstract as in pure science, nor highly specialized as in scholarship. These types of discourse are allowed in only when dressed down, reduced to a witty gentility first attributed to the "honest man" (*honnête homme*) in seventeenth-century French culture—a person, that is, whose rank or profession could not be discerned when he talked in polite society. When a cultured person writes or converses, you cannot tell his profession or background because, as La Rochefoucauld said, "il ne se pîque de rien." Or, to quote from the definition of the *honnête homme* given by the *Dictionary* of the French Academy, his demeanor is that of "un galant homme, homme de bonne conversation, de bonne compagnie," that is, "a courteous man, a good conversationalist and interesting to be with."

Certainly an appealing ideal, for today we are even less able to talk in a nonspecialized manner. The art of conversation has not improved. But if it has not, perhaps the older ideal was the wrong way of democratizing discourse or limiting pedantry and snobbery. Without the conversational style (still practiced in Oxbridge tutorials) our situation might be worse; yet it must be said that those who presently uphold the art of criticism as conversation too often stifle intellectual exchange. The conversational decorum has become a defensive mystique for which "dialectic" and even "dialogue" (in Plato's or Gadamer's or Bakhtin's strong sense) are threatening words.

In Pater the conversational ideal is the last refuge of a neoclassical decorum striving to maintain the mask of a unified sensibility. Yet it is merely a mask. Pater holds onto the beautiful soul, the *schöne Seele*. It is time to try something else.

What might that be? It is hardly surprising that English studies should resist the influx of a French *discours* heavily indebted to post-Hegelian German philosophy. Tea and totality don't mix. Something should eventually grow from within the English tradition, even if the pressure comes from without. Richards and Empson certainly made a beginning; and criticism did become more principled, more aware of the complex structure of assigning meaning and making a literary judgment. But the problem of style remained, that is, of communicating in colloquial form the theory or methodology developed. Today George Steiner and Frank Kermode are among the few successful translators of technical or speculative ideas into an idiom familiar to the university don brought up "before the flood." Yet it might be said that they are superb reviewers rather than an originative thinkers: their vocation is the Arnoldian diffusion of ideas and not a radical revision or extension of knowledge.

We seem to have reached an impasse. What alternatives are there to the conversational style if we grant its necessity as a *pedagogical* rather than *social* matter? Yet this shift of perspective, however slight, indicates that such a style is useful rather than ideal, and no more "natural" than other kinds. We know, moreover, that pedagogical tools can become merely tools: "instrumental reason," as the Frankfurt School calls it, may affect language by homogenizing it. The critic who uses the conversational style because of its propriety may actually be doing a disservice to language. However difficult Blackmur, Burke, Heidegger, or Derrida may be, there is less entropy in them than in those who translate, with the best intentions, hazardous ideas or expressions into ordinary speech. Kermode's translative skill is great; one admires how rebarbative concepts from German hermeneutics or French semiotics steal into the English idiom, but something can leak away.

We have accepted difficulty in art, but in criticism there is still a wish to "solve the phenomena." The irony and intricacy of art were fully described, not resolved, by the New Criticism; nevertheless, a sort of pedagogical illusion arose that codified the language of explication and exempted it from the very analysis it so carefully applied to art. It is not surprising, therefore, to find that Paul de Man's *Blindness and Insight* (1971) is subtitled "Essays in the Rhetoric of Contemporary Criticism." In the aggressively modern thinkers he takes up, de Man was concerned to show traces of a "Hellenic" ideal of embodiment that continued to privilege categories of presence and plenitude.[10] What was passed over, according to de Man, was the "temporal labyrinth of interpretation" with its purely negative kind of totality (Sartre had coined the phrase *totalité détotalisé*). But now, some twenty years later—these de Man essays were written in the 1960s—the situation has changed. It is no longer a pseudoclassical notion of *paidea* that needs scrutiny but a para-Marxist and utopian notion of pedagogy.

I mean by that a "dream of communication" that looks not only toward the transparence of the text or the undistorted transmission of messages from sender (writer) to receiver (reader) but also toward a social system that is supposed to create that language-possibility instead of merely enforcing it. Yet everything we have learned from politics or pragmatics has put the dream of communication in doubt. It is an ever-receding horizon like Hegel's state, where subject and substance, real and rational, concrete and universal, coincide. That end-state remains a *topos noetos*, a heaven in the form of a horizon, a glimpse of totality that converts every end into a means and so proves to be the moving principle it sought to arrest. Every style (stile) is also a Gate, to put with Mather; but a style is at once open and closed.

Developments in criticism since about 1920 show that language can be analyzed more closely than was deemed possible, but not purified by prescriptions arising from the analysis. The intimate alliance of writing with "difference" we find in Derrida, and such typical assertions that "language is the *rupture* with totality itself . . . primarily the caesura makes meaning emerge," are symptomatic of a cautious attitude toward both theory and the dream of communication. "The theory of the Text," Barthes has said, "can coincide only with a practise of writing." We are now as aware of our language condition as of the condition of our language.

Derrida is important also because he exposes the privilege accorded to voice in the form of the conversational style as it aspires to Pater's "inward dialogue." Derrida's deconstruction of course does not target a specific historical style but the dream of communication which that style, as the proprium of all styles, underwrites. The columns of *Glas* are cut by the arbitrary "justification" of the margins and the edginess of pages that interrupt, like a caesura, the words. *Glas* becomes a stylish reprisal against style—that word whose *y grecque* was hellenized into it during the Renaissance. Derrida rescues style from its confusion with Greek *stulos*, column, and so recovers its link both with stiletto, a pointed weapon, and *stiglus* or *stigma* that emphasize cutting, pointing, branding. Style is in fact short for *vertere stilum*, or turning the incising stylus to its blunt side, which was used to erase the impression made on waxed tablets; writing stylishly is thus to erase what is written and write over it.[11] The term "verse" takes up the other half of that phrase, as in Wordsworth's "the turnings intricate of verse"—although the metaphor accrues overtones of the turning earth, the turning of the plow, and so forth. Style is what cannot stand still.

I want to add a few remarks on a philosopher's recent attempt to introduce the conversational style once more. This attempt is a valiant throwback to the Age of Hume, when the conversationalists had won out, at least in prose. Yet philosophy remained under the imperative of not entirely forsaking the quest for a universal and immutable discourse. It honored the conversational mode for its virtues of social accommodation. It was philosophy for the salon. But subversively so, if we recall that it led to such strange conversation as *La Philosophie dans le boudoir*, which put nature out of countenance. The contemporary post-Wittgensteinian attempt to revive the conversational ethos and to use it as a critique of foundationalist perspectives in philosophy is that of Richard Rorty.

Rorty's *Philosophy and the Mirror of Nature* (1978) examines three modern thinkers who have had an immense influence on both professional and nonprofessional philosophers. The careers of Wittgenstein, Heidegger, and Dewey are taken to be exemplary. Each began with a project to make philosophy "foundational," that is, to discover a basis for distinguishing truth from falsity, science from speculation, and verifiable representation from mere appearance. Each of the three breaks free of this project (labeled as "epistemological" and "Kantian") so that their work becomes therapeutic rather than constructive, or, as Rorty also likes to say, "edifying" (in the secular sense of the adjective, that conveys the German idea of *Bildung*) rather than systematic. Indeed they warn us

69

against the very temptations acceded to in their earlier, scientific phase. Rorty ends with a section entitled "Philosophy in the Conversation of Mankind," alluding to Michael Oakeshott's well-known "The Voice of Poetry in the Conversation of Mankind," published in *Rationalism and Politics* (1975). He latches onto the idea of "conversation," which suggests an alternative to the rigorous terminology and analytic pretensions of epistemological inquiry. Contemporary issues in philosophy, he writes, are "events in a certain stage of conversation—a conversation which once knew nothing of these issues and may know nothing of them again." And he distinguishes between treating philosophy as a "voice in a conversation" on the one hand, and treating it "as a subject, a *Fach,* a field of professional inquiry," on the other. This denial of a special field to philosophers has an attractive Emersonian ring, and of course brings Plato back as our most edifying thinker. Yet Rorty stops short of exalting even Plato, mainly because "the conversation Plato began has been enlarged by more voices than Plato would have dreamed possible."

This conclusion is surprisingly close to what recent literary critics have wished for. They take back from philosophy what is their own; they are tired of being treated as camp followers of this or that movement in philosophy. When the privilege accorded to science spills over into philosophy, literary culture is considered a dilution of ideas originated by stronger heads, a crude and subjective application of those ideas. Literary critics are then deemed parasitic not only vis-à-vis creative poem or novel but also vis-à-vis exact philosophy. Their very attempt to think independently, intensely, theoretically, is denounced—often by other literary critics. They are said to be big with the "arrogance of theory" and accused of emulating a discipline that should be kept out of the fair fields of literary study. "Whereas a generation ago," we read in an issue of *Novel,* "fine American literary journals would devote complete issues to a Hardy, Yeats, Faulkner, or G. M. Hopkins, current journals devote whole issues to French professors." The complainant goes on to charge that it was Northrop Frye's insistence on criticism as a systematic subject that allowed the "pod-people, so many of them dropouts from technical philosophy, or linguistics, or the half-science of sociology, into the fair fields of Anglo-American literary study."

However comforting it is to have a philosopher like Rorty on one's side, and to have him appreciate the recognitive as well as cognitive function of words, a hard question must be put. Can Rorty's position do more than redress the balance between philosophy and literary studies by demystifying the scientistic streak in modern thought? Can it disclose also something substantive in literary study itself, as the distance between philosophical discourse and literary commentary is lessened by viewing both as "conversation"?

The term "conversation" is a metaphor. It slides over the question of style. Should we really name something "conversation" when it is written? There is "dialogue" of course; but Rorty's concept does not wish to be dependent on a formal or stylized exchange between persons. Perhaps he would say that all writing is internalized conversation, a select polyphony of voices. The problem is not adequately treated from a literary point of view; nor entirely from a philosophical point of view. Is Rorty arguing that thinking is possible in idiomatic language without special terms or neologisms? Or is he saying that noncolloquial language also, even when it seems harsh and abstract, as so often in Kant and Husserl— in all such Teuton-Titans—is figurative or inventive despite itself? Does he not in fact circle around two claims: that technical terms (which diverge from so-called ordinary language) are necessary for rigorous thinking; but also that ordinary language—vernacular, conversational— is more inventive or figurative than the language of abstruse, systematic thought?

To these challenges there may not be a resolution. What is important is the recognition aroused in us by contemporary philosophers like Rorty and Stanley Cavell that no order of discourse or institutional way of writing has a monopoly either on rigor or invention. Philosophy remains a "conversation" with unexpected turns that cannot all be predicted, though they can later be integrated by subtle adjustments or shifts in the way we think.

At the very moment that Rorty seeks to deliver philosophy from pretentiousness (both metaphysical and epistemological), literary study is seeking to deliver itself from the ideal he propagates: *conversation.*

In fact, the gentility of literary dons and the avoidance of theory are on the increase, because science has invaded literary studies too, and the older ideal is becoming, in reaction, more defensive. Many otherwise intelligent critics turn into bulldogs of understatement as they try to preserve an elegance, however moldy, and a casualness, however fake.

Even the best British critics succumb. In Christopher Ricks at times, a word-chopping, ordinary-language type of analysis is directed against all who attempt theory, as if the big words were naughty words we had to be shamed out of, and as if any inventive, elaborated schematism were a sin against the English sentence.

What is appealing about Rorty's position is how little difference there is between him and Pater in *Plato and Platonism* (1893). Pater did not wish to distinguish sharply between dialogue and dialectic; the same holds today for Hans-Georg Gadamer (an "edifying" rather than "systematic" philosopher, according to Rorty). Yet however attractive this Hellenic ideal may be, the results have often been dismaying. An Anglicized version of Greek *paideia* (tutorials pretending to be dialogue) has now become an unthinking attack on theory and is in danger of returning literary study to a supercilious kind of lexical inquisition that undoes everything we have learned from the largehearted stylistics of a Leo Spitzer, an Erich Auerbach, and others.

Yet it is also clear that to take back from philosophy what is ours cannot mean a method that applies specific philosophical ideas to literature. What does Heidegger really tell us about William Carlos Williams or Paul Ricoeur about Yeats? Or Derrida about Melville? Such mixing it up may have its uses. We write by assimilating what we read: we could therefore read philosophy as a sister-art; and philosophy in turn could consider literature as something better than time out for conversation. "Literature" here should be understood to include essays, and also larger scholarly structures in context: Spitzer in the context of German philology and the making of dictionaries; Auerbach in the context of Marxism and socioeconomic philosophies; Frye in that of anthropology and the ecumenical unifying of all fables; Empson in that of English, abdicating its political supremacy as a culture yet asserting itself as a "moral science" by constructing a new language-centered ethos.

As we pursue this institutional analysis, the thorny issue of whether we need an abnormal or special terminology (a metalanguage) becomes moot. Either we shall give up the idea that there is *one* correct way of talking about literature (in a terminology that is "logical" rather than "literary"), or we shall realize that all commentary is as much metacommentary (Fredric Jameson's term) as metacommentary or theory remains context-bound commentary. The real issue that will come forward is how skeptical we should be about *cultural translation*. Can the affairs of one culture (so dependent on a different text-milieu and not only on a different language) be understood by thinkers situated in another culture, even when the latter is a relative? (It may be easier to understand a culture when the distance is great enough to prevent easy rapprochement, or what translators call "false friends.") A creative skepticism about the crossover from culture to culture seems to me the right attitude. We need a "negative capability" that does not deny speculative criticism but engages with the highly mediated status of cultural and verbal facts. The basic question then is about the nature of understanding, and what sort of responsive style might articulate this understanding. Is a conversation between cultures possible? Or is such a conversation, as between persons, always mixed with imposition? Though we talk about "dialogue" and "keeping lines of communication open," it is hard to think of a conversation that is not forcefully interspersed with moments of appropriation and expropriation. The rules of language, the cunning of reasonableness, the sheer display of intellect or personality enter an unpredictable equation. The perfect English style, Orage said, will charm by its power; yet power and charm are precisely what the resistant thinker would like to keep separate.

t h r e e

_____

From Common to Uncommon Reader

The critical wars are fought today with very sophisticated weapons, and to a considerable extent remain war games rather than actual engagements. It feels as if one were sitting in a room watching scenarios on a videoscreen. My historical and conservationist bent may induce a strange sensation. I'm still playing a war game, but I take an older strategy out of mothballs and reinsert it into current thinking. Somewhat like refitting a Second World War battleship, with its lumbering monumental features and its inbuilt capacity to show the flag.

Yet let me add at once that none of us is, at his or her best, merely playing games, futuristic, formalistic, or self-dignifying. What is being done with language in literary circles may seem abstract, yet is no more so than in any advanced exploration of sign systems. The nature of the sign, the power of the sign; possibilities of misunderstanding; the prevention of misunderstanding; the creative and necessary side of error; the difference between understanding and agreement (consent)—these are still part of what I. A. Richards called "The Philosophy of Rhetoric," although as much work has recently been done on the Rhetoric of Philosophy as on the Philosophy of Rhetoric.

I take the prevalence of theory for granted; to define theory is another matter. It may be best to start where it hurts, at the level of style. That is where the insult or offense is often taken. The style of avant-garde criticism, like that of Donne's muse, is harsh; nor can it be excused by saying that the harshness is in the service of a new realism, a fresh contact with realities. For theory is felt to sin by its abstractness, its distance from relevant or humane matters, its tendency to cerebrate rather than celebrate. In short, its maddening vocabulary, the devices that lay bare the device. Without specifying what makes theory theory, I will say that it is prose with a noticeable proportion of technical terms. This presupposes the existence of a style relatively free of such terms—"criticism without theory," as Richard Rorty has called it. Any examination of the demand theory puts on critical style should begin by acknowledging that there is such a normative or classical prose. We also know that this prose emerged in England after 1660 and quickly achieved a hegemony that continues into the modern period.

An exact or featural map of this classical prose is beyond my scope; I must be content with a glance at *The Spectator* of Addison and Steele. Are their essays really criticism without theory; and if so, why is their style so different, in its energy and humor, from that of modern conversational critics who try to perpetuate the mode? After that all too brief glance at *The Spectator,* something must be said about the integrity of advanced literary studies. To view theory only in its effect on style, even as an effect of style, promotes it as a fashion, with rebelliousness and incivility as trademarks. Its claim to rigor could then be dismissed. Theory, however, is not just another style of discourse but raises the entire question of discourse-control to a level where our awareness of it becomes irreversible, and such antiself-consciousness devices as parody, sangfroid, or a stubborn emphasis on the practical side of things (kicking the stone) begin to appear stupid rather than commonsensical.

Jacques Lacan has remarked how many of Freud's pages are given over to a discussion of language, the role it plays in dreams or the life of the psyche. In returning to *The Spectator,* one is struck by a similar wealth of reflections on language, but as it enters the social life through conversation and writing. At times *The Spectator* appears to be a Courtesy Book for those who should not have need of it. Sportive and pleasingly didactic, it expresses the thoughts of the "honest man about town," the adventures of his soul in the demimonde of opinion, but presses no further claim than sympathy for the way it skirts the abysses of self-esteem or hypochondria. Conversation must go on.

Our interest, therefore, in this spectatorial blend lies in the area of morality of style. True, at its most frolicsome, a Swiftian vein emerges: then this essayistic melange of observation and speculation becomes inventive. Mostly, however, Addison and Steele write light prose satire in a Horatian mode, content to fashion a middle style that relishes while it admonishes such splendid vices as Cardinal Woolsey's egotism (*Ego et Rex meus,* I and my King) or Montaigne's. (Had this "lively old *Gascon,*" Addison remarks, "kept his own Counsel, he might have passed for a much better man, though perhaps he would not have been so diverting an Author.") The opposite of Egotism—a self-mortification for which we have no single name, and which leads to melancholy as surely as egotism leads to mania—is also gently reproved and dissipated.[1] True conversation, whether secular or sacred, whether taking place in the company of other people or in the soul as it inquires of itself before God, tries to avert blankness, silence, or the deeper implications of Terence's *praesens absens ut sies* (be present as if absent).

One episode in particular raises itself to Swiftian dimensions. A few days before Addison ceases to publish *The Spectator,* announcing his retirement and the dissolution of his imaginary Club, he pretends to wish to found a new Club in which he would put off his "Character of a Silent Man" announced in the very first number of his journal. Considering he and Steele had published by this time 550 issues of *The Spectator,* one is entitled to wonder what that claim of taciturnity, in its very jokiness, might refer to. What is it he has not said, having written so much? Is Addison a precursor after all of Roland Barthes, and the post-Mallarmean *absence?* "Who *speaks* is not who *writes* and who *writes* is not who *is.*"

"In order to diversify my Character," Addison proclaims on Monday, December 1, 1712, "and to shew the World how well I can talk if I have a Mind," he will proceed on "the first Meeting of the said Club to have *my Mouth opened in Form,* intending to regulate my self in the Particular by a certain Ritual which I have by me, that contains all the Ceremonies which are practised at the opening of the Mouth of a Cardinal." Moreover, he expects that foreign gazettes in their next articles from Great Britain, "will inform the World that the SPECTATOR's *Mouth is to be opened on the twenty fifty of March next.*"

It is a telling and delicious passage, disclosing in its contrast of Club and Church the incongruity of its conceit, and mocking in advance the very revelation that might break the silence. The suggestion is that one cannot have one's mouth opened in form. A mouth is not to be regulated: once open, it will not only break the silence but silence others, silence that polite conversation which was Mr. Spectator's aim. "Whoever wishes to attain an English style," Dr. Johnson said, "familiar but not coarse, and elegant but not ostentatious, must give his days and nights to the volumes of Addison." And just before signing off, Addison inserts a letter summarizing his ideal:

Mr. SPECTATOR,

In spight of your Invincible Silence you have found a Method of being the most agreeable Companion in the World: That kind of Conversation which you hold with the Town, has the good Fortune of being always pleasing to the Men of Taste and Leisure, and never offensive to those of Hurry and Business . . . You never begin to talk, but when people are desirous to hear you; and I defie anyone to be out of Humour till you leave off.

It is not sufficient, then, to view *The Spectator* as an agreeable effort to develop a magazine that could avoid political controversy aroused by Whig and Tory, or Puritan and Papist. For it is also a daily that aims to keep conversation going, as if Addison and Steele were shadowy prefigurations of Bouvard and Pecuchet generating endless copy. During its short, intense life *The Spectator* addicted the higher and middle ranks of society. As a supposed carrier of news it filled the emptiness it perpetuated. Addison may be less terrified by the silence of infinite cosmic space (yet see *Spectator* 565) than by a silence that persists despite speech, that permeates the mode of taciturn—written—conversation. The very dailiness of life now enters consciousness more thoroughly, also by way of the novels of Defoe, and then Richardson and Sterne. It is impossible to say whether the journalistic stream of conversation that arises to consume the silence of thought is incited by an intolerable sense of the vanity of all that factitious news or by a fear that fanatic ideas might once again enthuse from that void. Addison's Ode imitating Psalm 19, "The spacious firmament on high" (*Spectator* 465, August 23, 1712), is symptomatic. It depicts the gospel as a perpetual and omnipresent conversation, published day and night by the heavenly bodies, despite their muteness:

Th'unwearied Sun, from day to day,
Does his Creator's Pow'r display,
And publishes to every Land
The Work of an Almighty Hand.

Soon as the evening Shades prevail,
The Moon takes up the wondrous Tale,
And nightly to the listning Earth
Repeats the Story of her Birth:
Whilst all the Stars that round her burn,
And all the Planets, in their turn,
Confirm the Tidings as they rowl,
And spread the Truth from Pole to Pole.

Even an Age of Prose has its music of the spheres.

Where everything is news, nothing is news. Perhaps this classic form of disenchantment—that everything has been said or is being said again—is the surest way of keeping the social fabric whole, away from schisms, from tearing renovations. The punctual day, *ille dies,* is but a literary pang, dissipated by all the datelines in these Journals. A *nunc stans* seems as far away as the stars, or as belated as thought, or the post itself. Always already postponed.

Can we pass from Addison's era to our own? Those who complain of a modern "indeterminacy" or philosophy of "difference" are preferring a previous era's defense against enthusiastic or pleromatic expectations. Prose then was more careful, more self-fashioning than today; but it was no less aware of its potentially inflammatory relation to everyday incidents. Then as now the ordering of news is the preoccupation, as politics becomes the concern of a wider audience, as writing and literacy spread, and as the man of letters wields his pen with an increased sense of both power and impotence. Journalism is creating its rationale. Erich Auerbach would surely have interpreted the gentle humor and temperate didacticism of Mr. Spectator as evidence that the quotidian did not yet seem entirely newsworthy. It is thought about only in a conversational mode separated by a very thin line from satire on the one side and elegant trifling on the other.

There was good reason for eighteenth-century studies to assume a place of privilege in the academy. The relation between English society and literature became visible; we recognized in that era a franker, sometimes more exotic version of our own struggle to be critics rather than political hacks or evangelists. Reading journals, letters, even novels—an act that also catches the interest of painters—carries with it a special moment that is neither worldly nor unworldly, that is essentially in suspense. When René Wellek fixed a starting point for his *History of Modern Criticism* he chose 1750 because by that time criticism had detached itself (more or less) from theological and political controversy. This detachment, I am suggesting, goes together with a more reflective and tolerant attitude toward reading. The forces arrayed against the free exercise of literacy are lulled, though not disarmed, by an exemplary type of prose, which seems to have no one subject and therefore perhaps no subject; and which can touch lightly on anything at all and nothing at all.

Once a reading-culture has been created it faces new challenges, both from within and from without. But it must posit, if only as an ideal type, a Gentle or Common Reader. To get a Common Reader you must encourage the mind's capacity for a willing suspension of belief, or, what may be the same, a willing suspension of disbelief. The new prose evokes a mood of indeterminacy that hovers between light and grave. We begin to understand the critical frame of mind.

Today we realize that the Common Reader may never have existed except in the personified form of Mr. Spectator, or as part of a very small elite. Today also the reading-culture is more vulnerable than ever. "There is no Common Reader," Leavis says forthrightly; "the tradition is dead."[2] Even Eliot's suave, authoritative voice could not maintain the tradition. Leavis turns to university education in the hope of stemming the decline of the elite. "If literary culture is to be saved it must be by conscious effort; by education carefully designed to meet the exigencies of the time—the lapse of tradition, the cultural chaos and hostility of the environment." "It would not be," he significantly adds, "merely with the 'culture' of individuals that such an effort would be concerned." Some seek to expand the reading materials that make up what we conceive of as culture; others revise the very concept of reading in order to divest it of its culture-bound, ethnocentric focus. It is supposed to combine a highly specialized with a universally accessible method of analysis. All these factions have made the academy their battlefield, in which curricula clash by day, and reading (perhaps) takes place by night.

Fashioning a Common Reader involved a particular and contagious prose style. It may be that the Reader we are incubating today, let us call him or her the Uncommon Reader (a phrase I adapt from George Steiner), will also be projected by way of a certain style. The Uncommon Reader is not the opposite of the Common Reader but one who uses theory as effectively as the Common Reader used the Classics. It was Trilling who said that the study of the Classics gave thinkers like Freud the opportunity to escape being subdued to their culture. The very obsoleteness of that "other" world of the Classics fostered a humane equivalent to scientific detachment. The "beyond" of culture remained within culture. But it is hard for us to think of *theory* as a language, like the Classics, inside our own language. Theory seems to belong elsewhere, to some other part of the mind. Imagine a writer converting theory into as integral a style as Leavis claimed Ben Jonson did Latinity. "Jonson's effort was to feel Catullus, and the others he cultivated, contemporary with himself; or rather, to achieve an English mode that should express a sense of contemporaneity with them. The sense itself, of course, had to be achieved by effort, and was achieved in the mode . . . The English poet, who remains not the less English and of his own time, enters into an ideal community, conceived of as something with which contemporary life and manners may and should have close relations."[3]

Leavis' idea of a vernacular and defining tradition, which is the English charm against the dead hand of scientific and Classicist abstraction, is stated as fact rather than theory. But the fact still needs to be reenforced by an institution like the university: as fact it is neither self-evident nor self-enforcing. An "English School" is called for; and an essay entitled "The Idea of a University" invests that idea with something of a mystical body. Leavis argues that we should be preoccupied "not with the generalizations of philosophical and moral theory and doctrine, but with picking up a continuity; carrying on and fostering the essential life of a time-honoured and powerful institution, in this concrete, historical England."[4]

Surely this is a language-theology; surely what Leavis calls the English School is much like the English Church. The saintly, or at least guardian, energies of Shakespeare, Donne, Jonson, and Pope are still with us.

How different the attitude toward theory in an American contemporary, Kenneth Burke. Theory for him is a creative mode of resistance rather than what is to be resisted. Burke is unafraid of rhetoric and technical terms; they are inventive and competitive in the marketplace of all such terms. They are also Ancient. Burke relishes rhetoric or terms of art because they concentrate rather than dissipate the powers of language; and he recalls, like the Cambridge anthropologists, their possible relation to ritual speech acts.

Searching for a "desirable prose" in *Towards a Better Life* (1932), Burke subtitled the book "a Series of Epistles or Declamations" to stress its turn from "the impromptu" or "conversational style" (including the ability to tell a good story), toward the "re-erection" of the "structural" and even Jonsonian sentence. We see a philosophy of literary form in the making. What characterizes this form are "Six Biblical Characteristics" or "Pivotals"; "Lamentation, rejoicing, beseechment, admonition, sayings and invective." Interestingly enough, Burke cites Defoe as "our first great journalist" who tried, without quite succeeding, to get literary effects by giving up declamation for reportage.

What I want to emphasize is not Leavis' restricted literary pharmacy or Burke's larger understanding of the poet as a medicine man. Rather that both critics have remedies, though not simples, to resist the decline of the reading-culture into a consumer-type of literacy. For Leavis theory is part of the decline, a symptom of "the blind drive onward of material and mechanical development." For Burke theory is an interesting and inventive development of terminology, no less creative potentially than Blake's thuriferous namings. Leavis seeks the institutional support of the university as an ideal secular community to direct our reading; Burke's only authority is in the very rhetoric he revalues as a charged, dangerous, necessary part of speech. "In considering the past of English prose," he writes, "and in realizing by comparison with the present how much of the 'eventfulness' of a prose sentence is omitted from our prevalent newspaper and narrative styles, we are furnished with authority enough for a 'return' to more formalized modes of writing."

I suggest we view theory as participating in that return to a more formal criticism. It attempts to reach beyond the middle or conversational style, which has frozen over. The inventive use of terms of art and previously excluded colloquialisms are both means to this end. Burke shows their convergence; he follows Lawrence's *Studies in American Literature* and anticipates Olsen's *Call Me Ishmael*, yet mixes terminological and colloquial modes at will. Even the difficulty of reducing style to meaning or substance—always acknowledged in literature and sometimes defined as

81

the locus of literariness—may indicate a language-residue that cannot be *written out* or *theorized*. In the empirical, contingent realm, as in the literary, there is that sort of density which forms a perhaps involuntary alliance between the two. This density can only be "shown" (in Wittgenstein's sense) by the discourse of theory—however paradoxical it is to suggest that the untheorizable is the motive for theory.

Paul de Man adds that the resistance to theory is basically a resistance to reading, to the *lectio difficilis et potior*. When we confuse theory with ideology we do so to be absolved from reading. If theory were merely a version of ideology, then "practical criticism" or "criticism without theory" would certainly be preferable: it is far more liberal and productive than the terroristic casuistry which characterizes some of Lukacs' later essays. Against this confusion of ideology with theory, Adorno directed his provocative aphorism: "The empirical is the untrue."

For theory is inquisitive but ideology is inquisatorial. In countries where literature is considered an extension of ideology, and literary studies are politically answerable, even casual divergencies can lead to Kafkaesque interrogations. Theory should never be the application of idea to fact, unless it wishes to disclose that the *appliqué* method is just that. Theory does not fertilize itself by mingling with the empirical. It exposes the fact (Arnold's "object as in itself is") as the untrue—an abstract form of immediacy which can masquerade as the totalized "thing itself" by concealing a figurative or rhetorical operation: a part for whole substitution or exemplification as freely chosen rather than mediated and highly intentional.

Criticism, then, is mental fight as well as appreciation; yet it is useful to know what one is fighting for or against. There is no need to expend one's anger on unintended insults. The whole question of what gives offense in writing is interesting and must be related to what Leavis observes about the "confident maturity" of *Tatler* and *Spectator*. "Even the finest expressions of the spirit," he writes, "were to be in resonance with a code of Good Form . . . The characteristic movements and dictions of the eighteenth century, in verse as well as prose, convey a suggestion of social deportment and company in manners."[5]

Theory may strike one as Bad Form, but it is form. Leavis' style too is no less formal, and perhaps no less ideological, for all its avoidance of technical terms. His iterative and prejudicial, though always exact, use of certain words makes them carry a weight they can bear only as ritual chanting. They are no longer purely conversational but rather passwords, dictions. Their force is in the tradition they focus and perpetuate. Even the hardhat empiricist knows that the language of theory does not retain its tinge of solecism forever. Theoretical terms are often recycled and become literary. Terms of art generate forms of art. So Keat's "Ode to Psyche" is full of poetic diction, and Blake's longer poems provide, like Opera, a powerful setting for homeless visionary clichés. The language of learning, Leo Spitzer shows, is as much the source of etymologies as the *lingua del pane*. And think what a Ballanche and a Joyce do with Vico; or think of the new unnamed genre represented by Norman O. Brown's *Love's Body*, a cento of displaced quotations from theory and fiction. Roland Barthes's *A Lover's Discourse* also turns the language of learning, indeed, his own theory-infested metalanguage, into the language of love: everything becomes cantabile again; all special terms aspire to the condition of music.

It was always that way. Learning tends to precede the creative language that takes its inspiration, or at least its fuel, from that source. This is quite clear in the Renaissance, which is inconceivable without the scholastic sources of Dante, the copiousness of Erasmus, and the pedagogical fire of humanist editors.

My main point goes in another direction. What makes theory important to the Uncommon Reader is not only a modern sort of *contrafattura*. The importance of theory lies principally in its "critical" character. Yet theory too is often associated by us with the contrary of a critical position, with a systematic or ideological closure that appropriates one part of existence, or of language, at the expense of others. Theory is then accused of forgetting its own positivity, that it is not nature, that no natural totality exists, and that totalization should be in the service of a critical or comparative counter-perspective. Indeed, totalization, and its most obvious figure, prolepsis, cannot be avoided, because we are always situated. The domain of preunderstanding (what we have always already known) coheres us, makes understanding, in all its error, possible, makes dialogue and agreement possible. How can theory be critical? It is a paradoxical project.

That paradox, however, seems to overlap with the paradox of language itself as a "system of differences." I do not mean to suggest that Saussure's anti-foundationalist view of language was determinant. But semiotics emerged as a "critical theory" in the domain of linguistics and so kept alive the promise of an exact science. Critical thinkers on both sides of the Channel were, however, as deeply concerned with *parole* as with *langue:* with what was happening in the contemporary era to actual speech both in its educated and in its demotic forms. Is Heidegger's idiolect an obfuscation, or an extreme but justified formal turn from ordinary and overnaturalized speech? What of Paul Celan's sublime stutter? How do we value, if at all, the other extreme: street language, consumerist jargon, medialects?

"Critical theory," associated with the Frankfurt School, raises such questions. But the word "theory" remains a problem and leads me to an historical aside. While in Leavis' educationist pamphlets the possibility of resistance to appropriated or managed speech centered on the word "tradition," on the Continent "theory" emerged as the focus of critical vigor. The reason is that the European social order, however complexly traditional, had in fact either collaborated with or collapsed before the power play of totalitarian regimes. While the English way of life, parliamentary and practical, showed its worth, it barely escaped; and the Frankfurt School, in a revisionist view of eighteenth-century history, argued that modernization, rationalization, and the leveling effect of Enlightenment ideas were bound to lead to a totalitarian result. "Critical theory" was thus projected out of its academic base into an analysis of all institutions, especially their relation to language. Could any institutional arrangement oppose standardization and the drift toward a totalitarian mentality?

Let me continue, a moment, this historical aside. The situation of the intellectual after the Second World War was very different in Continental Europe and in Anglo-America. Anglo-American circles did not know that bitter sense of a *trahison des clercs* that inculpated both university and political life in Germany and France. There the importance or ineffectiveness of the humanities made an appeal to "tradition" impossible. Only certain heroes, resistance fighters like Malraux and Sartre, could begin to heal that breach. But the Era of Suspicion was now entrenched, and "critical theory" itself was attacked in the 1960s by students who had learned from it and saw the university system basically unaltered. They yearned for critical action—the negative in action—in the very years that

Gadamer's exemplary defense of humanism, entitled *Truth and Method,* appeared.

Those years of activism made it clear that the need to find a language for theory had two components. The students spoke a dialect that was meant to be disruptive yet proved to be a media-boon. The students also tended to leap over language altogether, as if reading and writing were rearguard actions of late bourgeois capitalism. A stronger defense of reading had to be formulated, together with a language that had its own critical life beyond the moment it aggressed or illuminated.

The gain of literary theory in the 1970s was a gain in thoughtfulness. Literary theory defended and elaborated the thesis that art was more philosophical than philosophy in uncovering the illusion of unmediated action or speech. There was always a text motivating the act, and a reading informing the text. The focus of radical theory shifted to identifying the social forces that made us believe speech and action might be liberated from what Lacan had called the "inmixing of the Other." Those forces, it seemed, wanted to have us speak only their language and so, in a sense, to silence us. It is always tempting to conspire with these forces (Left or Right) because they represent themselves as necessary ideas of order or as public conventions that prevent a deeper sort of alienation: that of social isolation and narcissism, on the one hand, and, on the other, being usurped by a heteroglossia from within, by compulsive fantasies in the form of spectral or inner voices. The decorum of accommodation is so strong that some of us scarcely remember how *isolating* it is to be a writer. Why should Virginia Woolf's learned father prefer her to dig in the garden rather than continue her studies? Why are writers persecuted in totalitarian countries?

It could be argued that to become aware of these matters through the hygiene of historical scholarship is enough. But it is not enough. We require theory because of our augmented technological expertise, our ability to shape and reshape the environment and have it conform to a program. History is now part of that conforming environment. In the early stages of the scientific enlightenment historical critics could still counterpunch that tendency. But the Enlightenment generalized from successes in physics to ethics and the world of nations, and glimpsed a millennial uniformity, an end to all but mental strife.

The contemporary polemic, therefore, which pits historical or social thought against "theory-mad" critics, is the product of a misunderstanding. The same suspicion of uniformity that inspires the antagonism to literary theory also informs literary theory itself. Theory of literature does not set itself against the "various light" of history but scrutinizes proliferating explanatory schemes that claim scientific status. Literary theory forms an alliance with art to resist cheap, verismo, versions of history. This critique of historical reasoning may still have to catch up with Foucault, whose history of epistemes and discourse-systems constitutes a critique of society but not of his own mode.

Our greater need for theory is thus linked to a change in the environment, though I risk simplifying history once more by such a claim. The change I refer to is the rise of propaganda, organized lying and ideological falsification. They have always existed; and when they lose their actual political clout we call them myths. What is different is our present capacity to enforce such myths by nonviolent as well as violent means—by, in particular, the pressure of the media.

However important history-writing will continue to be, it is clear that propaganda techniques took a giant step forward during the First World War. Hitler reminds us in *Mein Kampf* (book 2, chapter 11) that when he joined the German Workers' Party he immediately took over its propaganda. "I considered this department by far the most important, at that moment." More significant still is his assertion that the Allies won because of the "spiritual weapon" (*geistige Waffe*) of propaganda, and the harmful behavior of the German Press, whose effect on home-front morale he terms "psychological mass murder" (book 1, chapters 7 and 8). Propaganda is part of our modern mystery of iniquity. When, immediately after the war, Stephen Spender interviewed the great scholar Ernst Robert Curtius, he got no answer to his question how it could be "that the teaching profession, as a whole, taught all the Nazis lies about race and deliberately set about perverting the minds of the young." Curtius said simply: "The Germans always submit." But he had allowed himself, before that, a more aggressive remark that anyone outside Germany who maintained that it was possible for the German anti-Nazis to prevent war should make a serious study of the effects of government by terror, propaganda, lies and perverted psychology in modern scientific conditions.[6]

Let me narrow the focus once more to America, and literary studies. In the United States, where the experiment of mass education has been more seriously pursued than elsewhere, it is not a political catastrophe but an educational morass that obliges us to think about what reading involves as a form of life. Naive ideas concerning assimilation, modernization, and standard-language instruction are being questioned. We have learned that literature and art as civilizing instruments are not pedagogical simples. They raise all sorts of ambiguous feelings about the value of a reading-culture. Standard literacy leads to bureaucratic idealism; advanced literacy raises questions about the leveling impact of reading on other forms of creativeness: sport, performance, oral culture. Is literacy, whether basic or advanced, harmful to organic and regional patterns of life? Does it not corrode those patterns and undermine institutions which as such are never justifiable in rational terms? Will that subverting process result in new fundamentalist sects as well as countercultural communes, any of which could become the base of another totalitarianism because of the leveling that has occurred, and the discourse-control made possible by the media?

We need Uncommon Readers if the Common Reader is, as Nazism made clear, potentially a Coordinated Reader—coordinated (*gleichgeschaltet*) with a State ideology or an illusory Public Philosophy. If the past is heeded, even those who want to change rather than interpret the world cannot afford to be antihermeneutic fundamentalists. In this respect Althusser and Habermas are exemplary. Theory for both is not a hysterical symptom but a critical necessity, something with rigor, consistency, and extension, bearing on the need to find—in the past as well as the present—a language for theory through a theory of reading. How did Marx handle the problem of the future reader, of appropriation and institutionalization?

Althusser—a Marxist scholar, deeply involved in the question of how to deal with the insinuating and imprisoning character of ideology, which prompts action rather than putting thought in action—complains in *Reading Capital* about "the thin sheet of the [Marxist] theory of reading." As for Habermas, his heroically conglomerate style tries to save a "public philosophy" described by Walter Lippmann as springing eternally, like hope, from its own wreck. His theory of "communicative reason" resembles Kant's emphasis on the ethical value of open argument. "The art of critical thinking," Hannah Arendt wrote, in reference to Kant, "always has political implications," because it takes place, and even is dependent on, social intercourse. "Critical thinking is possible only where the standpoints of all others are open to inspection. Hence, critical thinking, while still a solitary business, does not cut itself off from 'all others.' To be sure, it still goes on in isolation, but by the force of imagination it makes the others present and thus moves in a space that is potentially public, open to all sides . . . To think with an enlarged mentality means that one trains one's imagination to go visiting."[7] So Habermas declares that critical theory is a form of hermeneutics, insisting that the former liberates the later within a form of discursiveness that is the precondition for public *Öffentlichkeit*. Critical theory, he writes, is "a form of appropriation no less than hermeneutics," but at the same time it also "dissolves validity claims that cannot be redeemed discursively." Without privileging tradition in the manner of Gadamer's hermeneutics, he wishes to release "the semantic potential" of that tradition.[8]

Let me touch back to the beginning of this chapter. Bonamy Dobrée, contributing in 1949 to a collection entitled *Pope and His Contemporaries,* remarks that these writers were all "masters of the middle style . . . men at that time prided themselves on speaking with the voice of society rather than with their own individual speech: it would offend against taste for a man to be known by the way he wrote." Dobrée, the historical scholar, reminds us that individualism is a new and perhaps transient thing, and how fine it was to give the self up to a tradition. But the Uncommon or Critical Reader finds a doubtful preachment in this pleasing thought. Dobrée's language ("masters," "men," "man") seems unaware that the conditions of consensus have changed, that a purely male orientation is now seen to be exclusive and unwarranted. "The voice of society" is not a single voice, and the idea that it can be so finely mixed that it appears to be unified may have to be resisted—by what Adorno called "the intransigence of theory."[9]

Most of the time, however, theory simply puts the reader on guard. It provides an alternative form of reflective speech to set against the seduction of a sentimental and dominant mode. The desire to converse, as well as the need for public discourse, make it inevitable that a set of high-minded clichés should continue to exist, in every age: passwords with little or no cognitive value, dead metaphors, obsolete concepts, tropings, that may or may not be retrievable by releasing, to quote Habermas, their "semantic potential." Critical writing, in brief, becomes a *strange conversation* in which archaic or repressed or accepted terms rebound—and even, exceptionally, creates new terms through a powerful moment of periphrasis.

A different essay would be needed to show how the conversational style, with its open and public character, can become the basis of a strange conversation—with the critic burrowing from within, or swerving into unexpected turns, or breaking the form altogether, as if that had been monologic not dialogic, and conversation had to be reconstituted at quite another level. This last and most radical revision of critical style is also what presently is least understood: midrashic exegesis, for example, with its elliptical interaction of authorities, or imaginary exchanges between God and this or that Biblical character, since the Bible's words are all God's words. Even in its day this mode was both free and constrained: *free* to quote synoptically any part of the text, *constrained* in that every secular gain, every interpretative yield, had to be drawn from the sacred text by hermeneutic skill or cunning. The *davar* remains within the received book.

Intertextuality in fact, as a heuristic theorem, encourages a view that the author is but a medium, or the editor of texts that continue to speak through the composer. The authority of authors comes from the way they deal with the intertextual situation; in this they are often close to being compilers, even if they do not always know it. Some theorists of course use intertextuality as a "technique of suspicion" directed against both the romantic myth of originality and the classicist myth of normative language behavior. But in all cases the awareness that writing is a fusion of heterogeneous stories or types of discourse—even while seeking the appearance of unity—restores the antiphonal relation between text and text, or text and commentary. It is this antiphonal relation that turns criticism into a strange conversation.[10]

f o u r

The State of the Art

Contemporary literary analysis exposes once more the ambiguity of language. It does so not to impugn words and induce new schemes for a "real character," a more stable and truthful language-structure, but to heighten our awareness of the complex resource already in place.[1] "Where the old Rhetoric," I. A. Richards writes in his *Philosophy of Rhetoric*, "treated ambiguity as a fault in the language, and hoped to confine or eliminate it, the new Rhetoric sees it as an inevitable consequence of the powers of language." Ambiguity, at least in art, confirms these "powers," and suggests that modes of reading which assert the possibility of literal or unmediated expression are terrible simplifications.[2]

These simplifications, however, enter a vicious cycle reactive to freer modes of reading. While it is liberating to celebrate ambiguity as indeterminacy, the very ease of doing so exacerbates the fever of fundamentalism that chronically ravages the body politic. The polemics of the situation do not work for the critical spirit unless we can make a case on behalf of the negative energy of intellect all around us. "The mind of man," Christopher Smart wrote, "cannot bear a tedious accumulation of nothings without effect." So we may ask ourselves: Is Derrida's "atheology" perhaps the equivalent of a negative theology? Are we in the presence of a "negative classicism," as André Malraux defined the unconventional strength of modernist painting? Should we accept a philosophy of history like that of the Saint-Simonians who took comfort in the fact that after each skeptical age there would arise an organic and myth-filled age? Do we credit Michel Foucault's insight, developed above all in his *History of Sexuality*, that all our liberated talk about repression and censorship is merely a way of extending and intensifying the directorial powers of church and state that now penetrate via our own "critical" claims into the innermost recesses of a private sphere they were intended to guard? Can even art escape being propaganda?[3]

I take it for granted that we remain in an age of criticism, but one traversed by a return to religious faith, to clear commitments and often to fundamentalist kinds of faith. Now it is hard to get one's historical bearings on the frequency of these cycles. T. S. Eliot announced in 1929 his return to religion and conservative politics; the same year Walter Lippmann published *A Preface to Morals,* analyzing the dissolution of the ancestral order and suggesting that neither modernism nor fundamentalism could lead to that "religion of the spirit" appropriate to a "Great Society." We also know too well that fascism expressed apocalyptic traits and a fervor of adhesion that have typically characterized the more fanatic religions. So that the evidences of a return from the 1960s on to either cultic or conventional religion need not surprise.

Whatever the complexity of contemporary reactions to "Whirl is King" (Aristophanes), the problems that affect literary and cultural criticism can be clearly defined. I will single out the problem of doing interpretations at a time when texts seem to be overly porous, that is, so ambiguous or variable in the history of attributed meanings that the cry is heard, why should we study literature? A time too when, obversely, the import of texts is decided by authority, with the aid of the idea that there is one meaning, often defined as "literal."

We can turn once more to Richards for a modern focus on this dilemma. He asks criticism to foster an "intellectual tradition" that "tells us . . . how *literally* to read a passage."[4] If he had said: how not to read literally, the emphasis would have fallen on the interpretive complexity of art. Yet a modern prejudice, linked to the change of hermeneutics into criticism, makes him put his statement the other way. He is of course a realist rather than a fundamentalist, one who admires that stubborn and commendable streak in us which links literature to life, not only to more literature. Like Wallace Stevens, he too keeps "coming back and coming back / To the real: to the hotel instead of the hymns / That fall upon it out of the wind."[5] Yet by the end of the paragraph what is deplored is not the loss of reality but the loss of interpretive flexibility. This is where theory comes in, as a supplement to the recovery of a skill. Our age, Richards suggests, is "losing its skill in interpretation" and "begins the reflective inquiry which may lead to a theory by which the skill may be regained—this time as a less vulnerable and more deeply grounded, because more consciously recognized, endowment."

Richards also posits a time near the beginning of modern English when we actually "read aright." He connects the adroitness of later sixteenth- and much seventeenth-century writing to social and religious causes that coincide with the flourishing of English: the wide circulation of sermons as well as plays, letters as well as poetry, controversy as well as fiction and translation.[6] By the end of this period certainly, the very prose Richards himself writes, as well as the genre of essayistic criticism, has been created.

But we have little evidence of how the literature of that period was interpreted (*Rezeptionsgeschichte* not having been invented); what evidence there is belongs to the history of taste and does not take the form of sustained analysis. Certain prefaces and some self-commentating sermons or works, like those of Donne, seem to constitute an exception, but is that enough to make up for the lack of a global view of seventeenth-century culture or a better grasp of the way art reflects on itself and its text-milieu? These questions point to what has in fact developed since Richards: (1) reader-reception theory; (2) a new historicism that wishes to ascertain the "episteme" (Foucault) of a culture by appreciating all its signifying *and* repressive practices, not only canonized works; and (3) a more general awareness of how cultures augment their fictions through interpretation and obversely their interpretive discourse through fiction. (Frank Kermode's subtitle to *The Genesis of Secrecy,* "The Interpretation of Narrative," could as easily read "The Narrative of Interpretation.") Together the three tendencies expand the definition of what literature is, redeem the isolation of belles-lettres, and shift attention to unfreedoms of speech challenged by forceful though oblique or marginalized cultural practices. A further movement, puzzling and influential deconstruction, is a critique of all canonical or new-historical schemes that put a bit of weight behind interesting allegories, turning them once more into comprehensive symbols or paradigms

I am trying to inch forward from Richards to the contemporary scene by constructing a historical narrative that avoids progressive claims. The loss of interpretive skill that Richards responds to, whatever its ultimate cause, is still with us. It obliges us to expand our view of the history of criticism, and to see that we cannot start it around 1700. What we call criticism is only the tip of the iceberg compared to the vast commentary-tradition stretching back to Midrash and Patristic exegesis, and beyond that to Alexandria, Philo, and the sopherim. The age of criticism is a distinctive though very late development. Yet one can hold to Richards' distinction between skill and theory, as between nature (that is, vulnerable endowment) and its conscious reinforcement (that is, a more thoroughly grounded, immunized endowment). Together with the utopian premise that attaches to Richards' notion of educability, there emerges a pragmatic caution that projects the skill to be grounded not as something given or gained once and for all but as a second nature, a habit of the flexible and reflective intelligence. Even though Richards uses one period as a touchstone for his conception of interpretive mobility, his attitude toward that skill is antifoundationalist. The literal for him always stands in relation to other modes of reading, and the critical spirit itself is clearly more than an auxiliary and subordinated gift.

It is here that I sense a real difference between our present work, which remains close to Richards, and that of others in Eliot's generation or the American New Criticism. As promoters of modernism, the New Critics brought contemporary literature into the university and linked it to what they called "the tradition." It was a pedagogically progressive yet culturally conservative movement. The New Critics were also surprisingly conservative in their attitude toward the critical spirit. Like Eliot, they stressed its capital importance in the work of creation but remained wary of its free-lance and sometimes autonomous character. They overlooked, as it were, Oscar Wilde's deflation of the artist. "I am always amused," he wrote, "by the silly vanity of those writers and artists of our day who seem to imagine that the primary function of the critic is to chatter about their second-rate work." In the Eliot tradition the critical spirit, when left to its own recognizance, was considered dangerous, corrosive, and too self-conscious. It was safer leaking from art as irony, paradox, or ambiguity. Uneasy about the creative potential in criticism, Eliot remarked in 1956: "These last thirty years have been, I think, a brilliant period in literary criticism in both Britain and America. It may even come to seem, in retrospect, too brilliant." What might he have said of the next thirty years?

The emphasis has shifted from integrating high modernist art into the canon, to the work of reading that helped to establish the canon and can therefore also modify it. Our picture of the literary universe is no longer that of great, autonomous, quasi-Scriptural books clustered at the center, attracting into their orbit satellite and epigonal works of Interpretation. That picture can never be entirely effaced; it has, let us say, a Ptolemaic value. But our concept of what is creative projects today a more eccentric, or decentered, map. It is not only that social movements, gathering momentum in the 1960s have overturned hierarchy, patriarchy, academy, monogamy, in the realm of letters. That is the surface, I think, of a tidal change that began when structuralism, joining anthropological and linguistic findings, reformed Western concepts of creativity by rationalizing episodic compilations, from folklore to South American myths. Using binary opposition as a structural principle, Lévi-Strauss explained how meaning was made and remade: how cultures dealt with contradictions in their belief-systems. So primary creation and secondary interpretation lost their rigid boundaries; though to expand the canon does not mean the proportional representation of every ethnic group but an acknowledgment (that must stand the test of time) of the devoted work of commentators and critics. The significant new work of art is gathered in, if at all, by them. We no longer maintain the image of the perfect work or objectified mind over there and the consumer or interpreter desirous of communion with that brilliant object over here.

In these matters Richards was in advance of Eliot, or more democratic and experimental. *Practical Criticism* (1929) showed that art was not all that available even to acculturated students; that education had to undo both mental simplification and cultural prejudice; and that especially in a competitive modern era, where consumables replace the more difficult experience of art, the culture had to find a way of "endowing" criticism. It may seem like a small thing, but despite recent complaints about bringing criticism into the university and so overinstitutionalizing it (as if each year the university were aborting Edmund Wilsons and Kenneth Burkes), to write and read critical texts with the same care that we give to literature—to bring, as it were, even the literature of criticism into the canon—is an achievement we are still working on.

Most of us, I have found, do not think criticism very productive, or read it with much pleasure. It has too many undeveloped allusions and ricochets. Within the casual flow of critical words there is a charged and overdetermined quality. Like pastoral, criticism seems always to glance at greater matters, and Richards' prose is a case in point. It evades fixed terminologies and never seems indebted to a central discipline, though it is steeped in the vocabulary of the social sciences. This absence of one fixed doctrine is crucial; it explains both the suggestiveness of criticism and the fact that there is this sort of writing able to avoid dogmatic resting points and explicitly systematized argument.

It is quite possible, then, even necessary, to subject critical prose to explication. The first who did so in a sustained manner, who took it to have a texture, was John Crowe Ransom in *The New Criticism* (1939), the title lending its name to the movement he discussed. Other New-Critical practitioners applied close reading exclusively to fiction, and insisted with Eliot that "you cannot fuse creation with criticism as you can fuse criticism with creation." Our recent, more acute awareness of intertextuality, which has lessened the a priori ranking of fiction over commentary and enabled us to see the mediated and redacted nature of all texts, even when a named author originates them, is making us more medieval and midrashic in studying criticism as a creative yet text-dependent activity.

Take Richards' opening once more: "Intellectual tradition tells us . . . how *literally* to read a passage." It sets up a shifting series of ideas. Is Richards raising the issue of what might restrain interpretation (the chapter is entitled "The Bridle of Pegasus"), or what might liberate it? Is he calling for the rediscovery of hermeneutics as a discipline, but within a nonreligious, that is, primarily intellectual frame? That is the direction Heidegger will go, with the difficult aim to depragmatize meaning and to explore (if not explain) why we cannot speak "being" at the present time, like a Scripture does or a few great poets. Is not "intellectual tradition," however, an oxymoron, since traditions are notoriously resistant to rationalization? Does "intellectual" intend "secular"—in which case the critic would be seeking an alternative tradition to the one that sustained the religious if unstable society of seventeenth-century England? The subject-phrase that opens the paragraph is impersonal, evoking as Eliot does an authoritative guide.

We are on a train that must switch from one rail to another, yet our journey takes us along both. It is essential (1) to explore the antagonism of theory and tradition, which Richards accommodates by the notion of

95

"intellectual tradition." It is also essential (2) to explore the question of critical style, that is, how to read *criticism* aright, which leads us to acknowledge a conflict between the essayistic mode and descriptive poetics.

Yet we can relate (2) to (1). The growth of a science of literature that looks down on the familiar essay replays the antagonism of theory to tradition. Essayistic criticism is held to be merely impressionistic or epigonic (parasitic) by scientific critics. It is accused of using the resources of figuration in a lax or self-contaminating way. From it, consequently, no rules can be derived for reading aright the auxiliary prose that exists to help us read literature aright. "Figurative language," a typical statement runs, "is a stereotype of 'essayistic' criticism. It is a symptom of its epigonic character: 'essayistic' criticism imitates the semantics of its object language because it is unable to develop its own descriptive language; therefore, it cannot rise above the level of paraphrase or parody" (Lubomir Dolezel).

Practically speaking, the contradiction between descriptive modes and essayistic ones is less formidable than it appears. For however inventive of categories and technical words the science of literature may be, it relies, like literature itself, on the critical essay to integrate and familiarize its terms. Is it not, in fact, a sin against literary science to forget that the social and pedagogical prose we use in most discussions originates in the essayistic criticism of the latter half of the seventeenth century and the beginning of the eighteenth? That prose was inspired by the proto-democratic ideal of the *honnête homme* (see Chapter 2), and it has remained almost totally stable as an ethos and a style from the time of *Tatler* and *Spectator* to that of the *New York Review of Books*. Indeed the return to technical poetics is often a protest, one of several, against the demi-intimacies of this style that pretends to be a conversational equality of author and reader and subdues class distinctions as well as the signs and trappings of expertise. Even Hans-Georg Gadamer is tempted to put his key concept of a "fusion of horizons" under its aegis. *Horizontverschmelzung,* he claims, is "the full realization of conversation in which something is expressed that is not only mine or my author's, but common."

In addition to a science of literature, or integral to it, we need a sociology. Important as the conversational imperative was in forming a communicative prose, it drifted into a bad gentility promoting chitchat or causerie even in professional circles. While not bad in itself, since one can only praise what James Boswell described as "gaiety of conversation and civility of manners," the habit was unfortunate in the way it censored both enthusiasm and the scientific spirit. Its decorum tyrannized over large tracts of French and English letters.[7] Richards' insistence on theory is clearly a provocation to the genteel and amateur tradition: it calls for research, protocols, professionalism, empirically tested principles. The title of his first book, *Principles of Literary Criticism* (1924), gains resonance against the background of the parodic Jane Austen opening of R. H. Tawney's *The Acquisitive Society* (1920): "It is a commonplace that the characteristic virtue of Englishmen is their power of sustained practical activity, and their characteristic vice a reluctance to test the quality of that activity by reference to principles. They are incurious as to theory."

Richards lifted a Cloud of Unknowing from the humanities at the risk of admitting scientific and artisanal ideals. *Chariots of Fire* (1981), the Hugh Hudson film about life at Cambridge University in the 1920s, renders the situation against which the emphasis on theory protested.

There surely is an "ordeal of civility" (J. M. Cuddihy) which the founders of the "sciences humaines"—Marx, Freud, Lévi-Strauss—and their followers had to undergo. The central tradition of learning was also a Gentile tradition; to jump forward a little, when Harold Bloom used Buber's *I and Thou* as a framework for Shelley's mythmaking, or Gershom Scholem's understanding of Kaballa to argue for this theory of misreading, the jittery dovecotes of English studies did not coo with pleasure. An eloquent article denouncing Bloom and one of his colleagues, entitled "The Hermeneutical Mafia: After Strange Gods at Yale," not only alludes to one of Eliot's most Christian books but makes it clear that something not quite gentlemanly was going on in the Old School. Essayistic criticism, in short, is not always part of the tradition but fights an internal battle by fashioning an iconoclastic style. When we read Coleridge on "the modern Anglo-Gallican style," which he despised because it was without "the hooks and eyes of intellectual meaning, never oppressing the mind by any after-recollection," do we not suspect that it was to redress such attenuation that Jacques Derrida—*enfin*—appeared?

A neglected aspect of the ordeal of civility concerns women. Though the conversational ideal is attached to the "gentleman," in France it is perpetuated by the salons.[8] The civilizing power of women over men was, in any case, a chivalrous cliché that came into the Renaissance via legends and books of courtesy. The cliché intimated also the other side of woman: her seductive potential that could lead men to break out of the bonds of conventional behavior. For Virginia Woolf the issue posed itself in terms of the domestication of women; and in that domestication, in the tying down of the wildness, in confining her to the role of consort, mother, housekeeper, the conversational ideal played its part. It was not gossip (often subversive) but social chitchat that kept the emotions in check, albeit at the cost of trivializing overt relationships.

Woolf's short stories *Monday or Tuesday* (and others published between 1921 and 1925) show that kind of conversation eating into a woman's soul. She even seems to cooperate with it: the Mrs. Dalloway figures in Woolf's fiction are as reticent about their true feelings as the men. So "Together and Apart" depicts the impasse of small talk as it unseals yet soon freezes a momentary affection. Words are frigid; they fail to betray (in the sense both of express and give away) persons who must hunt and haunt each other by these wary, destabilizing tokens. Alongside this Jamesian theme another prevails at the level of near-caricature: tags of poetry and gilded phrases rise up in the female soul—even identifying themselves as that soul—to create a prose poem that counterpoints an asthenic causerie. This rape by revery, by golden speech ("Thinking thus, the branch of some tree in front of her became soaked and steeped in her admiration for the people of the house; dripped gold; or stood sentinel"), is as disconcerting as the more prosaic impositions of society. Each stream of thought, color it gold or gray, is composed of clichés and keeps language within an airless realm of signifiers. Sasha Lasham, we read, "was glad she was with Bertram, who could be trusted, even out of doors, to talk without stopping . . . he chattered on about his tour of Devonshire, about inns and landladies, about Eddie and Freddie, about cows and night travelling, about creams and stars, about continental railways and Bradshaw, catching cod, catching cold, influenza, rheumatism, and Keats." For woman's soul, "by nature unmated, a widow bird," this distancing of the outdoors by pseudo-intimate talk at once preserves virginity and disastrously confirms its violation. "At that moment, in some back street or public house, the usual terrible sexless, inarticulate voice rang out; a shriek, a cry. And the widow bird startled, flew away."[9]

At this point I wish to propose a historical generalization. If the history of commentary spans more than two millennia, then the period René Wellek describes as "Modern Criticism" is dominated by closure and premature synthesis. From about 1660 to 1950 (I chose dates that should be modified by a knowledge of national traditions) a neoclassical decorum triumphed, despite traumatic breaks and perhaps because of them. Even when art was adventurous, criticism remained reactionary. It requires of course more than the pop sociology I can offer to indicate how many factors conspired to produce that loss or limitation of interpretive skill which is Richards' point of departure.

The closure characterizing that period involves an ethos of language refinement that goes back in England to Charles II and the Augustan age, and is still notable in Richards' mentor, C. K. Ogden, who published Bentham's incisive attack on legal fictions and wrote a tract against "word-magic" entitled *Debabelization* (the occasion was the Basic English project, which Richards too supported). Sacred hermeneutics are marginalized; there is a general weakening of multivocal diction and a consensus in favor of plain or common speech and whatever genres and formal unities could be derived from Aristotle. The "limitary tone of English thought," as Ralph Waldo Emerson called it, is formed.

There is nothing original in identifying such a period of closure. Nor in suggesting that a fear of enthusiasm, which leaves its stamp on Swift's greatness, is the scarlet thread that runs through an age in which a *via media* decorum spread to all matters in hopes of damping the fires of controversy and preventing a recurrence of bloody schisms. Mikhail Bakhtin, taking Continental rather than English literature as his text, sees a similar period characterized by the attempt to repress vernacular energies and popular—especially mocking and so potentially revolutionary—speech. My sense is that this period continues much longer in criticism than in art, and with fewer exceptions.

So decisive in any case is the disintoxication of prose and the suspicion of visionary poetry beyond Spenser, Shakespeare, and Milton that Somerset Maugham can assert of the King James Bible that it has been harmful to English prose. "The Bible is an oriental book. Its alien imagery has nothing to do with us. Those hyperboles, those luscious metaphors, are foreign to our genius." The latter consisted, according to

Maugham, in plain speech. "Blunt Englishmen twisted their tongues to speak like Hebrew prophets." He does not see how he passes from bluntness to refinement, as he concludes: "To write good prose is an affair of good manners . . . good prose should resemble the conversation of a well-bred man."[10] Though written in the late 1930s, these lines might have been redacted in Will's Coffee House where the Tatler held forth in the first decade of the eighteen century.

I am under no illusion that in pursuing the question of style, and pitting theory against gentility, I have resolved the larger issue of the relation of theory to tradition. My purpose was to suggest that in this area too we do not know we are talking in prose.

It is time to consider two influential positions—of George Lukács and of deconstruction—to see how they stand in the lines of thought I have followed: the question of critical style and the antagonism of theory to tradition. Tradition for Lukács is German idealist philosophy and its Classical background. What relation may there be between the literary theory of this thinker and philosophy, on the one hand, and German classicism, on the other?

The crucial link between theory and philosophy involves, as in Hegel, the notion of totality. It is only through a total and integrating view that knowledge of reality can come about. This sounds obvious enough, but it raises the question of why things do not appear as what they are, or do not fall naturally into place, disclosing their true relation to the whole. For Hegel the answer points to history as a gradual, laborious and dialectical fulfilment, an "Odyssey" of the human spirit. And for Lukács' *Theory of the Novel* (completed around 1915) that mention of the *Odyssey* is both relevant and ironic: the difference between Greek epic and the contemporary novel being a difference between the possibility of achieving, despite contradiction and heterogeneity, a total and harmonious view of things and the impossibility of such integration except at the level of philosophical method. Where art was, theory must be. It alone has the force to go from the fragmented, alienated nature of present fetishes and objectifications to a totalizing vision—one that integrates all things without reconciling them.

In Lukács' *History and Class Consciousness*, written only a few years later, but with the Russian Revolution and bloody German clashes on

Right and Left intervening, theory's unmasking function is emphasized, in addition to its integrative function. An instrument of the revolutionary consciousness, theory will make us see reality *de novo*—not unmediated of course but, on the contrary, informed by all the mediations that determine and overdetermine what we have naively accepted as natural. Through theory we gain the strength to "tear the veil" drawn by the ideology of the ruling class over the reification (commodification) of human relations in bourgeois society. The picture of modernity Lukács took from the novel is now applied to the condition of man under capitalism, a far more profoundly disturbed condition than in Classical culture. Theory, in short, is a totalizing perspective that unmasks another totality—capitalism's pseudoobjective, pseudoholistic way of life, which retains a power of untruth because of the ghostly objectivity created when we constitute the relations between people as a relation between things.

Lukács is aware that the unmasking change theory effects in our understanding is still allied to something imaginary. In that sense his concept of theory does not break with a traditional view of art. He is now interested, however, in the transformative as well as reflective power of art—transformative, I mean, of the subject (the consumer). We who are bewitched by capitalism must find a means of disenchantment, of breaking the spell, and from within our historical moment. Otherwise we lapse into a transcendental form of interpretation, whereby thought realizes only itself and does not change anything outside itself.

This crucial, thought-and-reality-altering potential of theory is described as follows. The dialectical method "destroys the fiction of the immortality of [bourgeois] categories," and with that their reified character. For in capitalist society even categories of thought are treated like things, and the thing itself is transcendentalized (as in Kant's "Ding an Sich"). The critique intends to destroy German idealist residues which had perpetuated an antihistorical, "eternizing" strain in Greek thought. More basically, theory unmasks capitalism by representing it in its purest form, that is, as a total and translucent phenomenon. By that visionary move, confused happenings and concealed appearances become intelligible, fully correspondent to a theory that enables the desired demystification. "No sooner does this strategy produce results, no sooner does this world of phenomena seem to be on the point of crystallizing out into

101

theory, than it dissolves into a mere illusion, a distorted situation appears as in a distorting mirror which is, however, 'only the conscious expression of an imaginary movement.' "[11]

Given this kind of world, can anything be read aright? Theory's imaginative error reveals but a second error: the unmasked social system. The theoretical thinker knows, at the same time, that his representation cannot be as true or total as it pretends to be, because by its very nature capitalism is not coherent. Theory discloses the full insufficiency of one (capitalist) system in the light of the unrealized reality of the desired (socialist) system. When Lukács describes theory as a distorting mirror that yields the translucent image of a denatured reality, he is doing something tricky and extraordinary with the reflection (mimetic) theory of art. He views art as the historically transcended precursor of theory, but he also views theory as a representational technique now fully aware of its imaginative force. It becomes an instrument of the class struggle that reveals the illusory and contradictory nature of capitalism; it cannot straighten its angle of vision or de-distort itself in order to produce a true image of socialism.

"La chose est oblique," Derrida writes at the end of *Glas* (1974). Obliquity affects the thing, that is, every effort to describe what is the case, every historical reconstruction, every representation of reality. The problematics of reading with which modern criticism is concerned, and the ambiguity or distortedness of signs (even as we pass from partial criticism to holistic theory) cannot offer more than the pattern of a rigorous subversion of idealistic, bourgeois, pseudoclassical assumptions—in short, of tradition as error. Hegel's key notion that mind reveals and grasps itself as a "labor of the negative" is set to a harsher music. Yet "labor" in Marxist thought denotes not a temporal, quasi-religious waiting in patience, but an actual if alienated force in social relations, and a negated value in economics.

The recovery of that negated value in the history of criticism—so negated that it can reappear only as a "negative" value—is what attracts us to the strongest and most theoretical thinkers of the present era: Walter Benjamin, Martin Heidegger, Theodor Adorno, Maurice Blanchot, Jacques Derrida, Paul de Man. We recognize that the negative form of their intellectual energy *is* an energy—that it can inspire, and without promising an edifying or progressive result. When we recall how parsimonious Eliot is about precisely this critical energy, and how much talk surrounds us concerning human powers being laid waste by the options, distractions, stimulus-flooding, alienating tempo, and endless semiosis of modern life, then we realize how difficult it has been to make that negated energy work *for* rather than *against* us. Indeed, Freud's classic analysis of the discontent in civilized life predicts that we cannot reach the stage where labor puts on a purely human face. It is doomed to produce collective relations that are a form of slavery as well as of love, and modes of leisure that drift toward passivity and nirvanalike regression.

It is fascinating that the problem of "economy" is always raised by Eliot in an aesthetic rather than a sociopolitical context. His critique of *Hamlet,* and his formula of the "objective correlative," repeat in another form his view on William Blake. The artist who lacks an authorized worldview has to expend too much energy in creating rather than adapting one. This anxiety about the energy required to meet the challenge of modernity is not a factor in Georg Lukács; for him there are untapped resources in the repressed working-class ethos, and the very tearing of the veil energizes, because it reveals something real, material, and labor-related rather than spiritual-ghostly.

At the same time this conversion of the negative into revolutionary energies can lead to coercive and totalitarian demands. An example is Ernst Jünger's *The Worker (Der Arbeiter),* a long, articulate tract of political philosophy published the year before Hitler came to power. Jünger attacks the arts as an intolerable luxury, the last refuge of bourgeois stability and fetishized traditions. He castigates their lack of productive power and predicts the development of great weapons of destruction to counterbalance this hoarding of cultural goods. He demands in fact a radical lightening of the baggage foisted on us by culture and education ("eine Gepäckserleichterung . . . die man sich gar nicht gründlich und umfassend genug vorstellen kann"). In words that are unbearably ominous today, because they express so openly the totalitarian coercion, Jünger asks for a complete mobilization ("totale Mobilmachung") whose task it is to "turn life into energy, as it manifests itself in business, technology and communications through the whirring of wheels, or on the battlefield as fire-power and mobility."

The disconcerting agility with which totalitarianisms of the Right and Left compete for the worker's soul, the way clichés like fetishism and totality are appropriated by both sides, yields a first perspective on the problematic "purity" of deconstruction. There is an awareness that to reverse values or oppositions is not enough, that it is only the beginning of an inquiry to disclose the mutuality of such oppositions, and a verbal vertigo as frightening as the vacuity it displaces. But there is also a question about the character of the intellectual and transformative energy claimed by revolutionary thinkers. Does that energy escape messianic or visionary sources of hope, the same often denounced as being at the root of our incapacity to live simply and humanely?

When de Man says, paraphrasing Walter Benjamin, it is not at all certain that language is human (or words to that effect), he cannot be going back to the thesis that language has a divine origin, since foundationalism is strenuously resisted by deconstruction. It is precisely language with its peculiar deferrals of meaning that undermines the metaphysical positioning of origin or end. Nor is it likely that the statement is a naive agnostic reflex. As one of those gnomic utterances by which de Man unsettles us, it reintroduces a worry about the nonhuman or transcendent impulse in language. That had previously troubled the question of the invention (origin) of words; now it returns as a question concerning the inventions (products) of language. For however practical and expressive our linguistic abilities are, they stand in a distancing, even renunciatory relation to phenomenal reality. Thinking and naming (un-naming), language and the labor of the negative, converge. One often senses an alliance between deconstruction's interminable analysis of texts (sometimes in the form of "plurisy" of verbal play that "dies in its own too much"), and the negative counsels of a theology that renounces worldly values and especially a possessiveness regarding the divine names. Deconstruction is still engaged in identifying and removing anthropomorphism from thought. It says no more, no less, than that language has no "proper" meaning, and so must, yet cannot, be appropriated.

What keeps deconstruction mysterious is only the opaqueness of its social or political motive. It seems to enact an intellectual scruple that serves no one. It therefore leaves itself open to the charge that it does not care to change things, that it is content to tease language and mind by its paradoxes and paranomasia. According to its detractors, it is at most a powerful critique of academic pretensions. And did we not know already, with their idol Nietzsche, that university culture is a mode of professional deformation, a *Gelehrtenkultur*? In view of the purity of deconstruction (which may be paradoxically related to its sense of the impurity or over-determined character of writing and politics) it is consoling to remember critics of the 1920s and 1930s who debated the fate of language and reading in modern society.

Yet deconstruction for its part also emphasizes reading. (That emphasis helped its acceptance in America.) Now, however, ad hoc concepts adopted by the New Critics to motivate their concentration on reading ("organic unity," "heresy of paraphrase," "intentional fallacy") are given a fully negative development. Theories of impersonality, of intertextuality, of an "inmixing of the Other," model the text as a field of forces in which writers inscribe their experience. The new model entails a questioning of masterful author, all-stabilizing ego, and incarnate world. A linguistic or semiotic critique arises of how language is prematurely synthesized and appropriated. Also how words take their revenge: Derrida's analysis of *pharmakon* in Plato shows that it means undecidably poison and cure, and that this in-difference affects the entire system.

In terms of reading, the handling of ambiguity is a very sensitive matter. Art in some sense speaks beyond the doubt and irony it subsumes, just as every ideology-critique is indebted not only to what it criticizes (which could produce political stalemate and leave everything, as before, open to schemes of violence) but to a unitive mythology represented by Northrop Frye as an infectious principle of structure. How is ambiguity to be contained? From the 1930s (especially after William Empson) and into the 1950s, the disclosure of ambiguity was often accompanied by a theory of archetypes, generally indebted to Jung and Kerenyi, that grounds polysemy as a positive value. There was a tendency to link myth and archetype to, in particular, Romantic art, as if that explained the residual magic of all literature, its recuperative and unifying qualities in an enlightened age. Movements like deconstruction not only revise this view of Romanticism by showing the latter's dialectical and ironic style—even when most "symbolic"—but keep an analytic eye on the otherness, rather than supposed therapeutic intimacy, of symbol and archetype. The post-Flaubertian nausea of Roland Barthes, when he senses a cliché, is also a reaction to *masked* otherness, to the insidious violence of stereotypes in both conservative and emancipatory thought. If "it is not at all certain that language is human," one reason is that these stereotypes are easily given the spurious (often politically motivated) authority of archetypes.

At every point, then, deconstruction prefers to develop the notion of critique as impasse. Take the question of discursive style: is deconstruction scientific or essayistic? We can reply that it belongs to the sphere of the essay, because deconstructive reading no longer aims to establish a master-code but undoes every totalizing perspective. Yet it also belongs in spirit to the science of literature. We certainly have cause to place deconstruction on the side of theory, since its largest effort is to see Western tradition as a totality, one that has erroneously promoted the closure of the commentary process by reifying canon and book. Taking a page from George Lukács, we could argue that deconstruction's totalizing view "distorts into purity" a tradition that envelops us, and which we cannot criticize from the outside—the more so as "outside" "inside" presupposes a dichotomy deconstruction views with suspicion. It cannot be classified disjunctively as a philosophy *or* as a type of literary analysis. It is both; and while it implies a theory of reading, that theory seems to be effective only as a set of practices, of actual readings, which revise and so revive texts in an "intellectual" tradition stretching from Plato to and beyond Mallarmé.

I sometimes feel that deconstruction itself is the impasse. The name stresses analysis, and *Abbau* rather than *Aufbau* in the wake of the grand spiritual narratives, the dialectical structures which *Geisteswissenschaft* built up after Hegel. Wilhelm Dilthey is the grand old man of those grand narratives, though Gadamer is a worthy successor. Theory for both Dilthey and Gadamer articulates the inner form of tradition, which is held to be its truth rather than untruth; and theory cannot triumphantly replace, only manifest, a rich historical evolution. To make of theory a critical rather than totalizing instrument—or totalizing in the service of criticism—motivates the extraskillful structuralism *(avant la lettre)* of Northrop Frye, which integrates William Blake's at once visionary and radical Protestantism. Perhaps the best one can do is to "place" deconstruction, and to show that it is not a foreign import but connects with English developments that had glimpsed the impasse of theory and tradition.

For this, curiously, we must return to Coleridge, and chapter 13 (an unlucky chapter) of his literary autobiography. That he wrote a literary biography is remarkable in itself and suggests the text-haunted character of his imagination. He adopts, in chapter 13, a "Constructive Philosophy" that tries to break from the entanglement of texts by identifying the role of imagination in the (mainly Fichtean) dialectic by which otherness is derived from ego. About to tie himself into a knot, he interrupts the chapter by inserting a letter from a prudent friend, advising him that this kind of talk is neither intelligible nor sellable. Coleridge then jumps to the famous definition of imagination (primary and secondary) every schoolboy can learn by heart. The characteristic virtue of Englishmen, their practical instinct, wins out, and Coleridge's autobiography has to compose itself of two rather than three types of discourse: a narrative of the readings that have determined him, together with (instead of the masterful paradigm of Constructive Philosophy) passages of practical criticism that disclose the unifying power in imagination—a unity which neither his life nor his philosophy could demonstrate.

Now Constructive Philosophy is a term applied to the work of Schiller, Fichte, and Schelling (today called identity-philosophy) that culminates in Hegel's effort to overcome the formalism of Kant. Prior to Derrida it received its strongest antithetical response in Heidegger, and the Frankfurt School (Theodor Adorno, Max Horkheimer, Walter Benjamin, Herbert Marcuse). Derrida moves away from the possibility of identity to a radical notion of difference that seeks to avoid any foundational or resolving concept. Difference is not difference in contrast to identity, as if we could base it on the experience of a self-identical thing. So *deconstruction* is a fitting name, if we recall that Schelling, while respecting the contradictions that open up in thought when it tries to recover "repressed resources" *(versiegte Quellen)*, defines *construction* as the resolving of contradictions *(Aufhebung der Gegensätze)*. Deconstruction is a twig that twitches for the *versiegte Quellen* of suppressed or sublimated contradiction in every system or text.

Indeed, it shies even from "interpretation" because interpretation-theory (hermeneutics) is traditionally engaged in a textual or conceptual harmonizing of contradictions. The neutral, even flat resonance of "reading" suits it better; and though reading means more than reading—though reading, in deconstruction, is raised to a second power—there is no suggestion that logical or grammatical or rhetorical forms can be moved to a higher plane when they clash with one another. The conflict of systematized modes of analysis is valued, even when it leads to an impasse in the construction of a single, unified meaning. That language works in this manner, always imperfect from a mechanical or totalizing perspective, that it must in fact use error (some call it tradition) as its energy, is what makes it so remarkable an instrument.

I have to end sometime, so let it be with two observations. One concerns the surprising antihermeneutic stance of deconstruction. It not only directs the notion of allegory against allegoresis but refuses to harmonize the text with itself or think of literary works as having a yummy, mysterious inside—a depth-dimension that would bestow existential pathos on inner division and ambivalence. The removal of this myth of depth also shows itself as a suspicion of psychologism, naive intentionalism, and essentialist views like the "Proper Meaning Superstition" Richards analyzed in his *Philosophy of Rhetoric*. Its play with the words of a text, at the same time, which is often—in Derrida—as consistent and extravagant as that of the midrashic rabbis, sets up an impasse in which an ancient interpretive skill is recovered yet cannot be grounded by either faith or theory. Like clowns or jongleurs, deconstructionist critics repeat the same act with language, obliging us to think of its negative, dismantling, as well as promissory, aspects.

My last observation concerns the residual "metaphysical pathos" in deconstruction. It is, more precisely, a methodological pathos: a mourning over the self-invalidating nature of all methodologies. A desire for rigor, in the form of a near-Pascalian hatred of egotism (the source of delusion and moral fallibility), remains. In an era where literary studies claim to be autonomous yet have absorbed the often minute and pugilistic intensity of religious kinds of exegesis, it is all too easy to put secular hopes on literature rather than Scripture. The working-out of this confusion—foreseen by Matthew Arnold—preoccupies most literary thinkers at present, and partially explains the puristic demeanor of deconstruction—which can become merely hygienic and mechanical. The larger issue here is in what sense we can lay claim to a Scripture, whether in the form of the Bible, or a secular canon (a national, privileged corpus of writings) or even to something special defined as literature in distinction to what is not literary. Deconstruction scrupulously points to the reversibility of hierarchical constructs or to foreclosures in the commentary-process. When it challenges, by close reading, assumptions about the unity of the work of art or discloses the drive in every type of discourse for unmediated expression, a drive that includes mimetic as well as mystical residues, indeed everything associated with the dew still clinging to the words "origin," "presence," "being"—then deconstruction is not a symptom of lack of conviction but a sane and sustained response to ersatz religions.

five

Placing F. R. Leavis

The astonishing importance of F. R. Leavis in the English academic consciousness does not seem to be a passing fad. The scandalmaker of the 1930s became, by a kind of self-fulfilling prophecy, part of the saving remnant on which the future of reading would depend. The photo on the cover of Denys Thompson's *The Leavises* shows him in a jacket impermeable to the insults of time and with the open shirt of a labor leader.[1] He looks indeed, as his wife wrote of both of them, "grey-haired and worn down with battling for survival in a hostile environment." Queenie Leavis stands beside him, also dressed simply, sharing his pursed lips and focused eyes that tilt only slightly toward a better world. Together they make a painful hendiadys, an icon of the threadbare, indomitable British intellectual. The snapshot catches something grim and mortal: an embattled uniformity, rather than their spirit active for half a century to save a culture that had lost, so Leavis wrote, "any sense of the difference between life and electricity."

That phrase characterizes the consistency of a career totally within the contracted sphere of the English university, and devoted to making it reflect a "human world" instead of lusting after technological improvements that "promised to abstract the hopes of Man / Out of his feelings" (Wordsworth). Cambridge was the right place for this pursuit: here the sciences were valued and, in Leavis's eyes, overvalued; here the first School of English took hold.

One cannot separate Leavis from his university environment. The man found his lair and never faltered in his attempt to conform it to a vision that was as simple in its outlines as it was complex in its outcome. He called for the "re-establishment of an educated reading public," which implied that there had been, once, such a public; that education, especially through the agency of the university, might restore it; and that "reading" English was both the means to reform and perhaps its best result. This concern for reading was drummed in relentlessly, and supported early on by Mrs. Leavis, whose *Fiction and the Reading Public* (London, 1932) provided an official version of the rise and fall of the class-integrated audience. It also pioneered a direction which social analysis was to take by focusing, like I. A. Richards, on problems of communication and reception.

Leavis himself wrote a Ph.D. thesis on the emergence of magazines like the *Spectator* and the *Tatler,* which inspired the ideal of the educated or Common Reader. Modern critical prose was founded by their periodical essays, which also prepared for the great English novel. Keeping up the pretence of a "correspondence" between equals, Steele and Addison, and a few others like them, removed matters of taste from the heat of religious and political controversy. Art, as Schiller was to argue in his *Letters on Aesthetic Education,* was not simply a higher form of play that restored the illusion of wholeness to persons fragmented by the specialized demands of the modern world. Art mediated between two distinct tyrannies that always threatened human freedom: the tyranny of nature or instinct, and the tyranny of the state. It would not be an exaggeration to say that for Leavis the University institutionalized Schiller's idea of Aesthetic Education. If there could be an organisational arrangement to sustain rather than stifle the "organic community," it was the university as Leavis envisaged it in *Education and the University* (1943).

While in the United States of the 1920s and 1930s the university became linked to democratic hopes for bringing literacy (both scientific and humanistic) to all classes, Leavis placed his trust in a small meritocracy of skilled readers. Whitehead and Dewey, who stressed the university's contribution to the quality of life as much as he did, must have been anathema to him. Their optimism concerning the huddled masses was far removed from his fears about pseudoliteracy, the herd instinct, journalism, the application of technology to learning, and unfounded hopes as to the "culture" of science. As Chris Baldick writes in his fine *The Social Mission of English Criticism,* the educational model of the Leavises "re-

111

volves around the opposition between society at large and 'society' in the eighteenth-century sense; between an unconscious mass and its conscious embodiment or guardian."[2]

Leavis' sense of the eighteenth century was indeed crucial. His views were not very different from those of Establishment scholars, though more nuanced and critical, as his deft comparison of Dryden and Pope in *Revaluation* (1936) showed. Eighteenth-century journals, in creating the educated or Common Reader, also laid the ground for what Leavis' early tract (1930) would call "mass civilisation" in contrast to "minority culture." A plague of words, unleashed by Grub Street scribblers and the proliferating tribe of virtuosi (comparable perhaps to university dons), prompted Pope's *Dunciad* with its climactic vision of the eclipse of culture and the triumph of an "uncreating word." Eliot's notion of a dissociation of sensibility from thought, accelerating after Donne and Shakespeare, seemed only to confirm Pope's diagnosis.

The Augustan virtues of gentility, correctness, and refinement were merely, in this context, "a sublime singerie"—to quote Voltaire on the art of the French dancing-masters. Leavis could not forget how quickly the vernacular genius of English declined, after Shakespeare, into a mannered language. There was, however, nothing deterministic or fatalistic in his view of literary history; he held no overt thesis on the precise causes of that decline. He may have regretted that an independent peasantry (also Wordsworth's desideratum) did not grow strong enough to survive the Industrial Revolution. But he relied less on social history than on his sense for the growth of an antiword. The decline happened once, and perhaps happens always. Literature betrayed itself in Milton, Leavis' favorite bogey, while prose, when not downright journalistic or crude, began to walk on Johnsonian stilts. "There is no Common Reader," Leavis declared in the 1960s. "The tradition is dead." Yet one wonders whether that tradition ever existed except as a compelling social fantasy.

It is strange that Leavis should seem so dogmatic, when he is merely didactic. With Shakespeare as the measure, he tests every writer, always looking for the emergence of a renewed vernacular energy, a canon of native classics. He begins by underestimating some Romantics and championing decisively the high modernism of such poets as Hopkins, Pound, and Eliot. Yet by the time he died he had considerably revised himself.

After the "Line of Wit" discussed in *Revaluation,* a new achievement is said to have entered English letters, going from Blake through Dickens to D. H. Lawrence, and centering in the novel. The admission of Dickens into the canon overturns the verdict of *Fiction and the Reading Public* and goes beyond the rescue of *Hard Times,* the one Dickens novel treated in *The Great Tradition* (1948). That Dickens was a popular entertainer is not held against him in this case; Leavis' increasing tolerance for "moral fable," especially when it tackles the subject of education itself—Mr. Gradgrind versus Sissy Jupe in *Hard Times,* or Blake versus the England of Locke and Newton—allows him to observe how a "poetically-creative" prose takes over from Shakespeare's dramatic gift. "Shakespeare," he wrote in *The Living Principle* (1975), "compels one to recognise that language is essentially heuristic." What is intriguing is Leavis' fidelity to that principle, and the gradual shift of allegiance toward Dickens and Blake. In the *Critic as Anti-Philosopher* it is Blake's language—and Wordsworth's—which is heuristic, while Eliot, a Urizen despite himself in his view of humanity as utterly abject, is championed only for his poetic creativity, for "doing impossible things" with the English language."

As is his wont, Leavis does not define "heuristic" except by example, by singling out this or that passage and displaying its resourceful, even equivocal texture. "You can't tell beforehand what liberties will justify themselves." Despite enormous differences in presentational method, Derrida's emphasis on the aleatory or chancy character of language (based not only on Freud and Saussure but also on Mallarmé and Valéry) has the same, radical focus. As it turns out, Leavis' insistence on judgment and revaluation is not the sign of a doctrinaire but of an open mind—with standards, to be sure, and lively prejudices, yet a mind for which excellence was never confined to a single writer, period, or "total upshot." His commitment goes beyond these to language, and in particular to English as the reservoir and result of the labours of genius—indeed, analogous to a biological acquisition. I do not admire his aggressive taciturnity, but neither am I alarmed by the fact that he can only jab words at us, to describe an "English language in terms of which the writer lives his creative life." The collective memory which anthropologists have tried to define at the level of *pensée sauvage* he locates at the level of high culture. The result can be a jargon of authenticity as unpalatable as Heidegger's. "The 'living principle' itself is an apprehended totality of what, as registered in the language, has been won or established in immemorial human living."

Did Leavis, then, escape the varicose veins of theory as it imposes a rigid or curious vocabulary? Once a socioelect establishes itself, only a mannered and idiosyncratic prose can achieve some distance from it. Such a sentence as "Essential or Blakean responsibility manifests itself in the full accepting recognition that the directing *ahnung* implicit in life and the *nisus* that has led to the achieving of mind and anticipatory apprehension and initiative are to be thought of as, in the world we know (Los's world), preeminently represented by humanity" is hardly a well of English undefiled.

Many learned books are now placing Leavis in an "English" line of social thought. Fred Inglis' *Radical Earnestness* has an explicit section on the English mind. He gets away with it because of his zany, fast-paced, name-dropping style, which puts Collingwood, Keynes, and Leavis together as "decent herbivores" who shun a "man-eating rhetoric," resituate their ideas in literature, and make common cause against "ruling-class Oxford and Cambridge . . . still deeply poisoned by the playboys of Brideshead." The earnestness of English Inglis does not always extend to his prose. His book, a swarm of lively, stinging words, is as beleaguered as Leavis was, being written, we are told, "at a time when, in Britain, intellectual life is itself once more openly menaced by the interest groups of the time-servers and gangsters who live inside and outside the gates of the academies." The desperate hope Leavis placed in the University has clearly become more desperate: but that "English" sense of how to speak quietly yet forcefully amid the noise of political and journalistic sloganeering has vanished, despite Inglis' claim that he "honours a line of men who kept up such language," and his own driving intelligence that exposes the "blank at the heart of the moral sciences."

Chris Baldick also deals with that blank or vacuum. He has written an important and clarifying work that traces the rise and rationale of English studies from Arnold to Leavis. To replace with "English" such different, often competitive disciplines as moral philosophy, social history, and political science entails ideological struggle, and loss rather than gain. Inglis enjoys the fray, and the energies released by it; Baldick analyzes an impasse. He shows that the claims made by Leavis for the centrality of a literary education are just too large and untheoretical. In the wake of Arnold, the crucial question was what might substitute for religion in English life—insofar as religion had proved to be, culturally, a cohering symbolism, making for wholeness rather than division. Could a literature of imaginative reason replace religion's unifying role? Could literary criticism, by renewing a scrupulous conversation between persons and between the private and public sector, retain at least the sensibility of the "organic community"?

This is the task insinuated by "practical" in "practical criticism"—a discipline which is obviously more than the exercise of a brilliant analytic technique. In Richards, "practical" scarcely conceals a wild utopian and scientific hope, the possibility of engineering a substantial improvement in communications and so in world health. Leavis, *contra* Richards, adopts a sense of "practical" that is opposed to "theoretical" and directed always to the text and person *at hand*. He shrinks the mission of social criticism into a reform of literary studies. Baldick concludes his book with an indictment: "The title of 'criticism' was usurped by a literary discourse whose entire attitude was at heart uncritical. Criticism in its most important and its most vital sense had been gutted and turned into its very opposite: an ideology."

A leader in the *Times Literary Supplement* of 5 March 1970 (devoted to the Social Sciences) voices a similar complaint about the social conscience of the English critic. It compares English with French responses to Marxist thought. English empiricism, the anonymous writer claims, "by destroying potentially useful ideas before they could be applied to new situations, has left an uncomfortable legacy. The bias of empiricism was largely responsible for preventing a whole generation of English philosophers from becoming familiar with important aspects of Hegel." And so of course with aspects of Marx. In France the challenge of Marxist thought was met by a typically national appropriation, much preferable to English neglect or Soviet orthodoxy. "A number of important French thinkers had the good sense to attempt to make the Hegelian-Marxist heritage relevant to their own problems. They thought of Marx as a western thinker, not in his eastern iconology."

Leavis, in this light, carries too great a burden. He must substitute for, or new-create, the social conscience of English criticism. Baldick's title-dates are ironic opposites: 1848 denotes the revolutionary turmoil to

115

which Marx responds, and 1932 launches Leavis' *Scrutiny*. Detaching criticism from any direct engagement with politics or theory, Leavis fosters a "culturalism" that removes all intermediate categories like class, sex, creed, and occupation, in order to focus exclusively on the genius of the language and the genius of the writer.

Unfortunately Baldick limits his view to the English scene, and so appears to confirm the existence of a separate "English Mind." That exacerbates the problem by keeping it in the family. Inglis too, despite his habit of breaking out in a rash of names, accepts the way English intellectuals have treated ideas by keeping them close to the tea table or a "domestic idiom." There is little ventilation: no reference (except nominally) to Lukács, who sets theory against alienation and fragmentation; no acknowledgment of the Frankfurt School's attempt to frame an ideology-critique; no mention of Ortega's *Revolt of the Masses;* no comparison of English with Continental reactions to the upsurge of propaganda, stock responses, and standardization.

The family perspective of a book like Baldick's is deceptively invigorating and contributes to the crisis it identifies. Yet it does begin to examine the question of "Englishness." What is at stake is the strength of stereotypes or "vital prejudices," their felt necessity in the active as well as the sluggish mind. They evade analysis, as if reflection were a hereditary enemy. Like role-playing, they have many useful functions (comic, cathartic, consolidating). Yet when the Nazis add the concept of purity to that of race or genius, stereotyping becomes sinister and a carrier of hate rather than tolerant humor.

The omission, therefore, of intermediate "social" categories—which throws all the emphasis on the relation of individual mind (talent) to race (tradition)—is a fatal simplification. In Eliot certainly Englishness functions as a mentality, a crucial pseudohistorical episteme. Englishness restrains a corrosive, out-of-control self-consciousness that destroys loyalties and produces rootless intellectuals. And what seemed innocent, or merely nostalgic, in the early publications of the Leavises—their wish for a national culture grounded in the soil and bearing with it "the accumulated and religious associations of a race" *(Fiction and the Reading Public)*—cannot be read today without misgivings.

Leavis participated, as critic and educator, in a historical paradox. The very notion of a racial or vernacular genius, which had encouraged the rise of diversified national literatures in Europe, becomes conservative and constricting once these nation-states have consolidated themselves. The "organic community" is then threatened by the continued momentum of a process of centralization. For Leavis, the word "central" is deliberately transferred to a university discipline; and English denotes, not an insular word and insulated canon, but the *destabilizing genius* of the Shakespeare heritage as it reemerges in Bunyan or Blake, or in the great tradition of the novel, or (one could add) in a critic more like Empson than Leavis.

Denys Thompson's collection, *The Leavises,* is not all that different from the ambitious historical placements of Inglis and Baldick. Together they amount to an extended family history in which Leavis plays a climactic role: the loner hero, the irreplaceably honest person who charms us with his stubborn, archaic habits. Leavis sticks to the personal essay and the tutorial encounter. Muriel Bradbrook speaks of him as "pre-eminently a teacher by the direct method . . . both orator and actor," and recalls contemporaries who still hear his voice when turning to certain poems. For all his influence, he did not have charisma, as Raymond O'Malley notes: "He listened. In particular, he always searched for the sense behind a student's seeming nonsense." O'Malley quotes one of Leavis' favorite phrases from Eliot to characterize the master: "the intolerable wrestle / With words and meanings."

A fit hero indeed for lament and admiration in the media age of the great communicators. Why then do so few of these candid portraits reproduce the *feel* of Leavis' supervisions and classes? Or simply record—reconstruct—his talk? One exception is Raymond Williams, who did not meet him till 1961. "I have never known a social situation in which a group seemed so obsessed by one man," he remarks of Cambridge. Even Williams can describe only Leavis's behavior in the university faculty. There is the time Leavis resisted having a set paper (for an examination called the Tripos) on the novel in general rather than on the English novel exclusively. It would be a misdirection, he claimed, to have read Proust and Kafka. Since the majority were against him, he turned to Williams as chairman:

> "I put it directly to you, Mr. Secretary. The coherent course would be the English novel from Dickens to Lawrence . . ."

"All right," I said, "I think it is a coherent course. But a majority of the committee want some foreign novelists included, and I think their arguments are strong. Part Two, after all, has that important extending dimension."

"No, I am putting it to you, directly."

"I could vote for either. They would be very different. But at the moment I am an officer of the Faculty, trying to get the committee's decision."

"To you," he repeated.

This *ad hominem* streak, opposing itself like a "conviction of genius" to systems and structures and the pressure of the majority, is not theorizable. "If the fool would persist in his folly, he would become wise" (Blake). Leavis was, Williams concludes, "all intense concern and conviction, at levels inaccessible to separated argument."

A century earlier he might have gone to a Utopian community on the banks of the Susquehanna or the Springs of Dove. A Leavisocracy might not have endured for long, yet Queenie would not have had to "cut" so many dear acquaintances. The sensibility of those two is symptomatic and extraordinary. They remain, somehow, within the English class system, embodying its rigidity by their hurt and reverse elitism. Despite Leavis' courtesy toward students, a talent for insult can emerge, which elaborately breaches the very code of manners it sustains, or loses itself in obsessive asides. The lectures collected under the title *The Critic as Anti-Philosopher* show much of that eccentric form.[4]

The very first essay, "Justifying One's Valuation of Blake," is a peculiar piece of rhetoric, more about Eliot than Blake, while insisting that its use of Eliot is a "means of economy." It is hard to concede that, yet the involution of the procedure adds a quasi-philosophical dimension under the guise of being antiphilosophic. The essay is basically a meditation on "genius" in its opposition to "positive culture," and seeks to expose Eliot's inability, even in an early, brilliant piece on Blake (see *The Sacred Wood*), to value that crucial antagonism.

It is not the judgment or verdict, Lukács remarked about the essay form, that is important, but the process of moving toward the verdict. Whereas a typical early piece by Leavis, in *New Bearings* (1942) or *Revaluation,* is almost purely gestural, a kind of flower arrangement in which much is left to the eye of the reader, here a repetitively assertive element has entered, and the maneuvering takes on a value of its own. It is as if Leavis envied Blake for "working creatively though unpossessed of any vision of an ultimate goal." In Wordsworth too Leavis associates a "vital equivocalness" with creativity.

Being a medley of public lectures from the final eight years of Leavis' life, to which some early pieces from *Scrutiny* are added (the attack on Joyce is of special interest), the essays contain few surprises. Dismissive judgments and complex evaluations mingle. Milton is quietly denied any influence on early Blake in favor of "the traditional popular culture and Shakespeare." Hardy makes "a style out of stylelessness" in his poetry. "There is something extremely personal about the gauche unshrinking mismarriages—group-mismarriages—of his diction." Tennyson is "an Academy poet of genius" who brought "English as near as possible to the Italian." We savor the hyperbole of "Dickens was an incomparably greater poet than all the formal poets of the age put together," and the fortrightness of the Old Presbyter who claims that Coleridge's "currency as an academic classic is something of a scandal" or denounces Eliot's "significantly non-sensical doctrine of impersonality."

Yet it is less the particular judgments than the style one is now aware of. What other critic can marshal so many honorific adjectives, bolstered by appropriate adverbs? "If not with the Laurentian astonishingness, the clairvoyant, deep-striking and wide-ranging genius, [James] is, as critic, finely and strongly central." Some might find this bullying or hectoring; I too find it so in the abstract. Yet it does keep alive a certain vocabulary; it makes us think again before discarding those words and trying for a less overt joining of the aesthetic and the moral. The late prose is, nevertheless, too mannered and qualified, too Jamesian in its self-allowance.

Only the pieces on Wordsworth and Wittgenstein are memorable. Since the critic presents himself as an antiphilosopher, let me dwell on his "Memories of Wittgenstein." This is a concise portrait of the man who had peremptorily enjoined him to "give up literary criticism." While making no excuses for Wittgenstein's callous or disregarding behavior, Leavis intuits him as his double: what he might have been had he read philosophy. Yet here the person is the text: Leavis does not engage with the philosopher's written work. But the quality of consideration is exactly the same; *ad textum, ad hominem,* as Williams writes in his memoir of Leavis. For once there is economy: what the essay shows is that Leavis was always thinking of being "just." Not perhaps in the religious sense,

119

though Williams talks of Leavis' "true sense of mystery, and of very painful exposure to mystery, which was even harder to understand because this was the man of so many confident and well-known beliefs and opinions." I mean rather Leavis' attitude that greatness is greatness, whatever a democratic egalitarianism might allege as it infects and weakens judgment. So on behalf of those he considered great, or who acted out of their conviction of genius (even if they did so offendingly), Leavis intervened in order to restore a sense of their basic humanity.

Yet he never forgave philosophy's relation to language. His antipathy is related to his rejection of a non-English mode of talking and thinking. The intrusion of philosophy as a "subject" was like taking up a foreign literature. It promoted a *modern* dead language under the guise of saving English studies from parochialism. It led away from what was at hand, and fostered, not a fuller human perspective, but a disguised solipsism, even *solecism*—a sin against English as "a discipline *sui generis*, a discipline of intelligence" that fused with the language it kept up.

Leavis has become the prisoner of a context he helped to create. If we cannot free him from it, his work will increasingly appear to be a caricature of Englishness. For a time Coleridge furnished us with the keys to his deliverance. His excursions into Continental philosophy (Kant, Fichte, Schelling) may have added nothing to an indigenous talent, one that absorbed Greek as easily as German, yet it allowed readers to spot the limits of the empiricism prevalent in England then as now. "Already in the time of Queen Elizabeth," Count Keyserling wrote in *Europe* (1928), "the German spirit . . . was to the respectable Britisher a horrid spectre; even then intelligence as such was already regarded as an unhealthy product made in Germany." There we see the spirit of caricature at work, although in the service of making the "incomprehensible islanders" understandable, so that they may be brought into a projected European Union.

Leavis' relative neglect of European letters (though he read in them) may be less significant than his attitude toward the American scene. Is there another critic of his stature who has been content to stop with Eliot and Pound? These were early loves of course; and Henry James, a third expatriate, comes often into his thoughts. But what Baldick chiefly holds against Leavis—that he drops out all mediations except language in order to gain the sharpest picture of "the creative conditions"—is peculiarly American. It is there in Thoreau, it is there in Melville, and it is certainly in Emerson, who cannot get away from defining and redefining genius, from brooding on its "original" relation to nature or national character.

Such comparisons, it may be said, are unfruitful: they merely prove the wisdom of Leavis' nativism. If he discovers Emerson's subject or for that matter Dante's (the illustrious vernacular) from within his own tradition; if he replicates Herder's view of Shakespeare (that integration of popular and learned elements which prevented a class-oriented separation of levels of style, as in French neoclassicism); if his ideas on wholeness and harmony seem to repeat a dialectic worked out by Schiller and Hegel—is that not a corroboration of the vitality and virtue of English?

The comparatist in me is silenced, but not completely so. There remains a nagging question: does American literature count for Leavis, importantly, centrally? "America *has* a classical literature," he writes in *The Critic as Anti-Philosopher*—but then he throws a curve ball. Though distinctly American, it is also "part of the greatest of all literatures." Cooper, Hawthorne, Melville, Henry James—yes, even Mark Twain— "may be said to be the distinctive American way back to (or away from) Shakespeare."

This is a moment of self-caricature, worthy of Scrooge. There is no awareness of Americanness as a different type of contextual thinking, one that might see the United States as a portion of Latin America (in the manner of Waldo Frank), or could allow such literature its own language-ethos—which, because it is so deliberate, even extravagant, drives us toward a new anatomy, to echo Hart Crane.

Nothing in Leavis' "heuristico-creative" stance compels such lack of generosity. His fear of the United States is the problem. It seems greater by far than his disinclination to take up European works; in this book there are two short pieces on Eugenio Montale that are sensitive and even, within bounds, comparative. The determining limitation shows up whenever Leavis suspects the presence of a "religion of equality" enforced by an emphasis on "economic considerations" or some other mode of standardized comparable worth. He rejects the America of Robert Hutchins' "Great Conversation" and all such abstract if marketable egalitarianisms. Leavis finds what difference he needs within his own tradition. The only way to bring him out of that corner is to match him with

121

the *fact* of another critic, a contemporary counterexample like Kenneth Burke.

When one reads Leavis' last essays it is easy to forget his supple early achievement, which brought to poetry and then to the novel the most "tactical" of literary-critical gifts. Though he rarely shows that gift in these essays, he can still describe it, and so restate a problem that was there from the beginning. How does a critic (but the question holds for any literary mind) get beyond "the mere assertion of personal conviction"? For someone imbued with a vision of decadence, and with salvational ideas about culture, this is a troubling and permanent concern. It explains in part why Leavis is so wary of theory, which he conceives to be rigid and assertive, incapable of discerning the intensely local life of words. His reticence vis-à-vis theory brings him closer to Keats's "snail-horn perception" when it comes to analyzing poetry. Theorymaking is already a symptom of "the blind drive onward of material and mechanical development." Yet for a Kenneth Burke, unafraid of technical terms— which are a part, so to say, of the American vernacular, competitive in the marketplace of all verbal forms—theory is an interesting and inventive flowering of terminology, or a strategy against gentility. Leavis, with his penchant for vehement social prophecy, found it preferable to work like a mole, seeing through the skin, or to leave him the last word, the fingers:

> The process of "getting beyond" [assertion] is tactical, and its nature is most clearly brought out in the "practical criticism" of short poems. But what is brought out in this way is the essential critical process. Putting a finger on this and that in the text, and moving tactically from point to point, you make at each a critical observation that hardly anyone in whom the power of critical perception exists . . . wouldn't endorse . . . When this tactical process has reached its final stage, there is no need for assertion; this "placing" judgment is left as established.

s i x

_____

Judging Paul de Man

There are times when abstract-sounding issues take on the most urgent and concrete reality. Literary studies, for example, are always assessing the relation of life and letters: what the biography of a writer tells us about his work, or what the work reveals about an author's character. The moral and intellectual aspects of such an inquiry are almost impossible to separate. Though we try to understand before we judge, and though not every judgment bears on character (when we say a work of art is good or bad, is it not clear that these terms are moral rather than aesthetic), some judgment as to worth is always being made.

This issue of judging a work, or the person behind it, is posed in a direct and painful way by the disclosure that Paul de Man, eminent Yale critic, influential teacher, and a founder of the controversial theory of deconstruction, wrote cultural commentary for the collaborationist Belgian newspaper *Le Soir* and a Flemish-language magazine, *Het Vlaamsche Land*.[1]

The articles cover two years, from December 1940 through November 1942. De Man was twenty-one years old when he began his *Le Soir* career; before the fall of Belgium in May 1940 he belonged to the editorial board of a decidedly non-rightist publication at the University of Brussels, *Les Cahiers du Libre Examen*. This journal tended to support democratic institutions, though not uncritically. Nothing in its editorial policy or contents prepares one for the de Man who contributed 170 items (some of them very short) to a paper whose politics and culture-politics (however nuanced, in de Man's case) were at best passively collaborationist, and at worst pro-German.

A storm of denunciatory comment broke out in the United States after the discovery of de Man's wartime's journalism. I am writing this a year after it was brought to public notice by the *New York Times,* followed by longer but equally hearsay reports in *The Nation* and *Newsweek,* yet the storm has spread rather than abated. The anger directed at de Man is remarkable in its intensity. It is also remarkable that many composed their denunciations without having seen more than a few extracts of the offending pieces. In this case, the literary rule that reading should precede judgment—reading all the texts in question, rather than quotes from them—did not survive an explosive resentment. A letter from *Newsweek* (March 14, 1988) speaks for itself. The professional attacks use a different terminology, but are not in a different vein.

> The Paul de Man scandal (IDEAS, February 15) should serve to remind us all that intellectualism can sometimes go so far as to divest itself of its own intellect. Deconstruction seems almost designed to hide a hideous past; it also tries to rob us of the beauty and passion of life and of our hunger to communicate our deepest thoughts and feelings, now and for posterity.

In order to discredit de Man's later work (texts written in the United States between 1953 and his death in 1983), an assumption had to be made not only that the journalism of 1941 and 1942 was reprehensible but that it contaminated the mature essays on which his reputation was based. It is alleged that the early writings are Nazi propaganda (or similar in their barely veiled ideology), and that later criticism is either a disguised fascism or an expression of the same authoritarian, antiliberal, and even nihilistic stance. One ingenious critic (associated with *Commentary*) claimed that deconstruction was actually a product of latent authoritarian trends in the 1960's New Left, and that the uproar about de Man was an attempt by aging Leftists to find an alibi for their own sins.

De Man's personal character has also been questioned, both because of the ideology of the wartime writings and because he had concealed their existence. Thus three indictments, if not judgments, are delivered: against the early, collaborationist journalism; against the later work; against de Man's character, early and late.

Having been de Man's colleague and friend for many years, I found the American reaction, in its rush to judgment, as hard to take as the original revelations. That I was a refugee from Nazi Germany, a Jew targeted by the ideology that spoke from some of de Man's articles, did not make my response easier. I wrote an essay based on the actual reading of a large amount of his journalism, to get beyond hearsay, to characterize elements of fascist ideology, and to describe the style and tenor of the one sustained anti-Semitic article.[2] I said that a rereading of the mature work was inevitable, and that the issue of whether it was related to the articles in *Le Soir* could only be answered by such a rereading. I did not think that de Man's later critical power could be reduced to his continuing in a deceptively new form (that of deconstruction) early and unoriginal ideas. Without his distinguished career we would not have paid heed to articles which have no claim on our attention except for an elegant and complicating twist of thought.

My first attempt to read de Man after the fact came to the conclusion that the mature work did relate to the earlier, not as a disavowal of its ideology (that would have been simple enough, and the question stands why de Man did not *also* take that path) but as an impersonal critique centering on the seductive power of a rhetoric of identity (organicity). This relation between the mature work and an unacknowledged earlier seduction seemed to involve a belated act of conscience, although I regretted the fact that he had presented such a pure—impersonal, or historically unspecific—picture of his position.

The intensity of the reaction to de Man (it soon implicated my own essay) has continued and become a significant fact. I want to analyze it and then comment on the issue of judgment, which is at the heart of the matter.

The American Reaction. An opportunistic whittling down of deconstruction's reputation—the popular caricature of it as a nihilistic bonbon did not help matters—may have played a part. But if there is something excessive here, something bordering on *Schadenfreude,* the emotions are serious ones, and the unusual publicity shows that literary criticism, separated by the academic mainstream from politics and ideology-critique, is breaking out of those limits.

Yet as we venture into an era of the "politics of" everything, differences of style or decorum should not be dismissed. There is a difference in the way Europeans and Americans handle disputes about the past. In Europe such disputes are far more common: men of letters, in France especially, often participate in the political process.

From the Dreyfus Affair to the *épuration* of 1944 through 1946, and still in books and films about French behavior during the Occupation, battles rage around the issue of national honor. No such passion invests similar disputes in cultural America. As a country without a foreign occupant since its independence, it never suffered the stress of deportations, bombings, and the legal pressure to collaborate. Even if it is charged that the United States abetted these, say in Vietnam, their immediacy is not in the guts or the memory of most literary combatants, but has to be reconstructed. The de Man case was a sudden invasion of the American consciousness by a reality most Europeans lived with for a long time and may be trying to forget rather than revive.[3]

We seem to have, again, a scandal involving the uncovering of a past. Usually these revelations affect civil servants who rose to high positions in the New Germany despite their Nazi background. But professors and journalists did not generally escape public notice; they were known through their writings. Guilty or not, the postwar purges dragged them into the limelight, and we have learned that de Man too underwent a judicial interview of some kind. It had no consequences, however, and his journalism was totally forgotten, perhaps because of the writer's youth. Yet when the past caught up, it appeared as if a "high intellectual" had been unmasked.

In the United States such *unmasking dramas* usually focus on a sexual rather than a political transgression, except during the time of the McCarthy era, which seemed to implicate a number of intellectuals. The de Man case may have brought back that fear—of a betrayal of national ideals in the name of some abstract, intellectual cause. The treason of the intellectual here is not literally a foreign allegiance but the importation of an alien mode of thought, one that is distinctly unhistorical with regard to American practices, if not unhistorical in essence. The irony, if this fear of the intellectual enters, is that fascist ideology displayed the same distrust—intellectuals were charged with having no roots, no settled loyalties—and that the young de Man himself emphasized in his articles the *âme particulière* of national (German) and paranational (Flemish) traditions.

But the most obvious and poignant factor in the anger at de Man's political sin is the link between fascism and the Holocaust. What appealed to many intellectuals in fascism, what seemed idealistic to them, has been utterly disqualified and tainted by the criminality of the Nazi regime. Anyone associated with fascist thought, even if the link did not go beyond intellectual sympathy, will share that taint, all the more so if there was no disavowal.

When *Newsweek* juxtaposed a photo of de Man (the same that was chosen previously for a *Yale French Studies* number in his honor) with a photo of marching Nazi troopers, that taint was conveyed in sensational fashion. When a graduate of Yale's English department, writing in the *Village Voice*, asserted that de Man would have continued to compose his dense, difficult essays if his students had been forced to wear the Yellow Star, the distrust of the intellectual and that inescapable taint converge as a suggestively powerful indictment.

Everyone who "touches" the de Man affair without outrage or a formal denunciation, runs the risk of that magnetic taint. Does this reflect the fact that during the Nazi era the bystanders *failed* to intervene? Our conscience is now so sensitive to remaining passive before any evidence of anti-Semitism, or accommodating to it in the slightest way, that the suspension of explicit moral statement, which characterizes most historical analyses, is impossible.

Indeed, an intellectualizing response seems too much like the trap into which de Man fell. There were forces at work in Nazism which made the intellect irrelevant, or subordinated it to irrational ends. There is, even now, something unbelievable in those criminal actions, something the mind cannot absorb. Revisionism feeds on that disbelief. My own anger at the killing of defenseless people, at the deportation and extirpation of entire communities, mingles with a subtler hurt. The appalled rational self wants to discover an explanation and not give in to the unnatural and irrational event—one so nearly victorious that it threatens belief in the discourse of reason.

Is there a rational discourse about anti-Semitism after the Nazi era? That issue is all the more central since in the context of history of European intellectuals de Man figures only as a minor incident. The case of Heidegger is far more significant; the case of Mircea Eliade (an ideologist of the Romanian Iron Guard) is only beginning to be known. And dozens of French writers could be cited. As I say this, I hear the objec-

127

tion: you are relativizing. No, I am describing what is the case. To contextualize is not to condone, although the objection really asks again what kind of discourse could make the darkness of that era visible.

The Early Articles. Making a judgment about de Man's journalism is complex also for another reason. It is difficult to be sure of his line in the *Le Soir* pieces. There is no brutal use of Nazi vocabulary, yet he not only accepted what he named the *ingérence de l'actualité* (the intrusion of the present hour); he accepted it with a kind of *amor fati.*

I will not enter here into a detailed analysis of de Man's political thinking but summarize it as follows. (1) He viewed collaboration as a necessary phase that could renew Europe after the collapse of discredited democratic regimes. (2) A spiritual revolution was taking place and the intellectuals, especially in France, were only just awakening to it. (3) He welcomed an era of German cultural hegemony in a Europe previously dominated by the French. (4) He envisaged a "New Europe" forced to think about its unity because of the German Occupation, but in which each country would continue to develop its national character. (5) He kept open the issue of the status of Flanders, but encouraged the Flemish to cultivate their own, German-oriented heritage. (6) In the notorious article of March 1941, part of a cultural page on the Jews, he denied that Jewish writers have dominated European letters, but added that this reflects the fundamental health of a culture which resists foreign intrusion, including the *ingérence sémite* (compare *ingérence de l'acualité*). (7) He insisted that art had its own laws of evolution and that cultural health depended on not forcing a "totalitarian" coordination of art and politics.

The difficulty in evaluating these positions is that, with the exception of the last, they could be soft propaganda serving a strong pro-German stance,[4] or they could be a seriously nuanced political philosophy that saw collaboration in the context of developments like the fall of liberal (parliamentary) democracy and the postwar rise of a European Community. Even if we decide that nuances should be set aside, and that de Man's articles are soft propaganda, a further judgment would have to be made on their effect, on the actual harm done.

Can we recover that effect? In a powerful indictment, which reconstructs de Man's "intellectual practice," John Brenkman seeks to demonstrate that de Man was "at that time a fascist and anti-Semite as well as an active collaborator." The words "practice" and "active" indicate that his journalism fostered Nazi rule and thus Nazi crimes. "In a context," Brenkman writes, "defined by continual confrontation between Nazi rule and Belgian resistance, de Man . . . supplied rationalizations and legitimations for the repressive measures the Nazis took against armed and unarmed acts of resistance, against journalists and civil leaders, against workers, and against Jews."[5]

The pernicious effect posited here depends on the recreation of a context. Brenkman does this by underspecifying, as when, in the above sentence, he sees everything in terms of Nazi rule against Belgian resistance, and puts actions against the Jews on the same plane as actions against other groups. In such a context any collaboration, however vague and qualified, must be guilty of helping a murderous repression. It would be hard to make any distinctions. But his point about supplying "rationalizations" is potentially an important one.

More often Brenkman recreates a context for de Man's writing by overspecification. He points out that in March 1942, when the Germans announced their intention to introduce compulsory labor, de Man in a book review summarized approvingly the author's contention that the workers' mentality was fundamentally warped because it had lost "the notion of the collective." De Man adds that "If [the worker] could succeed in recovering this sentiment he would soon be led back to a more joyous and more harmonious state of mind." Brenkman interprets this intervention as follows:

The phrase "a more joyous and more harmonious state of mind" was used to justify repressive measures [the German policy announced in March]. In this instance his vision of workers participating in harmonious social cooperation entailed more immediately the abolition of workers' most basic rights. And his lament against selfishness and individualism served the call for discipline in the service of the German war effort. Indeed, workers were eventually forced, first into mines in Belgium, and later into German factories.

A book review becomes sinister by this determination of context. De Man appears as a fascist contributing actively to the German oppression. The juxtaposition of de Man's review with the announcement of a new

129

German policy toward Belgian workers is significant on the face of it; the apparent coordination bears following up to see whether other cultural articles appeared together with new German policies. But equally on the face of it—or in the text of it—the statement quoted from de Man is a commonplace that, if it bears emphasis, echoes an idea associated with his uncle, the socialist leader Henri de Man. It is to say the least unscholarly, if not a historical distortion, to use a common idea about restoring the link between work and pleasure, which Henri de Man had disseminated for fifteen years, and claim that in this review the idea is necessarily used to back a compulsory labor scheme of the Nazis.[6] It is probable, at the same time, that Paul, like Henri, was attracted to the ideal of a corporate state with its supposed harmony between social classes, rather than a perpetual class war linked to Marxism and its uncompromising emphasis on economic over cultural interests.

To cite Henri de Man as part of the context does not disqualify Brenkman's charge (Henri de Man was condemned after the war for acts that included dissolving the Belgian Socialist Party in July 1940), but shows his reductive use of context. What does disqualify Brenkman's finding, as it stands, is the obvious gap between de Man's language and the specific political intent attributed to it. To argue that all of de Man's statements are culture-politics is to evade the very question raised so consistently by Henri de Man about the role of culture in politics. The basic flaw in Brenkman's method is that it instrumentalizes everything in order to gain an "incontrovertible" clarity. It empowers de Man's rhetoric by referentializing it in a certain way, by insisting that it addressed only the Nazi oppressor and his policies.

Placing every book review or cultural reflection in a determinate political context is a powerful mode of reading. Its interest for us may go beyond the particular case of de Man, because it is a mode that is now invading literary interpretation. I have no problem with it as a mode, only as an exclusive and "incontrovertible" mode. That it is reductive is not against it in areas which reduce themselves.

For instance, by joining the staff of the "stolen" *Le Soir*, de Man worked under Raymond de Becker, the editor-in-chief. That Becker, though Belgicist, was a strong Nazi sympathizer belongs to the context in which de Man wrote, together with the fact that he continued his *Le Soir* association for a long time.[7] His opinions, moreover, as Brenkman rightly notes, do not change perceptibly during the two years (except for an increased emphasis on art's resistance to the merely contemporary, a change ignored by Brenkman). Indeed, de Man goes very far in justifying the suffering around him as a spiritual necessity, as well as a punishment for Europe's disastrous parliamentary politics. Such justifications of suffering belong to theodicy: it is strange to see them in this context. When de Man's articles are read carefully, and the length of his association with a paper headed by Becker is considered, it is impossible to see him as only an opportunist. There was a deeper identification.

But what identification? The question of de Man's identity, then and later, is at the center of the controversy. Before I turn to it, I will conclude as follows on the question of early guilt. To condemn the articles on the basis of their ideas would mean we had clarified what was called *délit d'opinion* in the French purges after Liberation. In a democracy we do not prosecute ideas as such. Proof is required that they directly incited criminal or treasonous actions.[8] Despite Brenkman's effort, I do not think we have that proof. The essays stick to cultural issues and do not support particular measures of the occupier or denounce individuals or groups. The worst article, that on the Jews, is not a denunciation; it disclaims their cultural influence, and its reference to Madagascar or a similar "solution"—sending the Jews to a "colony" isolated from Europe—could as easily be understood to say that it is not necessary to do that. Our shock at this article comes from its cold, practical mention of the idea, without demur, and simply to reinforce an argument. It shows behind the suave language a coarse ideology. Such "solutions" to the Jewish "problem" (Palestine, another "colony," was one of them) abounded in Europe and intensified with the advent of Nazism.

In the case of this article, context *is* fatal as history overtakes theory: the solution de Man alludes to in passing was soon to turn into the Final Solution. De Man played into the hands of the Nazi occupiers with their announced policy of excluding the Jews from the professions and public life, a policy abetted by *Le Soir* as early as the first anti-Jewish legislation in late 1940 in Belgium. The link between the Nazi regime and the Holocaust makes it impossible to see either fascism or anti-Semitism as belonging simply to the history of ideas: they belong to the history of murder.

The Lineage of a Murderous Idea. Let us pause to ask how the idea of the Jews as aliens, basic to de Man's article, took hold. What supported it, what made it so murderous, and what role did intellectuals have in elaborating and disseminating it?

When de Man labels the Jews a *force étrangère,* the young intellectual displays an insidious xenophobia. He has constructed a harmonious or fully integrated entity at one level, anticipating (like Henri de Man) a European community rising out of the ashes of the postwar world. Yet at another level he employs a scapegoat mechanism that projects an indelible foreign character onto the Jews. How perverse that is in the circumstances of 1941 can be seen by asking: who was the *force étrangère* in Belgium at that moment? Was it the Belgian Jews, and the refugees from Nazi persecution, or was it the German armies who violated their commitments and entered that country by force in May 1940?

In 1941 de Man was blaming the victims. At the same time, in the "rational" or "nonvulgar" vein of the intellectual, he perpetuated the stereotype of the Jew as an alien in Western culture.

Though de Man's type of anti-Semitism is not at all demagogic, a massive and ultimately murderous prejudice underwrites it. Particularly among intellectuals a complex justification of anti-Jewish politics arises, whose elements are all known but not—sufficiently—the structure connecting them. An important clue to that structure is the assumption that the Jews have remained aliens despite more than a century of emancipation. If de Man were describing only the unassimilated Jew, who refuses to give up his way of life for that of the majority, the Jewish problem would not differ from that of any ethnic minority, but de Man's remarks aim primarily at the assimilated Jew, who seeks full participation in modern society. The suggestion is that, even when assimilated, Jews are marked by alienation, detachment, coldness.

The emancipated Jew, in short, has adjusted but not integrated; he remains an outsider. Richard Wagner's 1850 pamphlet on "The Jews in Music" *(Das Judentum in der Musik)* is symptomatic in this regard. The Gentile, we read, especially the liberal who fought for Jewish emancipation, when he actually comes into contact with Jews feels an involuntary and invincible repulsion. Wagner sets out to explain and justify this instinctive response.

"Our entire European civilization and art," he writes, "has remained a foreign language to the Jew." Culture is the work of a collective *(Gemeinsamkeit)*; the Jew, however, "has stood outside such a collective, alone with his Jehovah in a splintered, landless community." He did not participate in the evolution of European art; at best this "unhappy, homeless person" was only a "cold and hostile observer." I don't want to pain the reader by quoting too much; but the theme of Jewish frigidity is varied throughout Wagner's attack on the judaizing *(Verjudung)* of modern art. "Whenever we hear a Jew talking, we are unconsciously wounded by the lack of purely human expression in his speech; the cold, trilling indifference in it never rises, whatever the occasion, into the excitement of a loftier, glowing, heartfelt, passion." As with speech, so with music: song is speech roused to highest passion, and music the very language of passion. Jews like Mendelssohn and Heine are, paradoxically, the conscience of Wagner's epoch insofar as they disclose its decadence. By revealing their own inner lack of life *(ihre innere Lebensunfähigkeit)*, they also reveal whatever is artificial and lifeless in their society.

A disastrous complex of ideas is developing to justify a prejudice and represent it as a healthy instinct.[9] Ideologically we are but a step from the Nazi argument that ice must be fought with ice, heartlessness with heartlessness, and that is a matter of self-worth to deny life to those who are *lebensunfähig*. At the end of Wagner's polemic there is an extraordinary summons that must have haunted Thomas Mann's obsessive renderings of the German passion for music and its metaphysics. It is a call for art's orgiastic transcendence of every element of inner reserve and coldness, but it could also be a call to eliminate whatever is Jewish in the German character. "Take part, ruthlessly, in this self-annihilating battle, and we will be united and indivisible! But remember that only one solution *(Erlösung)* can redeem Ahasverus: *Der Untergang!*"

I cannot claim to know what makes an idea like this murderous. Is the decisive factor its interaction with other ideas, or a rhetorical slippage from figurative to literal, or ignition in a particular social context? Perhaps all of these.[10] What is certain is that analyses like Wagner's play a nefarious role in depicting—and *planting*—anti-Semitism as an "instinct." Nazi science was to give this instinct a biological foundation by inventing a racial theory of the Jews' difference. De Man's article does not go that

133

far, and contains no vicious, volkish, or demagogic rhetoric, but it depends on a climate of opinion that attributes a negative identity to the Jews, typecasting them as aliens in Europe.

Without a massive ideological complicity on the part of intellectuals acting as publicists, so settled a group of citizens as the Jews could not have been disenfranchized and then driven out or deported. For so large and dehumanizing an enterprise, for organized actions of persecution leading to mass murder, doctrine was necessary. The intellectual provided the rationale, a mental and emotional hygiene that desensitized those who carried out the Nazi program and those who were merely bystanders.

How could so many intellectuals lend themselves to these crimes? The clue, I think, is in their very projection on the Jews of an identity that is a feared nonidentity. This projected, essentialized nonidentity merged two antipathies: against the unassimilated Jew, or his "Asiatic" character, and against the assimilated Jew, whose Westernization is not trusted,[11] and whose distance from both cultures is thought to produce a cold, skeptical, faithless, and unpatriotic intelligence. The cosmopolitan qualities, at the same time, of many educated Jews, a long tradition of merchant trade, and the dispersal of the Jews all over the world abet the image of an international conspiracy.

Now in fact it is the intellectuals who have most to fear from the accusation of nonidentity. It is they who question and criticize, who keep alive in the midst of nationalism the transnational or cosmopolitan idea. So one of the most persistent strains of thought in Henri de Man is the conversion of socialism into a cosmopolitan culture. He seeks to persuade the workers that their economic and class interests are not jeopardized by culture. Without it, or with material gain the only yield of class conflict, the worker will imitate the burgher, and *embourgeoisement* will block every move toward national or even international harmony. (A hatred of bourgeois materialism is common to both the Right and the Left.)

The immediate aim of Henri de Man was the cooperation of workers and intellectuals under the banner of socialism. The ultimate aim was a new state structure, with a greater degree of organic harmony. The socialist leader argued that a distrust of intellectuals ("elitists") by the worker, and the intellectuals' own sense of inferiority vis-à-vis the worker, could not be overcome on the basis of Marxism; moreover, when the issue of identification with class or country was carried into the geopolitical sphere, it became mired in the struggle between national socialism and communism.[12]

The younger de Man seems at first to have no connection with this problematic of the socialist intellectual: his article is a defense of literary modernism that denies any influence of the Jews on it. Yet what is at stake—the art of Gide, Kafka, Lawrence, and Hemingway (and Proust, Woolf and so on), an art that clearly challenged conventional notions of identity (based on class, nation, religion, sex)—tempts him, as a defensive intellectual, whose own character or affiliation might come under attack, to support a politicized identity that is far more vitiated. It would not be unusual if someone who rejected modernity, or modernism, were to display anti-Semitism traits. But here a cosmopolitan writer, free of the usual prejudices, furthers what Thierry Maulnier had called "rational anti-Semitism." I am forced to think that in order to present Modernism as a healthy movement, despite its psychologism, individualism and Nazi suspicions, de Man accepted a crude alignment of Europe and the West and of the Jew and the East. This well-known politics of culture refigured Jewish identity as a subversive nonidentity or failed (hypocritical) assimilation. In the more vicious journals the Jew is caricatured as a maladjusted Asiatic whose "face" cannot be trusted, and whose *Kulturbolschewismus* must be exposed.

Intellectual work is not easy to define because it is often a labor of the negative. Social and political pressures, as well as suspicions about the reliability of the intellectual—he is detached, alienated, solipsistic, a *Luftmensch*, a charlatan, or even the enemy within—exact their toll. In this light it is interesting to compare Brenkman's and Derrida's treatment of de Man's "commitment." For Brenkman, it is crucial to solve the question of de Man's identity, and to solve it along the axis of his relation to work, in particular to a fascism that is clearly opposed to the workers' movement embodied in socialism. The nuances, therefore, in de Man's position are held to push him deeper into the culpable web of fascist ideology. They do not modify, but strengthen his flight from reality. Yet for Derrida these nuances are part of intellectual work, reservations or contradictions that deconstruct the fallacy of identity (racial, national, geopolitical).[13] All the false, and falsely evaded, dichotomies, centering

135

on ideas of cultural health, foreign force, and so on, rise to the surface again. The moral judgment of these two is antithetical, yet each is effective in exposing what can happen in the struggle to align identity and ideology.

First Summation. What kind of intellectual, then, or what kind of intellectuality, is found in the young writer? We can say with some certainty that his early production was a far from admirable compromise between ideology and nonidentity. He did not dare to defend Modernism on its own terms, and though he often suggested that art and actuality evolved along different lines, he failed to pit contemporary literature against the ideological pressure or *ingérence* of an actuality that demanded a total commitment from him.

My objection is not to his wish to extricate Europe from the hegemony of French culture. German writers had often tried to achieve some independence from it by a Northern or English turn (the latter not possible in the Europe of 1941); obversely, even noncollaborationist French authors did not abandon either German literature or German philosophy because of the war. Sartre, in fact, came under violent attack after Liberation for maintaining his philosophical interest in Heidegger.

Nor do I see evidence "beyond a reasonable doubt" that these cultural articles are mainly pro-Nazi propaganda. It depends on what one emphasizes: the careful style of a thinker interested both in the new political culture and an independent literary heritage, or his accommodation to themes and books promoted by the occupiers. What I find clearly reprehensible is the exploitative use (if only once) of anti-Semitic ideology in a self-protective article on Modernism. It decoys reader or censor by projecting on the Jew the intellectual's own "cerebralness," his "ability to assimilate doctrines while maintaining a certain coldness toward them." Despite an ironic twist of argumentation, it supports a crude notion of racial and geopolitical identity that was not only anti-intellectual, but deadly in its historical consequences.

Judicial criticism of the kind we are attempting here is not juridical inquiry or a posthumous trial, though some, like Brenkman, have insisted on a prosecutorial stance. In Brenkman's case, the stance is carefully motivated: it will make for clarity (like taking one side or another in a formal debate), but, above all, it is necessary because de Man "participated in fascism publicly, but did not abandon it publicly." Despite Brenkman's protestation that he proceeds fairly, there is an assumption of guilt in the way the charge is formulated. Others are much less careful than he and act as judge and jury in one, even as hanging judges. I will return in a second "summation" to the issue of judgment; I want to signal here the difficulty of avoiding terms that are metaphors for a moral discourse we do not have, judgmental terms that give an (immoral) impression of self-righteousness.

Would it be better to stop fussing and dismiss the early journalism as immature and relatively trivial? But trivial causes can trigger significant reactions. Something has been touched in the collective (especially American) psyche. While a solitary opinion like de Man's would simply be shocking, his cultural anti-Semitism reflected widespread assumptions that made Nazi policy toward Jews and "aliens" more acceptable, even among intellectuals. It therefore raises the question of a betrayal by the intellectuals, by the cultured class generally, including "Hitler's professors" (Max Weinreich). This betrayal is a piece of our—not only of de Man's—unmastered past. The active as well as passive participation of that class in the Final Solution is known, but not all the myths and collective representations that abetted it. Denunciation at this point is not enough; it tends to foster a paranoid style of localizing evil that removes the issues too far from our time.

Early and Late (1). De Man's wartime journalism displays an ideological engagement conspicuously absent from the writing on which his fame rests. The suspicion arises of "once burnt, twice shy." But that has little explanatory power, given the formidable energies of thought in the mature work. The most genuine attacks on de Man have come from those who credit the power of his work and fear its indirect political effect. They accuse him of seeking intellectual authority and suggest that an authoritarian bias from his "fascist" phase is carried over this way. But what can "intellectual authority" mean except that if this player entered politics he would be formidable, but that he uses his analytic powers to raise the intellectual stakes, to make potential activists hesitate?

Yet after the *Le Soir* articles de Man is attacked for not having hesitated, for having entered the fray as an opportunist. In pointing that out, I am interested in the situation of the intellectual, not in a defense of de Man.

137

For if we learn anything from his career, it is that the role of journalist or critic vis-à-vis the *ingérence de l'actualité* remains precarious, that the pressure of politics never lets up. But the suspicion that I *am* defending him raises in displaced fashion a basic issue: that of the apologetic nature of intellectual activity. However detached or scholarly de Man may have been, was his later work free of self-serving or hidden motives?

That question jumps to our eyes after the fact, especially in de Man's elaborate studies of Rousseau's *Confessions* and on the "figure" of autobiography. De Man explores the link between writing and self-justification or what is involved in confessing an identity: the transparence of psyche and language (of psyche to language, of language to psyche) identity presupposes.

His emphasis on the "muteness" of the written character, and on everything that complicates or displaces the identity of meaning, self, and word, may also not be disinterested. For many, indeed, these matters become interesting for the first time, under the sign of pathos and bad faith. His work now amounts to an involuntary confession or autobiography after all.

I would prefer to describe the links between late and early de Man as symmetries rather than identities, and leave their valuation open. Are they in the later essays because de Man was wishful as well as conceptual, effacing his error, struggling toward a saving doctrine of discontinuity, of dis-attachment from his past? I do not know how to resolve such a question. There is de Man's analytic of nonidentity, and there is an issue concerning its self-serving character. Several additional symmetries can be mentioned.

The first involves an ironic reversal and a sort of poetic justice. Deconstruction has provoked charges of antihumanism and negativism not unlike those lodged against Jewish intellectuals in the 1930s. A suspicion to which he once contributed eventually targets de Man himself. Consider the following comment by E. R. Curtius, a foremost scholar of the Romance Languages. Though Curtius deplored the narrow cultural program of the Nazis and the racism behind it, he found it necessary to write in 1932: "Our quarrel is not with Judaism but with the spirit of negativity *(Negation)*." German Jews, in particular, "have made a covenant with scepticism and deconstruction. The Jews have lapsed from the idea of Judaism itself, from belief in a Chosen People, but they are not ready to open up to or accept Christianity, Humanism, or the German spirit *(Deutschtum)*. For them only negativity is left, in its two forms of deconstruction and cynicism. We defend ourselves against this, for deconstruction in so split a nation as the German is ten times as dangerous."[14]

I admit tampering with the text and translating *Destruktion* as "deconstruction." *Destruktion* is impossible to render into English, and to understand it as deconstruction respects the latter's partial derivation from that concept in *Sein und Zeit*. Heidegger employs *Destruktion* to describe the process of clearing away Western metaphysics from life and institutions of thought.

The word is also used by Karl Mannheim, Curtius' direct object of attack. Mannheim supported the necessity of ideology-critique and the crucial role of the uncommitted ("free-floating") intellectuals. The latter, while not strictly speaking a class but rather an interclass stratum, can challenge—because their interest is dynamic rather than classbound —uncritical nationalisms, demagogic myths, and other idealistic-seeming absolutes. He saw that the utopian mentality (of which we all have a spark) could be captured by irrationalism, and he proposed—in a passage Curtius quotes—the "transformation of Utopia as it becomes an object of scholarly thinking, a *Destruktion* of self-deceiving ideologies that do not stand in an objective relation *(Deckung)* to reality *(Seinswirklichkeit)*."[15]

A second symmetry also involves a reversal, even more uncanny. The articles with which de Man addresses us from the dead put in doubt his antibiographical method. The direct relation of life to letters returns vengefully. At first it was the detached or difficult, the "inhuman" intellectuality of de Man that was questioned. After the *Le Soir* discovery, however, things become all too human. He had complicated our sense of the referentiality of linguistic signs; now a restored context of reference disturbs us like a fall from the sublime to the pathetic. The articles allow the motivation or pseudomotivation of an intellectual mode that had kept strictly to a labor of the negative. The very purity of the method, that it criticized others not from a competing ideological (or "subject") position but from the point of view of language itself, could now be seen as an evasion, a flight from a past that catches up and supplies the missing reference point.

This "descent of de Man," as Martin Jay has called it, leaves us where

139

we were, with an unresolved contradiction between a reductively referential explanation and what clearly exceeds it in intellectual force. Phrases
and paragraphs in de Man's later writing do light up with a self-referential
pathos, as when he suggests that Rousseau's language is a "silence act."
But even if we have a positive identification, as they say in police proceedings, it is good to remember that it is *we* who need it. By linking up
not only the early and the later writing, but both of these bodies of work
with a totalizing figure that claims to unify everything (his life, his writings, his writings with his life), we exhibit the very drive that led Adorno
to the aphorism: "The whole is the untrue." I do not think that the two'
de Man's should be collapsed into the one or the other.

There is a final symmetry to mention. It may be the most significant,
and it leads to the theme of how history—or better, the philosophy of
history—enters. It is quite clear that the young de Man accepted an idea
which the mature thinker not only refused to credit but saw as a basic
fallacy. That idea concerns the use and abuse of historical knowledge.
The journalist viewed the events of 1939–1942 as a history lesson, even
as a judgment. The scholar, steeped in Nietzsche, and a good deal older,
took history out of philosophy and the philosophy of history out of
interpretation.

My view is strengthened if Paul de Man's ideas resembled those of
Henri de Man. In his memoirs of 1952, *Against the Stream,* the socialist
leader describes how in the summer of 1940, shortly after the Nazi
occupation of Belgium, he welcomed the thought that the century-old
battle between France and Germany, which had impeded peace in Europe, was over. This development, he continues:

> was certainly purchased at a high price; but one was able to take comfort in
> the speculation that history seldom operates in a different way. I said to
> myself: History's decisions are beyond inquiry, and she makes use of the
> people and instruments suitable for her purposes. It has rarely happened
> that large territorial expanses, when fragmented through the rivalry of small
> powers, were unified except by the military victory of a great conqueror. It
> lies in the nature of things that the immediate result is a work of annihila-
> tion; the labor of reconstruction that follows requires different methods and
> is taken on by a different kind of person. Our Western culture would not
> have been able to receive and fructify its Latin heritage had not the Bar-
> barians first attacked Rome.[16]

We recognize here the tragic flaw of many intellectuals: after much thoughtful and painful hesitation, they overidentify with a particular historical urgency. There are many places in the nephew's journalism where we come upon a similar attempt to figure the European collapse as a judgment of history that opens the way to spiritual and political rebirth, a New Order unifying Europe by removing the old kinds of petty and disastrous conflicts.

Seen in this context, Paul de Man was a doubly mediated person: swayed by the ideas of his uncle, but also, specifically, by a teleological idea of history. Such mediatedness may later have seemed a more serious matter than the particular views he adopted. Yet from the perspective of the victims there can be no greater guilt than that which justifies their suffering in the name of history.

Early and Late (2). More symmetries will doubtless be found.[17] But what mainly strikes one in comparing the early and late de Man is the *asymmetry.* It is hard to bridge the gap, to transform by a recreative procedure the categories and reticences of the young author into the categories and intricacies of the deconstructionist.

Let us consider—also to meet Brenkman more directly on his ground—de Man's comments on two pro-German writers: Paul Alverdes, editor of the literary review *Das Innere Reich* (*Le Soir,* April 20, 1942), and Drieu la Rochelle, brilliant fascist writer, and editor of the *Nouvelle Revue Française* under the Occupation (*Le Soir,* December 9, 1941). De Man points out that while artistic merit remains the criterion of works published by Alverdes, the German collaborators have also another aim: to show that artists can draw their inspiration from the present war. Although "expression is a form whose beauty constitutes an eternal value, independent of present contingencies," both Alverdes' writing and that of his contributors succeed in their aim. In the case of Alverdes, "there is no incompatibility between complex and violent themes and a work of art of a quasi-feminine finesse"; in the group project, "to isolate oneself completely from the enormous military effort Germany is undertaking and shut oneself up in a poetical ivory tower would have been a real betrayal of national feeling. On the other hand, to disdain from one day to the other values of style established by the genius of several generations, in order to serve only the present moment, would be to stray into the worst excesses of propaganda."

De Man works here with a conventional dichotomy of form and content. One is free to claim that he uses "eternal beauty" to dignify the collaborationists, or else that he uses it to strike a balance and save literary value from being totally subjected to present concerns. I could say that his position is "undecidable," except that the instance is so trivial and that words like "trimming" or "balance" are more appropriate. There is nothing really complex or intensely theoretical here that anticipates the dizzying emphasis on oppositional and contradictory structures later on.

The review of Drieu's *Notes pour comprendre le siècle,* while appreciative, is decidedly more critical, but again deploys purely conventional terms. De Man reminds the reader that Drieu's antirationalist thesis on the culture of the body ("vertues sportives," "vertues animales") is not entirely new. He connects it with an "aesthetic" tendency already visible in D. H. Lawrence and Giono, who reacted to psychological analysis carried to its limit and to a growing separation of man from nature. The greater part of the review, however, is devoted to a critique of Drieu's use of history. He is called mistaken in blaming contemporary problems exclusively on rationalist philosophy of the last few centuries, first because sociological factors are more determinant, then because "One cannot consider history as a faithful image of abstract philosophical thought." De Man's main point, indeed, is less a correction of Drieu's reductive image of history than a more radical questioning of his use of *literary* history. "From the moment that we no longer look at literature from the angle of art but attempt to see in it an ongoing ethical evolution, we can make it demonstrate just about anything."

These methodological sentiments, which limit ideological appropriation, also caution against the use of literary history as an ordering or demonstrative discourse. But compared to any of his later essays touching the same subject, they remain feebly propaedeutic. De Man makes no effort to theorize the contradiction between Drieu's historicizing narrative which he rejects, and the antirationalist élan which he commends— except to point to neglected "sociological causes." What seems to matter at this moment in time is the independence of literary history, and a philosophy of vitalism, supported by Drieu, which promises (in "a country that has fallen as low as France")[18] "a radically new type of human being."

Judging from these two typical pieces, the young de Man sees aesthetics and politics as separate values. Aesthetic value, the "angle of art," is neutral rather than oppositional: it can coexist with ideology but cannot be taken over by ideology. One might say, sardonically, that de Man treats artistic value as if it were still as neutral as Belgium before the Nazi invasion. His purely formal and unproblematized opposition of art and actuality cannot lead to a critical or dialectical interaction, and the result is that when he reviews a fascist author, this separation of "poetry" and "belief" (to use 1930s categories more common in the Anglo-American domain) permits him to acknowledge, though not necessarily approve, fascist ideology and its aesthetic potential. We also see, however, a *limit* to his collaborationist ethos, based on what Martin Jay has defined as "aesthetic modernism," which kept the realm of the literary apart from corrupting influences.[19]

So different is the later theory of de Man that even my previous hypothesis (in the *New Republic*) along an action-reaction model, namely, that his critique of totality was a belated movement of conscience, seems like a doubtful guess. What remains correct, I think, is that the relation between language and identity is relentlessly analyzed. The line of resistance, separating art from the demand of politics or immediate relevance, is no longer located in the aesthetic as a formal angle of perception or a traditional (even eternal) value. Language moves to the center as a limit on positive knowledge. New oppositions become visible between the literary and the aesthetic, or within the literary itself. Literature is as self-divided and "unhappy" as other types of activity. It is the place where a "negative knowledge about the unreliability of linguistic utterance is made available."

The critique of what de Man late in his career named "aesthetic ideology" began as an opposition to literary theories that viewed art as an incarnational or reconciling structure, and literature as fuller speech, as a language reflecting a lost yet recoverable logos. He denied any claim (including Heidegger's) that saying and meaning could coincide; that there was, in great poetry, a possibility to "speak Being." Later, an opposition between the category of the moral and the aesthetic states itself

143

as an opposition between autonomous language and the aesthetic. Yet this analysis, however scrupulous, does not amount to an ethics, even a "negative ethics." The link between literary criticism and ethical reflection remains largely implicit.[20]

Nor do de Man's later reflections offer a formal philosophy. Everything is phrased in linguistic terms that break down larger classifications and seem to deconstruct philosophy itself. It he were a theoretician of language clearing away, like Russell, Carnap, and others, vestiges of metaphysics, one could understand. These philosophers saw literature fatally implicated in metaphysics. To amend the understanding, to straighten thinking out, meant for them a methodical purification of language. But this, de Man and Derrida set out to show, cannot be done: the idea of a correct language is itself metaphysical.

The end of metaphysics means nothing more for Derrida and de Man than accepting a linguistic predicament. There is no language formally different from the language we have: no metalanguage, no purified— basic or universal—structure of expression. The ethical implication here is linked to a denial of absolute linguistic authority. So de Man's analyses withhold any sort of transcendence, or authority based on transcendence, from both author and reader. In the central essay of *Blindness and Insight* (1971) he objects even to Derrida, who is said to deconstruct Rousseau by a "philosophical intervention from the outside of the text. It is better to work with the hypothesis that the text *knows* what it is doing, that it is self-deconstructive." The way *knows* animates the text, or the pathos with which de Man elsewhere speaks about language as such, suggests that literature is where a nontranscendent ethics is being formed.

Kafka wrote: "The positive has already been given: it is up to us to achieve the negative." We accept such "nihilism" in Kafka (though Lukács did not) as intensely ethical. Perhaps because it underwrites the powerful fictional rendering of a world that requires both passion and interpretation. Or perhaps because the negative task mentioned by Kafka is actually a negation of the negative—a negation of transcendental perspectives that aim at a world beyond this world. According to Nietzsche, such perspectives negate the world in order to intensify our will power over it. They too are a form of instrumental reason. De Man suggests that literature is more aware of this fact than philosophy, that it deconstructs both the positivity in transcendent moralities and its own linguistic hybris.

Second Summation. It is necessary to distinguish between the ethics implicit in de Man's critical theory and the ethical situation of de Man himself. De Man's failure to disclose his past now obstructs his work. It will always be possible to charge that the complications he brings to reading are so extreme, so beyond common understanding, and so "mute" concerning vital questions of morals and belief, that they function as intellectualized evasions of guilt. Some public acknowledgment was necessary, whatever the causes behind his silence. For de Man to disclose his past would have been morally courageous and clarifying. At issue is not just the silence about his past, but, as in Heidegger, about an ideology implicated in genocide. It is not disavowal alone we look for, but an open reflection on the error (whether personal, collective, or both) that led into an enormous human and moral catastrophe.

The ethical situation of de Man differs from that of Heidegger in that there was no retrospective falsification, unless his silence is taken to be that.[21] The question, in de Man's case, does not bear so much on the politics of the earlier work (despite differences of opinion on how collaborationist it was) as on the nature of his later work. I have argued that there was no contamination of the later by the earlier writings, or any but a superficial and general relation between them.

Yet the comparison between de Man and Heidegger must be carried one step further. De Man's "turn," like Heidegger's, included a more powerful orientation to literature. For Heidegger certain great German-language poets became an alternate history of being when the Nazis disappointed his hopes. Though de Man was a critic of Heidegger's use of literature (as he had been, more trivially, of Drieu's appropriation in 1941), that critique substituted for a direct reflection on both Heidegger's turn and his own. By deconstructing Heidegger's (and then everyone else's) poetics—by concentrating on the "prosaics" of linguistic expression—de Man removed from literature a false authority that made it into a "house of Being" and the only authentic form of speech. Yet his intellectual motives remained opaque, and even increased in power by removing themselves from the vulnerabilities of a confessional analysis.

The question of de Man's identity, therefore, has remained alive. Not so much "Who was Paul de Man?" as "What is an intellectual, and how did Paul de Man fill that role?" His dismantling of the positivities in literary theory is part of a negative achievement, yet gnomic utterances

145

("Death is the name for a displaced linguistic predicament"), when the *bona fides* of the critic are in doubt, revive latent suspicions about intellectuals as cerebral, tricky, and socially unproductive. The furor surrounding him is a danger signal and tells us that there are lots of people out there, academic and nonacademic, who do not think literary theory is either useful or disinterested.

Deconstruction is singled out, but the feeling that difficult writers have something to hide, that their language is obscurantist, covering a personal or intellectual fault, is widespread. Among journalists too a search-and-destroy mentality prevails, which spreads easily from deconstruction to literary studies generally. "By now," an article in the *New Criterion* informs us, "Professor de Man's teachings and catch-phrases are parroted in departments of English and Comparative Literature across the country." "No graduate student or assistant Professor reads books anymore, he engages in 'strategies' of textual interpretation." "It is easy to forget that we are not talking about Keats' *To Autumn* but a collection of reviews and articles that appeared in pro-Nazi publications . . . How comforting to know that the atrocities we read about are merely literary phenomena." It would be hard to find more misrepresentations packed into a few sentences. But the animus is clear: literary theory has become the opium of the intellectuals.

I am not putting forth a claim for the moral adequacy of contemporary critical writing. On the one hand, deconstruction has not made its situatedness clear enough or developed terms for moral questions in a way that is systematic or free of linguisticity. But is it just, on the other hand, to displace careful reading by a moralism that levels everything? One of the reporters after the news broke about de Man's articles was incredulous that I asked him to learn something about fascism and European intellectuals before writing that de Man had been a Nazi. "How can you make fine distinctions?" I did not think they were fine. I thought that to respect rather than flatten or falsify history was important. Karl Jaspers writes in his courageous little book of 1946, *The Question of German Guilt (Die Schuldfrage)*, that the victor limits his power through the (democratic) legal process. "Distinctions remove the burden of totality and set a limit to the formal complaint."

We need a moral rather than moralistic discourse, and literary criticism has not provided it. Part of that moral discourse would be a consideration of how history affects our acts of judgment. Do we have only two gears when it comes to judging: accusation and apology, denunciation and defense? Brenkman feels it is important to adopt a prosecutorial stance. Yet Jacob Taubes, in a case surely far more serious, that of Carl Schmitt (*Die deutsche Rechtswissenschaft im Kampf gegen den jüdischen Geist*, 1936), refuses to judge: "You are not the judge, for as a Jew you were not led into the Nazi temptation. We were mercifully spared having to make a decision about joining . . . You [the non-Jew] can be judgmental because you know about Resistance, I can't be sure about myself. I can't be sure about anyone, that he would not have caught the infection of that nationalistic exaltation."[22]

The shadow of the Nazi era continues to lengthen. The participation of intellectuals (and the professoriat) in that era is only one aspect of the tragedy, but it should concern us, in the academy, especially. To untangle all the issues will take more time than the pressure of single, notorious cases allows.

The role of historical experience in the process of rendering a moral judgment is crucial and complex. Whether we apply to the past secular criteria or identifiably religious ones, the context of the event under consideration, with its relativizing pressures, has to be heard. Then, even if our judgment goes wrong, it will have recorded a factual and thoughtful opinion which the future can evaluate in its turn.

No judgment is purely historical. To achieve an integrated view of the life and letters of writers who interest us—by deriving a character from their written legacy and adding elements of their biography—means accepting at some level the "metaphysical" assumption that identity is personal, stable rather that intermittent, and transparent enough for scrutiny. The challenge of accumulating all the biographic material so that a clear picture can emerge also involves a more than strictly historical projection, for even should we find the necessary texts (for example, letters possibly exchanged between Henri and Paul de Man), would they clarify or complicate? Might we not quarrel about how to interpret them?

There is, in short, no guarantee that when research assembles a total picture, it will reconstruct rather than deconstruct personal identity. The latter may become less clear, drawn into a deeper conflict of interpreta-

147

tion than that which prompted the research to begin with. My conclusion is not that we suspend judgmental or moral reflection, but that we think more about the aims of this kind of discourse. The aim of judgment in historical or literary-critical discourse, a forensic rather than juridical sort of inquiry, is not that of determining guilt or innocence. It is to change history into memory: to make a case for what should be remembered, and how it should be remembered. This responsibility converts every judgment into a judgment on the person who makes it.

Meaning, Error, Text

Meaning, despite the effort of *maîtres-penseurs,* does not remain stable. (The meaning, for example, of this French phrase is shifted when Foucault applies it, ironically, to German thinkers like Hegel and Nietzsche, who reappear in Nazi doctrines about the master race.) Unforeseen historical events and their interpretation keep meaning nomadic, though the instability does tempt us toward projects of codification or canonmaking.

Let me take a simple case and then go to a much more complicated one—complicated because it involves a tradition spanning twenty centuries. The simple case is the trial of Hitler, Ludendorff, and their associates in March 1924. The *Boston Transcript,* under a dateline of March 14, entitles its column "Trial Farce" and begins as follows:

> Alice in Wonderland's classic courtroom remark, "Nonsense, you are nothing but a pack of cards," is a perfect comment on this year's most important political process—the trial of Ludendorff, Hitler and their associates for high treason—which continues in comic fashion in Munich.
>
> As the trial proceeds it becomes apparent that the protagonists, including the military hero Ludendorff; the would Mussolini [sic.], Hitler; ex-Dictator Von Kahr, once described as the "strong and silent," like Alice's Queen, are collapsible when not taken seriously.

Obviously the unpredictable career of one of the defendants, Adolf Hitler, puts these judicial proceedings in a new light. Whether or not the trial was a farce, deserving, as the paper says in closing, "international volleys of laughter," one cannot but wonder how long it took for the world to take Hitler seriously. Not to take him seriously was a tactic that might have worked, but did not; and it raises peculiar questions concerning our failure to interpret especially political events. We seem to be unable to measure them, to guess at their future resonance. We underestimate or overestimate, dismiss or slander, shrug or fly into opinionated fits of rage. Hitler is not an inept example, since the height of overestimation always produces a Messiah-figure and the extreme of underestimation the deceiving image of a buffoon or trickster.

The more complicated case spans the tract of time named after its founder. I refer to the Christian Era, which has its first trial transcripts in the Gospels. The Gospels, as a New Testament, look back to the so-called Old Testament. That a carpenter's son should be the Messiah is a scandalous event not predictable by any soothsaying text. Yet the text about that event, the "new" testament, turns previous scripture into a prediction, degrading it as blind while investing it with a missed (or dismissed) capacity for illumination. The new text at once confirms and disconfirms the older one, which remains extant.

Two questions arise from this pattern. The question of error: if the Synagogue is blind to a truth it reveals, how is this state of affairs to be explained? The question of originality: are there texts which affirm themselves without the twofold structure of "new" (enlightened) and "old" (blind)? Do we know a type of writing that appropriates traditions so effectively that we cannot recover what was there, what is radically, permanently displaced?

Let me start with the second question. It is the Hebrew Bible, the "Old" Testament, that evokes the possibility of an original appropriation. Modern scholarship has been trying to reassemble the appropriated traditions for well over a hundred years by positing an alphabet soup of sources and redactors. The importance of transmission in a more than technical sense—of *traditio*—is crucial here and can lead to diametrically opposite evaluations. The Hebrew Bible, as it has been shown, tries to receive, censor, or reconcile various traditions. But it also replaces them, so that the originals disappear into an authoritative scripture that has become their only source. So the Hebrew Bible can be praised or blamed, depending on one's point of view toward tradition. We may admire the fact that it incorporated so much, or regret that it displaced so much, and by becoming the original made us forget other origins. The same kind of reflection could be applied to the New Testament. We can admire it for struggling with the incumbency of what it calls "old"; we can also blame it for trying to liquidate a precursor text by degrading it as the shadowy prefiguration of its own truth.

The impossibility of making truth and text coincide is what threatens all writing as it strives to transmit definitively a "body" of knowledge. We try to prevent that body from becoming a corpse, or losing its coherence and being scattered, dismembered, disremembered. The study of meaning, therefore, is coextensive with studies of textual embodiment and verbal incorporation. We learn how the commentary-process is related to works that want commentary to cease, or to revolve around them like satellites.

My main concern, however, is with error. Can we talk of meaning and error together, as if error were part of the structure of meaning? Why is it so difficult for truth and text to coincide? Or, what is equally surprising, why should anyone think they could come together?

It is not clear that there was ever a belief in an absolute Scripture. The Hebrew Bible, though divinely inspired, is held to speak in "the language of man" by the early Rabbis. There is accommodation or condescension (to use the Christian term that alludes to God's taking on human form). The Hebrew Bible, moreover, is really two books: the written law, and the oral law (commentary), both given to Moses on Sinai. A beautiful Rabbinic story has Moses attending a seminar of Rabbi Akiva's and not understanding what is being said. In a related story God intervenes in a debate about His law by means of the *bat kol* (echo-offspring of the founder's voice). But the Rabbis dismiss its authority in a postprophetic age, and God accepts their argument: "My children have defeated me." It is the equivalent of a voice coming from heaven to declare that there is no longer such a voice. Or a voice that says, in effect: "The results of your exegetical labors is my Law, in which I am pleased." Even the Protestant return to the plain text of Scripture and the rejection of Catholic safeguards, express not an idolatry of the letter but a precarious and spiritually burdened view of the relation between letter (text) and reader. Faith comes through hearing: through the internal echo, through the responsiveness of auditors to Scripture. The authority of belief resides in that transactive relation. The truth of the text is the text, but only as it inspires such a relation.

The Synagogue, nevertheless, was depicted as blind, and judged cul-

151

pable. It failed to see what it transmitted: it could not read its own message of deliverance. The Church considered this failure an act of God, similar to when He hardened Pharaoh's heart. The Exodus, the liberation from Egypt, becomes in Christian interpretation a "type" or "figure" of the very release from spiritual bondage effected by Christ and not fully understood by the Hebrews.

This concept of error, which combines an idea of inevitability with a judgment of blame, is indeed a scandal. However, it proved effective in fashioning a triumphant mode of interpretation, masterful toward the Hebrew text and consoling toward historical time, which remained, even after Christ's advent, a "waiting in patience." Figural typology, the instrument of the Church, enriched that time and sustained the believer. But just as there are two testaments, there are two modes of interpretation: Patristic, chiefly typological, and Rabbinic, which stands in a "negative" relation toward the Messianic event as a fulfillment of time and of the Word. The second mode has reemerged in recent thought but has not generally been recognized as having an affinity with a major Jewish tradition of exegesis (Midrash).[1]

What we learn from and against typology is the temporal complexity of the text-reality nexus, even the temporal complexity of signification generally. The meaning of signs is always being displaced or revised by the mythical and seductive image of a *grand temps* (Eliade) or the latest realism. While realism is demystifying and myth is restorative, they are functionally similar in positing a realm of error made visible by haunting ideas of reference. (I find the psychoanalytic connotation of "ideas of reference" useful in this context.) The drive toward reference is a kind of terminal illness, with us from the beginning, or from "In the Beginning." Reality itself, rather than its signs, is the desideratum, even when reality may turn out to be the dark side. Error is identified with unfulfillment; and there is an assumption that with fulfillment the language of signs— including the Great Code itself—will change utterly or disappear.

What the Church holds against the Synagogue is not so much its blindness as its stubbornness; its continuance in blindness. The people might have seen the truth, belatedly. It is not God who limits their role; they limit themselves until their vision becomes opaque. Israel, then as now, refuses to be mature, to emerge from its self-imposed minority. Its position in providential history is a judgment it has passed on itself.

Such self-humiliation is hard to explain, since the basis for group consciousness is rather the opposite: self-glorification, the sort of motive furnished, for example, by the idea of being a chosen people. The "error" attributed by Christian typology to the Old Testament is just not believable, except from the perspective of Church propaganda. A more likely view is that interpretation, when problematic rather than doctrinaire, is always involved in such "error." Its main feature is an imbalance or oscillation between self-humiliation and self-glorification, between an underestimation and an overestimation of private capacities or public actions, as my first example, that of Hitler, demonstrated.

In typology, exaltation—and exultation—are based on the humbleness of the subject being transfigured. This structure reminds us that, on the level of individual psychology, delusional ideas of reference may clothe every detail with an aura of ultimate significance. The simplest happening becomes a sign, a clue, and the indifferent or unconscious person, the "bystander," is drawn into a plot of divine or demonic dimensions. Similarly, on the level of political or group psychology, almost anything (a "straw") can precipitate conflict.[2] Indeed, the expressed reason for violent action, including war, is generally that of avenging a "humiliation," of restoring national or class pride.

In the Hebrew Bible this reversal from low to high, as well as the opposite movement of dejection, is less marked than in Christian story. One need only compare Hanna's "psalm" (I Samuel 2:1–10, perhaps interpolated) with Mary's *Magnificat* (Luke 1:46–55). The words are not unlike, and both women rejoice, having been freed from childlessness. The verbal and domestic contexts are very similar. Yet the Christian story emphasizes the humility and the humiliation—the humility of Mary herself, as a woman, and the pastoral and realistic world of the manger; while the humiliation, linked to this circumstantial frame, is that of religious persecution.

In the Hebrew Bible too there are famous reversals of fortune, as in Joseph's career, or that of Moses. Yet neither man enters the vision or the Holy Land. Fulfillment is withheld. Joseph's bones are returned to his country, and Moses is vouchsafed only a Pisgah-peek. This reserve, especially toward the leader, whose humanity is not associated with humility but with fallible pride, is what teases typological interpretation and allows it to "complete the figure." Typology, as an instrument of inter-

153

pretation, is forcefully anagogical, expunging the reserve of Hebrew Scripture as if it were blindness rather than insight. This blindness is the "wilderness error" that alienates God from Israel, though it also draws Him closer to mankind through the visible condescension of the Incarnation. A more temporal or temporizing view, however, marks both normative Rabbinic exegesis and deconstructive literary criticism. The impossibility of speaking the truth once and for all, of stabilizing meaning or memory through canonized textual closure, is the issue. Not to acknowledge the validity of commentary, or of interpretation generally as it reenters the primary, even the sacred, text and discloses that the latter too is layered, stratified, mediated—a "temporal labyrinth"—is to neglect the secularity of literature. Only the literalism of fundamentalist faiths could serve as an excuse for this neglect. Such fundamentalism in a postprophetic age is, however, too much like messianism in its furor and intransigence.

Advanced Literary Studies

If there were a phenomenology of literary studies, it might take for its starting point a reflection by Virginia Woolf. She is thinking about her "so-called novels," and she describes her achievement in this disobliging way because she cannot resolve a contradiction. "Every day includes much more non-being than being," she writes; her time divides itself into moments that are conscious and intense and others that seem nondescript—embedded, as she puts it, in cotton wool. "One walks, eats, sees things, deals with what has to be done; the broken vacuum cleaner; ordering dinner; writing orders to Mabel; washing; cooking dinner; bookbinding." A novelist, moreover, should convey both sorts of being. "Jane Austen can and Trollope; perhaps Thackeray and Tolstoy; I have never been able to do both."[1]

It seems good to start with so elementary a reflection, because it has a bearing on the profession of literary studies. There is an unusual amount of drudgery in such work: checking, double-checking, footnoting, a dutiful surveying of "the literature"—our kind of good housekeeping. These moments of nonbeing are as necessary to advanced studies as is the automatic round of things to a novelist. Moreover, we cannot be sure that this faithful, commonplace activity may not ignite a sudden-enough illumination. Yet we, like Virginia Woolf, regret the preponderance of the cotton-woolly state, both because it tends to expand and because there is a natural and misleading reaction to it: a desire to get out of this secondary state, out of "the literature" to literature itself, or even to some poignant reality without which none of this novel-writing or scholarship makes sense.

Such a reaction can undermine the idea of advanced scholarship. There is a temptation to substitute utilitarian and curricular questions for intense textual or interpretive study. Let me first discuss textual scholarship. Yale is one of the great depositories of unpublished literary manuscripts; yet how many students there have seriously tried to transcribe and edit even one page? We are losing the excitement, the wonder, that attends the discovery and publication of such manuscripts. It is foolish to pretend that most scholars today are still recovering ancient sources, or that this activity, insofar as it continues, is as important as it was during and after the Renaissance. Yes, there do exist manuscripts that must be restored and books that should be reedited or redeemed from obscurity. James Joyce continues to play posthumous textual tricks. But I think the important work, in this area, with a few exceptions, has moved away from English.

It is nearly incredible, for instance, how ignorant we in the universities are of Hebrew literature, not only of known sources but those recovered from a "Geniza" that extends far beyond the secret chamber of a Cairo synagogue that yielded its precious scraps in the late nineteenth century. Goitein has published five volumes from this one Geniza alone;[2] the Dead Sea Scrolls have been known since 1947; yet the "Wissenschaft des Judentums," the scholarly movement initiated by Zunz in the 1820s, has barely begun to influence the curriculum of an academy still fixed on that other, Greek and Latin, Renaissance.[3]

Arguably this latest renaissance, the Hebrew, could have a reforming effect on our concept of what literature is, as powerful as that of the classical Renaissance—given enough time. The case of feminist or black scholarship is both similar and dissimilar and returns us to native sources. Though we suspect that many such writings have been lost or assigned to obscurity, it remains unclear whether the imagined future library will be different from the old patriarchal mausoleum. Yet the animus (or anima) of these projects also matters, and it may test our critical faculties as severely as the influx of Hebrew texts may test the discourse of Christian humanism. Feminist scholarship will also have the problem of keeping the found text from a masculinist mode of appropriation that may now come from within its own need to build a tradition or canon.

Granted that various renaissances may be preparing themselves, and granted that there are always lost voices to be found, I doubt that we will approach the enthusiastic scholarship of the first Renaissance, which turned manuscripts into a print culture and founded the humanities as we know them. That upheaval, seconded and expanded by historicism, introduced us to the historical sense. Its very success made us the mortal drudges we now are, surrounded by a pantheon of cultural documents that all have a claim on our intellectual sympathy. It gave us so many new sources that once the technical work of authenticating and fixing them was over, the work of reading that ensued was bound to be critical in a different sense. At first that reading was combined with "illustration," as it was often called: reinscribing and exploiting the text in terms of a vernacular and contemporary idiom. (Just as today the film industry can do remarkable as well as unremarkable things with the fiction we used to read.) But modern criticism does not seek to illustrate, that is, enrich or refine, a source text. At this point I can cross over from textual concerns to theories about interpretive response, which have become central to literary studies.

Contemporary criticism is an affair of high tension. The expanded canon, the demand of each new or recovered work, and the liberation into pluralism lead, in reaction, not only to the character-armor of our conservative colleagues but to an ascetic practice on the part of our nonconservative colleagues. Even the most notorious of recent reading shows the refluence of a motive of purification. Deconstruction is a way of allowing us our own mind among all these competing texts: recognizing the ambition but also the improbability of hermeneutics—of gaining access to the "otherness" of person or text—it involves a rhetorical and linguistic rather than psychological and divinatory model of understanding. A truly radical thinker like Paul de Man puts in question the coincidence of reading and understanding, and we are obliged to ponder the fact that no discipline—logic or rhetoric or grammar—has been able, even when exquisitely developed, to assure "truth in language." Yet de Man insists that we know about those disciplines, for it is all that we may get to know.

In the posthistoricist market of genial productions, moreover, pedagogy itself becomes a topic of advanced study. How do we develop and defend reading, which used to be linked to a select, canonical body of works? Now reading begins in a relative vacuum, with very few shared texts, or in a plenum, where no book can act for long as the intellectual's

157

bible, as a classic with the freshness of a reborn ancient tongue. The ideal impact in the Renaissance of culture on nature, of learning on a vernal linguistic moment, may be the one thing that is not recoverable, though as a crucial phase in literary history it is a "moment of being" that keeps haunting every scholar's memory.

It is hardly surprising that, like everything else, literary studies should change. Today no mode of discourse may safely be disregarded. For the advanced student, methods of study have become part of the *Erlebnis,* not simply a preparatory phase, a scaffold to be discarded. As advanced readers we stop being consumers and assume our role as producers in a difficult, prolific, and competitive arena. We put away childish things, as Leo Spitzer learned to do. He was drawn to philology by his love of French culture, which pervaded Viennese life around 1900.

> I had decided to study the Romance languages and particularly French philology, because my native Vienna, the gay and orderly, skeptic and sentimental, Catholic and pagan Vienna of yore, was filled with admiration of the French way of life . . . The moment when the curtain rose on a French play given by a French troupe, and the valet, in a knowing accent of psychological alertness, with his rich, poised, voice, pronounced the words "Madame est servie," was a delight to my heart.

A shock awaited him at the university.

> No picture was offered us of the French people, or of the Frenchness of their language: in these classes we saw Latin *a* moving, according to relentless phonetic laws, toward French *e* (pater > père) . . . never would I get a Ph.D! It was the benignity of Providence exploiting my native Teutonic docility toward scholars who knew more than I, which kept me faithful to the study of Romance philology.[4]

How Spitzer integrated his immense learning, how it was put in the service of establishing the psychological profile of artists as linguistic innovators, is another story. Our question is, what today will draw gifted minds into advanced literary study? Teutonic docility is gone, and can we rely much longer on such nostalgic watering places of the learned imagination as the Florentine or the Elizabethan Renaissance or fin-de-siècle

Vienna? "Madame" is no longer "servie," and language no longer seems reducible to some redolent essence—as that other Viennese, Wittgenstein, demonstrated in his *Philosophical Investigations*.

It appears that we are a remnant. We do not motivate the best minds and attract them into advanced studies. Many will argue, defensively, that we have always been a small group; so, what is new? Yet I must state my belief that our profession, in trying to cope with its greatest challenge, to democratize education and demystify literacy, has exaggerated the separation of advanced studies and elementary concerns. Anything difficult today is subject to the charge of elitism, as if the manifest destiny of literature professors were to sacrifice their intellects and devote themselves to remedial gymnastics. Yet surely we have learned that literacy must be matured by the study of literature. Otherwise it will atrophy, like any undeveloped faculty of body or mind. How can we attract good minds if we are not intellectuals as well as pedagogues, if we cannot make the case that our discipline has a progressive dimension and a sense of new frontiers? Mathematics, often called a language, continues to think about itself and evolve. We alone seem to stay at the level of arithmetic, and we can't even agree on the necessity of finding a theory for what we have. I am often asked how theory relates to classroom practice, especially on the undergraduate level, as if theory had severed its connection with intelligibility, as if it were removed from the familiar world and its basic concerns as Blake's visionary epics were, before modern interpretation showed their all-too-human relevance.

We had to learn how to read Blake, and we have to learn how to read theory. Reading, in any case, is the middle term between elementary and advanced studies. Let me suggest, therefore, something of what reading—close and critical reading—involves.

A major obstacle to the appreciation of what we do is our very concept of literary study as an inferior or auxiliary exercise. In totalitarian countries it is taken for granted that literary study, like literature itself, has an ideological dimension that must be kept in line with national doctrine. We claim a greater freedom for both criticism and literature; yet when it comes to teaching we try in just the wrong way to avoid the suspicion of advocacy. We accept the low-grade repression implied by becoming purveyors of a skill, who, like the sophists, sell a certain technique: the

159

forming of adequate sentences and the ability to chat about English and American classics. We'd like to think of reading and writing as neutral activities.

Yet to esteem literary studies we do not have to overestimate them. The experiment of mass education has taught us that literature and art as civilizing instruments are not pedagogical simples. They raise all sorts of complicated feelings about the value of a reading culture, the leveling impact of literacy on other forms of creativeness, and the fostering of sophisticated (that is, skeptical) habits of thought that could be harmful to organic social structure. It is symptomatic that Louis Althusser, the Marxist scholar, should deplore our lack of thinking about reading, decry "the thin sheet of the theory of reading," and demand that even Marxists pose the question: "What is it to read?"[5]

There are presently two fallacies that prevent an appreciation of critical reading. The first is the belief that we can read at sight, as if reading were a visual ray, sight at a higher, more penetrating level. Yet reading is not the same as imaging; it may even go against our ingrained and understandable urge toward giving everything a visual sort of definition. All avant-garde theories seem to contain a critique of representational aesthetics. Reading at sight is a sexy ideal. So is reading aloud, when urged as an antidote to the semiotic or Derridean emphasis on the complexity of verbal signs. Both reading at sight and reading aloud are metaphors for a desired immediacy of understanding (Allen Tate once dubbed it "angelic") that can never be total, that is always to be recovered and elaborated. Though criticism, as the work of reading, should be enjoyable, the mind remains in labor. The real question is what kind of labor this strangely absorbing work may be.

The second fallacy touches on superficial concepts of writing. It again derives from an attitude that oversubordinates criticism to literature. Critics are asked to simplify themselves and cultivate a highly accommodated prose. The devices that perplex and enrich the creative writer must be exorcised when it comes to critical style. This decorum of accommodation is all around us. It is innocent enough when it objects to pedantry or esoteric terminology; it is not innocent at all when it dictates an anonymous sort of prose in the name of some democratic or pseudopopulist ideal. When James Fallows, a Rhodes Scholar and Jimmy Carter's chief speech-writer, left the White House, he had warm words for his boss but said that his experience with the anonymous art of ghostwriting had left him "beaten down" and "cured forever of the desire to work in the White House." He was leaving to "find my own voice."

To make what I am saying a bit more concrete—to pass from the theoretical to the practical plane—I return to Virginia Woolf as she thinks about "being" rather than "non-being." In her "Sketch of the Past" she recalls three special episodes. Two of them ended in despair and a sense of powerlessness; a third, however, was accompanied by an explanatory formula that made her confident rather than passive. "I was looking at a plant with a spread of leaves; and it seemed suddenly plain that the flower itself was part of the earth; that a ring enclosed what was the flower, and that was the real flower; part earth, part flower."

Where other epiphanies left her frightened and passive, this did not seem like "a blow from an enemy hidden behind the cotton wool of daily life." It was "a revelation of some order"; moreover, she was able "to make it real by putting it into words." What she experiences is not nature, but nature and words in tandem: a holistic structure because of the way a flower relates to its ground but also because of the way this grounding (in the sense almost of grounding a shock) relates to a verbal utterance, "That is the whole." Her ability to utter a demonstrative of such extreme generality—compare Stevens "the the" or Hegel's (self-sublating) "the this" ("das Dieses")[6] provides, as she says later, a "rod . . . that would stand for the conception."

Woolf's "rod" brings back a hint of chastisement, eliminated from the present moment compared to the others. But she means a measuring rod, a standard of reference that can pattern and integrate even the sense of nonbeing, whose very nothingness enables the blow to come more unsuspectedly—as when, waiting for dinner, she overhears that a recent visitor is a suicide. Nature by itself is unable to ground the impact of that casual disclosure. "The next thing I remember is being in the garden at night and walking on the path by the apple tree. It seemed to me that the apple tree was connected with the horror of Mr. Valpy's suicide. I could not pass it."

Interpretive work on these few lines of prose has barely started: Woolf keeps explaining the experience to herself, and we continue the task. For advanced readers, interpreting such a passage is as exacting as having written it. Scholarship recovers a text from unpublished materials in the archive of the University of Sussex; it passes as a legacy to readers who ignore, squander, or continue the work Woolf initiated.

If we accept the challenge of the text, if we agree to earn (in the strong sense of Goethe's *erwerben*) what is handed to us, further questions arise. Does "rod" have a sexual as well as a disciplinary meaning? Is the consolation of the flower passage—or opposite feelings of being struck at by an enemy from behind a screen—related to the author's inability to mourn her mother or to realize how possessed she was by the mother's voice and image, until after the writing exorcism of *To the Lighthouse*?[7] Does the very simplicity of the prose, which makes it readable, reflect a Victorian decorum, described by Woolf as all intellect upstairs (in her father's study) and all conventionality downstairs (in the drawing room)? Or is she dismantling that dichotomy even as she uses a conventional "language of flowers"?

There may be no answer or possibility of verifying it. Yet every interpreter is situated, and the contemporary pressures focus on the role of words, of *denomination,* in a type of experience that is often called intuitive. Virginia Woolf's "moment of being" discloses the necessity of verbal concepts such as "That is the whole," even though she keeps seeking her organizing principle not in words but in nature or in an art like painting that seems closer to nature. The reference point she finds, the grounding, is linguistic not phenomenal: her supreme demonstrative, "That is . . . ," can accrue only through language. To insist on the moment of being as a fixed, embodied intuition must lead to a pathological and unsustainable rapture. Such rapture is suggested, yet it merges with an analytic flow of words, a writing that runs on beyond consummation and reveals the unreliable if evocative nature of referential modes of expression.

Woolf, in short, has helped me to illustrate the anti-intuitive bias of contemporary literary theory, whether the theory derives from Wittgenstein, from Derrida's critique of Husserl, from de Man's uses of Hegel, or, as in Woolf herself, from those whose intuitions are most verbal—the poets. The theory holds that thinking is verbal thinking, however inward or imagistic it appears to be. It rejects a model of interpretation that says we must disclose what is hidden by turning, as it were, the inside out, by reversing an achieved or imposed internalization. This does not mean that we never rebel against being mediated or intermixed by words. The elemental—and sometimes, more dangerously, the fundamental—continues to beckon, in the deceptive shape of nonverbal experience or of a recuperative language that could speak Being, or point to it directly: "That is the whole." It is the literary thinker who is critically in touch with language, who applies, to echo Virginia Woolf, the "rod" of words at every level: from elementary English to the larger and demanding uses of language found in philosophy, in religion, in law, in politics, in literature itself.

The Philomela Project

For most people literary criticism is something of a mystery. They hear of the latest turbulence in those skies: for example, that deconstruction is shaking things up and has been claimed by a faction in the law schools or an eccentric group of architects. Or a new battle of the books makes it into the *New York Times Magazine,* after conferences at Yale and Princeton on the "canon" and a big curriculum fight at Stanford. What it adds up to is not easy to explain.

Critics face, on the one hand, a simple, down-to-earth task: books must be reviewed, courses must be taught. At a time when shelves are filling up, when more and more subjects are competing for prestige and attention, decisions have to be made not only about what to study, but about what every educated person, irrespective of profession or specialization, should know. Can we prescribe a "core" list that might contain, at least talismanically, what should be read by all? Are there books that could be shared by everyone—when even the Bible today is no longer the passion or obligation of every person?

On the other hand, the issues debated by literary critics are far from down-to-earth, because they involve not particular books but *how to read them.* The point is made that it was less the Bible as such, or the Classics as such, that inspired or oppressed, than a certain kind of reading, an enforced mode of interpretation sanctioned by a religious, cultural, or political elite. This elite not only chose the books to be read but limited the way they could be understood. Once we shift emphasis from books to the mode of their interpretation, we cross into an uncertain and disputatious country.

Interpretation is notoriously unstable. Its history is full of swerves and reversals. Reading different critics we sometimes can hardly believe they are dealing with the same book. Yet the distinction between a canon of books and modes of reading is not absolute. New books have the power to change habits of reading; they not only follow, but create, methods of study. Our idea of artistic greatness and the English language itself have been influenced by Shakespeare. Obversely, a hermeneutic discovery like Freud's can stimulate a new type of representation: psychoanalysis gradually changes the way we depict character, motivate what goes on, and even what we dream, or record as dream. Alfred Hitchcock's movie *Psycho* can serve as a popular emblem of that change. That there is an interaction between reading and representation simply increases the difficulty of identifying the one reading list everyone should consult.

Not that literary criticism—the formal study of books *and* methods of interpretation—brings order out of chaos. Criticism is often part of the problem rather than the solution. Indeed, skeptics say that whatever the pretension of critics who promote new readings or renew older ones, they remain in the service of a dominant ideology, even if as uncomplicated as consumerism. From this perspective, literary criticism is not an independent science or field of study but a byproduct of the culture—a surplus verbal and cerebral energy that leaks from the art of the period and has to be blotted like excess ink.

A more flattering view is that literary study, as it reviews and sometimes creates methods of reading, enters the cultural scene as an authoritative voice rather than as a dubious byproduct. Books, films, and paintings require an interpretive field of force to sustain themselves, and then to become traditionary: to survive beyond a "generation," "decade," "movement." Art does not have its axis of influence only in itself; a certain type of reading may have contributed to its formation, and certain habits of interpretation facilitate its reception. Culture depends on this interaction of "primary" text (Scripture or artifact) and "secondary" text (the work of reading that edits, interprets, mediates).

In the last hundred years there has been an accelerated shift from art to sophisticated theories of art, sometimes even abetted by the artists themselves. Mallarmé's poetics are couched in a prose as subtle as the diction of his poems. At once self-advertisements and adventures, his pronouncements have their own curious and inwrought integrity. Authors begin to market their very nonconformity. They recapture what they feel was

165

alienated from them by theorists and critics. The aesthetic imperative of a Mallarmé, Proust, Rilke, Stevens, or Borges acknowledges that a prosaic world, a tide of opinion and theory, is threatening to overwhelm or dilute art. These writers seek to preempt or transform that world by their own, highly self-conscious practice.

The astute critic does not automatically take the side of art against the tide of conversation, gossip, or commentary elevated into theory. The reason is twofold. First, the fetishized artwork may be as damaging to cultural life as an overelaborated criticism. Second, for culture to be participatory, artworks must circulate, by passing from private houses to public museums, and being widely thought about, talked about. There may be a greatness in *not* being monumental but in disappearing into the stream of life, the stream of language. I don't quite believe that myself. The real harm, I think, is done not by monumentalism, or haunting ideas of greatness, but by a hierarchical prejudice which holds that creativeness can be achieved only in certain genres, to which other genres are subordinate. In theocracies or totalitarian regimes, both art and criticism serve; in the epoch often called modernism, criticism serves art. A dichotomy reestablishes itself in modernism, with great art idolized despite or perhaps because of the skepticism of the age.

I have been identified with a position that urges a "creative criticism," but that position does not entail a confusion of art and critical essay, or a reversal of values. Rather, it says that we cannot restrict the locus of creativity. A critical essay, a legal opinion, an interpretation of Scripture, a biography, can be as inspiring and nurturing as poem, novel, or painting. The prejudice that separates the creative from the interpretive reacts to the fear that the creative element in culture is being swamped by institutional or commercial forces. The wildest paradox in this is that criticism, though considered by many on the side of institutionalization, in fact allies itself quite often with the new or the popular. Both criticism and innovation are outsiders, and usually a wave of art, sophisticated or demotic, breaks in together with upstart critical ideas.

Yet can that anxiety about the atrophy of creative genius be dispelled? Some such fear runs deep in every age. Today it fixes on criticism, because that really is a force to contend with. A culture of criticism is developing, one that inspires as well as depresses, one that breaks down media and genres in favor of "discourses." Yet our problem is not, I think, hypercriticism or commercialism, or even the burden of the past in the form of institutionalized Western classics. It is a strange inertia in our progressive thinking.

The heroes of a previous generation—modernists like Flaubert, Proust, Mann, Henry James, Joyce, Virginia Woolf, Yeats, Lorca—fostered an art-ideology. They attacked bourgeois values rather than the concept of Great Book or Masterpiece. The artwork becomes, if anything, more of a sacrificial idol. Have we really jettisoned the modernist art-ideology? Doesn't it keep sticking to us, even in this "postmodern" era?

The problem I discern is the spread of that diluted modernist ideology to every text used as a wedge to "open the canon." Though postmodernism seems to assert the opposite by deprivileging the acknowledged work of art, it may simply be privileging the yet-unacknowledged work. The very notion of criticism is threatened by a proliferation of "significant" or "representative" works, not just by a proliferation of theories. Critical judgment, which had been austere and exclusive—in theory, if not always in fact—is asked to be compensatory and restitutive. The vitality, but also the confusion, of literary studies reflects this double burden: multiplying theories of reading, multiplying works that claim a share of greatness.

To question, as I have done, the prejudice that keeps criticism out of the literary system does not help either the canonizers (the art-ideologists) or the decanonizers. It presents, rather, a conundrum, and challenges an inside-outside or hierarchical way of thinking. Criticism has its own strength; even commentary, as French anthropologist Dan Sperber points out, does not disappear into the Code or Scripture it interprets, but must itself be interpreted. A salient example of this is the Jewish Oral Law, the Talmud, and adjacent compilations called Midrash. They cannot be reduced to a purely exegetical function. They extend or reenvision the original, the "primary" text.

Midrash has always been exemplary for me. I am intrigued by its liberty and autonomy as well as by its strict adherence to proof texts. My interest did not start in the 1980s; I tried to develop a secular parallel in earlier essays. *Beyond Formalism* allowed itself the remark:

> Great exegetes . . . have always, at some point, swerved from the literal sense
> of the text. This text, like the world, was a prison for Rabbinic, Patristic, or

Neoplatonic interpreters, yet by their hermeneutic act the prison opened into a palace and the extremes of man's dependence and of his capacity for vision came simultaneously into view. I feel the poverty of our textual imaginations compared to theirs. The very idea of interpretation seems to have shrunk.[1]

Anthropologists, more skilled in the devious relation of Code (which can be a corpus of stories) to interpretation, especially in oral cultures, may have some sympathy with what I am saying.

I do not argue there has been no advance, but with advance comes loss or disregard. We live among restitutions, yet the rabbinic mode of reading (or religious exegesis generally) is still disregarded by most secular critics. My plea is not for Midrash as such but for an enrichment or even reconstruction of the literary-critical field. If there is a symbiosis between a discipline and what it seeks to recover, it might be said that criticism today is engaged in a project of *self-restitution:* that Midrash is more important for criticism than literary perspectives are for Midrash. By including Midrash or older types of exegesis, criticism would exercise its power to revalue an alienated practice and enlarge itself at the same time.

As we look across the entire expanse of literary history we find many moments of revaluation and recovery. The greatest of these may have been the Renaissance. Despite the fact that Europe remained Christian, it brought back a repressed heritage: the Pagan Classics. By an artistic amalgamation we are still trying to fathom, religiously alien forms blossomed again, fusing with a Christian content. A Jewish medieval tradition, similarly, is only now being retrieved for the nonorthodox world. We have something to learn from a religious culture in which the creative energies went almost totally into commentary, and the same basic method of reading was used for law (halakhah) and lore (aggadah). But while a lost masterpiece, once recovered, is like an *objet trouvé,* a neglected tradition requires decades of research and absorption. In an era of restitution Midrash still needs finding: as a cultural achievement, as a work of the social imagination, and as a distinctive mode of reading.

What is all this talk about Midrash? You're supposed to be a deconstructionist! Well, there was life before, there is life after, Derrida.

The foolishness of labeling aside (about which deconstruction has things to say), the problem facing us is that this age of restitution is also an age of resentment. There is no end to the demand for "identity," as something available to groups or individuals, yet denied them by the social order. The new emphasis on identity is like a rash left by movements that have rigorously questioned it in philosophy, fiction, and social thought. We seem to be passing from exquisite scruples about the "question of the subject" to a credal insistence on the "subject position." To confess "where one is coming from" is no longer a modesty topos but a required affirmation.

Something about this flight to identity is utopian or visionary. In Blake's words,

All Human Forms identified, even Tree Metal Earth and Stone, all
Human forms identified, living going forth and returning wearied,
Into the Planetary lives of Years Months Days and Hours, reposing
And then Awakening into his Bosom in the Life of Immortality.[2]

Restitutive criticism has absorbed this type of liberation theology. Its secular career began with historicism's "resurrection of the past." The massive research inspired by historicism showed how little we knew of other cultures and how much in our own had been marginalized and suppressed. When Herder (only somewhat older than Blake) characterized the neglected poetry of ancient peoples as "voices," the metaphor was just: it indicated an oral source that was effaced by print culture, and it pointed to something that *cried out* to be heard.

Yet this Philomela project (the restoration of voice to inarticulate people) has had a strange result. Retrieval of the past produced a conspicuous increase in feelings of guilt about culture as such. This guilt operates both at the level of intellectual consciousness, as we become aware of how much overhead (Nietzsche called it culture-debt) we must carry along, and at the level of moral consciousness, because history is no longer seen as the story of liberty, of progressive emancipation, but rather of denial, censorship, repression. What can be said for a civilization that exploits its poor, prosecutes bloody wars, and invents genocide? The philosophy of history—the attempt to find a meaningful, progressive pattern in the passing of time—is a dying discipline because a quickened sense of social justice does not allow us to forget realities discounted by

169

previous generations. History, it appears, was always written from the perspective of the conquerors. ("What were the conquerors but the great butchers of mankind?" Locke observed.) Contemporary historical research has become, especially in literary circles, a sort of protest against history: the use of the past to incriminate both past and present.

Walter Benjamin saw that the Renaissance model of restitution was flawed: it merely joined Roman triumphalism to Christianity. Though we are moved by the sheer magnificence of the monuments this combination produced, Benjamin was correct in charging that such achievements may be tainted by barbarity. Are they not built on the blood and sweat of anonymous masses, on victims whose history is ignored? The New Historicism wishes to recover that history (primarily the story of everyday life), and so restore the "material base" of art. It too, however, faces the problem that the material base has largely vanished, and that the process of restitution, of righting wrongs, seems endless.

The task remains visionary or utopian, insofar as a voice must be given to the anonymous, even if there is no voice. "The plaintiff becomes a victim," Jean-François Lyotard writes in *The Differend,* "when no presentation is possible of the wrong he or she says he or she has suffered." We can retrieve, for instance, only a portion of women's experience; the rest has disappeared, or lost its gender-specific aspect.[3] The archives yield something, in the form of letters, unpublished efforts, and legal depositions. Great epics, novels, or dramas also yield something, when imbued with the vernacular zest of a Dante, Rabelais, Cervantes, Shakespeare, or their modern successors. Yet historians or critics must often construct a legal fiction—invent, that is, a persona for absent presences.

What, finally, of deconstruction in relation to this protest movement and its visionary program? Though deconstruction seems negative rather than affirmative in its posture—compared to a curricular politics that *represents* minority interests against the canon—it did set in motion a close questioning of concepts of privilege. Nourished by sources in philosophy and semiotics, it dismantled such essentialist values as origin (genealogy), intent (original intent), and identity (nature), by a study of the temporal aspect of human existence (how our truths remain contingent, how we are never present or transparent to ourselves), and a method of reading that showed an unresolvable doubleness in language. The drive of language toward unmediated expression or sheer transparency of thought could make words superconductive. (Think of merging telepathy and telecommunications, or of a universal sign-system to overcome the babel of tongues.) But there is also the historical and analytic fact that every language is a system of differences, one that defers even while it anticipates meaning—"Success in Circuit lies" (Emily Dickinson). In deconstruction the emphasis on difference rather than identity is not essentialized. The challenge becomes how to support Third World writing, say, or the "minor" literatures, without counteridentifying them so strongly that we reinstate once again the contested notion of privilege, as well as essentialist, and at worst racial, slogans that have bedeviled an era of catastrophic nationalism.

There is of course an anti-restitutive bias to deconstruction, both in its concept of dissemination ("that which does not return to the father") and in its claim that voice-metaphors, as in this essay, are intellectually suspect. One supporter of the movement, after hearing me, complained that my emphasis on the Philomela project, although socially valid, undermined itself because, for deconstruction, the problem is "too much voice." Derrida, especially, insists that our thinking has been vitiated by equating voice and presence, an equation that reinforces a metaphysics of presence and leads to disastrously false, even apocalyptic, expectations. "Too much voice" means that we are swayed by rhetoric, that we respond to it literally rather than critically, that we allow ourselves not only to be moved, but moved to action, by the mimetic and promissory thrust of language. We neglect the semiotic aspect of words, which is more perceptible in writing, when writing is not considered as simply a pallid transcription of voice, or a script that points to a reality whose sensuous presence must be restored.

I find this critique of mimetic representation an important *spiritual* move akin to the antitheatrical prejudice that restrains, usually within the context of the major religions, the attempt to achieve a quasi-Dionysian identification with the divine, here and now. Deconstruction's methodical suspicion of the privileging of voice may also have been influenced by fascist uses of radio and film to restore a lost and unifying word. Still more relevant overall is Benjamin's understanding of what follows from the fact that our capacity for mimesis has progressed radically in a technological era. That the mechanical powers of reproducing simulacra are

171

at the point where everything can be re-presented (where presence can be achieved through representation) degrades, according to Benjamin, the unique, in situ "aura" of the valued object. Benjamin saw that the "aura" was commodifiable, and that fascism (or for that matter communism, in its own way) could appropriate it through technological means. The sacred or epiphanic notion of embodiment suffers, as absence and presence become less absolute and enter a dialectical process leading to their indistinction. It becomes harder to discriminate between false and true representations, and this added burden on our powers of discernment, this incentive to distrust and suspicion, can intensify a reactive desire for charismatic closure, and so the movement of a metaphysics of presence into the political process. It is not restitution that is attacked by deconstruction but the use of restitutive pathos, of a politics of desire once associated with messianic religion and now responsible for political theologies.

The problematics of restitution are never simple. Let me turn to a movie, Wim Wender's *Wings of Desire*. It enacts a pastoral version of the mimetic dilemma I have described. Wender is never naive about place or its phantom relation to presence: *Paris, Texas* is a classic on that theme. The quest for emplacement or embodiment that he portrays in *Wings of Desire* is necessitated by Germany's guilty relation to a past it has destroyed no less than twice: through the war, which abolished monuments and sites (the setting of the film is Berlin); and through a repression of memory, which obliged Adorno to ask as late as 1959: "What does it mean to come to terms with the past?" The Germans—but they are only the extreme case for Wender—must learn to experience their past without evasion, and this the film translates as *to experience for the first time*. This "first time" is a purely mythical event. To exemplify it Wender appropriates the theme of the angel who falls (falls in love) because he envies mortals their fully sentient being. He renounces angelhood (hearing and seeing everything without being heard or seen) in order to enjoy the earthly pleasures of a finite body.

Despite this brilliant joining of historical and mimetic issues, the movie does not rejuvenate what it touches on. It collapses under the inner quotations it recycles: the weight of culture—the reproducible culture of film—militates against the allegory of a repristinated nature, a "first time" tasting of the fruit of mortal experience. For the viewer, ironically, there is more abstractness, more stereotyping in the colorful reality and pantomimic legerdemain of the circus which is the object of the angels' envy than in the monochromatic and voyeuristic existence to which the heavenly homunculi are doomed before the film switches to color. The object of the angels' desire remains obscure, and the reduction of the world to the love-clichés of one man and one woman, with which the film ends, indicates a retreat from words that is more forgetful of realities than the reality-loss the film addresses.

Perhaps only one thing is certain after such movements as deconstruction and the Frankfurt School ("Critical Theory"). Essentialism is instrumentalism in disguise; and instrumentalized reading has been the norm. Yes, we hunger to engage literature, morally and politically; we want to escape Lukács' contempt for the Western intellectual's "permanent carnival of fetishized inferiority." But this cannot be achieved by turning up the volume of moralistic pronouncements through affirmations—or denunciations—which act as the equivalent of loyalty tests. Today the entire landscape of moral philosophy is in motion, shaken by events that hardly seem related to questions of language, yet are not separable from an inveterate pattern of verbal abuse that has come to light.

There are signs that the challenge to create a new moral criticism is being taken up. The impact of John Rawls's *A Theory of Justice* and the way contemporary thinkers are engaging issues of literature in relation to moral philosophy are among those signs. Let me single out Charles Taylor's *Sources of the Self: The Making of the Modern Identity*.[4] It holds that we are living beyond our moral means because we pretend that contemporary life has overcome theism (or religious worldviews, however vague), Romantic expressiveness (or some belief in an organic connection with Nature), and similar "sources." More, we actively deny them. This "stripped-down secular outlook" is not the product of an irrational denial, but is based on experience and prudence. "We tend in our culture to stifle the spirit—after the terrible experience of Millenarist destruction in our century." Spirit has acquired a bad name. There are other causes too, in addition to this prudent reaction to the knowledge that "the highest spiritual aspirations must lead to annihilation or destruction"—obvious causes such as partisan narrowness and less obvious ones such as the creed of naturalism. Yet Taylor refuses to let his diagnosis limit our moral and philosophical options. To accept spiritual impoverishment—to be ashamed of one's explicit religious and spiritual motives—is simply a countermutilation, and so an evasion of the dilemma.

What makes Taylor of particular interest in the context of this discussion is that his book provides not only a richer moral phenomenology but also an attempt to redress the situation. He seeks to *restitute* the denied sources—resources—of the self. Modern analytic philosophy has been propositional in its approach, seeking a stripped-down truth; Taylor puts analysis in reverse gear to recover by his account of intellectual history (Hegelian in its confident sweep) the problematic of invalidating a quest for the good because that too has led to suffering. We may bridle at his effort to narrate history once more, after so many thinkers, analytic or anti-Hegelian, have deflated that tendency, and we may regret his resuscitation of the concept of a "modern identity," however critical he is of its anemic texture. But his challenge to rethink issues in moral and not just political terms, and to reconsider a superficially transcended past, demands consideration.

Restitutive criticism requires serious debate. It is something old rather than new, and still a sharp turn on society's path toward the recognition of collective as well as individual rights and talents. The classic analysis of recognition in a situation of social inequality is by Hegel: a famous section of his *Phenomenology of Mind* traces the aroused consciousness of master and bondsman, as they grow aware of their interdependence. Recognition is the key rather than restitution, though restitution is often the acknowledgment of an achieved recognition. The end is not righting wrongs as such (there may be several rights in conflict), nor a reversal (which serves a retributive rather than restitutive end), but a new, spiritually as well as politically effective, respect.

Turning back from political philosophy to literature, it is important to recall the recent emergence of oral history. Popular traditions challenge as well as inspire high culture; they question the confusion of art with ideas of order by revealing the heterogenous and often folkloric elements of canonized books like Homer and the Bible. Literature grows from traditions rather than tradition, as the ballad collectors knew; and literary criticism is restitutive by helping to honor such sources. The Philomela project, giving a voice to the voiceless, a name to the anonymous, merges at the literary horizon of history with another myth: Orpheus compelling Acheron to yield and restitute a lost object of desire. That Eurydice is twice-lost suggests, however, that the magic of art is limited to the recovery of the story rather than the object itself.

Literary Criticism and the Future

My subject has been literary criticism, not as an institution but rather as genre and mind-set. I *could* say that my interest has been in the institution; but that seems unsatisfactory because it is not certain that criticism has enough authority (in the form of rules or settled conventions) to qualify. The term "specificity" is more appropriate. It allows me to describe a significant difference between literary criticism and a mode of cultural propaganda obtrusive enough to suggest a distinction.

I have argued in the opening chapters of this book that early in the eighteenth century Addison and Steele fostered a prose whose decorum had social and ethical implications in excess of its explicit content. Their gentle and humorous commentary touched on matters that in other arenas—politics, religion, pamphleteering—had a divisive and inflammatory potential, but which they defused by adopting slightly eccentric personae and the genre of Letters to the Editor, often composed by themselves. This Journalism was a development of the epistolary mode assigned by the *genera dicendi* to the middle style. The formal informality of letters, or their extension as the "familiar" essay, addressed the public as if it were a peer group—an ideal public (even republic) assembled from different classes and professions, yet considered equal for the purpose of intellectual exchange. Though a tension between private and public style remained, as in intimate correspondence addressed at once to a personal recipient and a posthumous audience, the stage was set for the Common Reader. The contemporary and influential French concept was that of the *honnête homme,* the honesty involved being that of congeniality, especially of not insisting on rank or profession.

Such honesty required leaving one's habit (sword, pistol, other emblem of privilege or trade) at the door, and joining the discussion on terms of equality.[1] Influenced by developments that cover more than a century, honest prose did not become associated with a particular ideology. It aimed at the middle rather than at being plain; it was highly variable in tone and even somewhat unstable; however, it always sought to avoid mannerist extremes and to maneuver between satire and sublimity.[2] Its temptation was gentility on the one hand and false wit on the other; and its enemy the treacherous depths of "enthusiasm." The authors of the *Spectator* surprise every movement of their mind, subjecting it to an editing ethos that reinforced a *via media* kind of sensibility.[3]

From Dryden to Donoghue this honesty, also called civility, is recognized as the characteristic of a critical style originating together with a mock-heroic savagery (think of Swift and Pope) whose major target is the same: enthusiasm, religious or secular, private or collective. The moral calculus in this critical style involved a restraint that infused common words with an intelligence less ostentatious than wit (see Note 1). The birth of the New Prose, moreover, acted as a moderating event at a time when the production of *news* became a potentially explosive spark, a rumor with slanderous or revolutionary or messianic force, aided by the spread of print as a popular medium. *The Spectator* newspaper extended the power of the familiar style; though it ostensibly brought news, it was really a form of antinews and tempered evangelical and enthusiastic flights.

Crossing from that period to ours, I want to suggest that as cultural history succumbs to cultural prophecy, this civil and critical prose grows in importance. The more pressure, the more it becomes a *style* as well as a medium, one that remains deliberately anti-inflammatory and resists futuristic generalizations of both the optimistic and the pessimistic kind. In the era between the World Wars nationalistic and intellectual demands increase the pressure and begin to sideline that courteous and reflective prose. Having become routine rather than self-renewing—Goethe would have called it a manner rather than a style—it was vulnerable. While in certain areas of the social sciences the "ordeal of civility" still meant something, the donnishness and academicism of most literary criticism was in danger of foundering under the didactic fervor of various philosophies of action. Criticism had to compete, or else snipe tweedily from the rear. The cultural propaganda I refer to and oppose to the *mentalité* of this critical prose is typified by Spengler's *Decline of the West*, but is active whenever ideas of the end of the West or threats to a cultural outlook provoke aggressive alarm and advice for a regenerative fix.[4]

It may not be prudent to generalize about a style whose variety in the field of criticism is very great. There is less of a risk in defining what that style, even in its variety, generally opposes: manifestolike culture-critiques, linked by Fredric Jameson to an "apocalyptic vision of the end of Western civilization to which Spengler gave representation." Jameson adds that "the exhilarating pathos of this decline of civilization conceals the more prosaic realities of the crisis of a class and of the disastrous inflation." In his socioeconomic interpretation this manic-depressive pathos is seen as the cover-up for an inflation that threatened to wipe out the middle classes and to create a mass proletariat, a prospect that increased conservative fears about culture. By a similar reduction, Terry Eagleton links the *Spectator* papers to a rising mercantile class attempting to maintain its hegemony.[5] If Eagleton is correct, the honest style is anything but honest, for civility would have been acquired at a price, that of suppressing a class war that is heating up. And if Jameson is right, my generic understanding of critical prose as antienthusiastic is likewise an evasion of basic social facts.

Wyndham Lewis, the subject of Jameson's inquiry, was a protofascist culture-critic, and anything but civil in his prose. Like Carlyle, Nietzsche, Pound, and Lawrence, his style enjoys its own extravagance against the background of what it attacks: the atrophy of the organic and energic elements in society, the increase in bureaucracy and reification, and a general feeling that life had become alienated and abstract. These were symptoms also denounced by the Left. The symptoms of cultural decay are described in similar ways by both sides; it is the interpretation and the remedies that differ. What was common to these culture-critiques was a heroic—or mock-heroic—vision of society's power to transform itself. Lewis' style, for example, is mock-heroic: Bakhtin might have classified it as carnivalesque. It is prose conceived as a counterenergy and viciously satirizes wrong forms of vitalism. Lewis lumps together Bergson, Croce, Stein, and Joyce as antispatial "time trotters" who merely contribute to a dying culture. Their artificial commotion, he claims, makes us aware how enfeebled Tradition has become, how much deadness it exhibits. Something is rotten in Europe, and the writers flayed by Lewis are part of the problem, even if they think themselves part of the solution.

What is clear from this account (other than the complexity of the situation) is that we face a chiasmus: the heroic propagandists want to remove what is deadening in the culture by a scheme of revitalization, and the nonheroic practitioners of criticism object to naive and inflated polarities, seeing *them* as debilitating, and placing the possibility of cultural renewal in art's verbal and visual discrimination. This chiasmus, in which the two parties live each other's death, brings public and political discussion to a dangerous impasse.

The title of this chapter, "Literary Criticism and the Future," means to indicate neither the future of literary criticism nor a future it might help to achieve, but an attitude toward the future which the critical temperament, in the form of literary criticism, carries within itself. Though conjectures about modern decadence (as well as milder theories on a "dissociation of sensibility") had a salutary effect by restraining excessive hope in progress, they also fed a cultural despair traced by Fritz Stern via German thinkers to its terrible culmination in the vaunted rebirth of KULTUR promulgated by the theoreticians of National Socialism. This fixation on decadence, on the part of Right or Left, led to ideological ravages greater than the severest religion. The question arises: is there no other way to signal the seriousness of a thinker than the apolcalyptic tone or the sweeping cultural statement? Must we always talk in "Big Think" terms about the Modern Dilemma or the Destiny of the West?

A solution adopted by many writers was to abjure "philosophy" altogether. They cultivated the book review or brief essay. T. S. Eliot's "Tradition and the Individual Talent," perhaps the most influential statement on literature for half a century after its publication, was but an elongated review in size. Leavis and *Scrutiny* magazine institutionalized this tendency, opposing to the sound and fury of propaganda and disembodied ideas an education whose centerpiece was close reading and the unpretentious honesty of the essayistic mind.[6] This reaction to heavy speculation also targeted what Nietzsche had denounced as *Gelehrtenkultur*: a pedant culture with increasing dependence on narrow specialization and an unavowed though virulent ideological investment.

Such a rejection of speculative thought was based, nevertheless, on a simplification of the cultural picture. For philosophy too suffered such pressures as affected literature and history. In the period between the World Wars these pressures came from opposite quarters: from science, with its neutral and objective stance, and from the politicized scholarship fostered by nationalism. The turn to literariness, in scientific Formalism, or field-centered and defensively aesthetic New Criticism, or many literary reviews flourishing at that time, was paralleled by the linguistic turn in analytic and ordinary language philosophy. Even philosophers began to abjure philosophy—at least metaphysics or "ontotheology." Descartes' exemplary stripping away of every uncertain certainty was pushed to the limit. A thin man emerged from the speculative fat.

On the issue, then, of philosophy's relation to literary criticism, one should distinguish between a pseudodevelopment that could be called *culturology,* which is ideologically aggressive and projects ideas of national, social, or racial destiny into the future, and the inventive schemes of empirical thinkers with world or text before them.

There has always been some competition between the disciplines—between philosophy and theology, for example, or philosophy and literature. A grand poet like Wallace Stevens, when he relaxes the spirit in his prose, is intent on overcoming such competitive distinctions and dissolving the narrow institutionalization of activities he considers fundamentally poetic (see the "Prose" collected in *Opus Posthumous*). Stevens does not confuse the disciplines but insists that there is a magnanimity of effect which issues from a poetic mind whatever its field-specialization. So Leibnitz, despite his imaginative way of thinking, is said to be a poet manqué, a "poet without flash" who was limited, as so many philosophers are, by fear of ornament and horror of metaphor. Stevens suggests that there is a "call to poetry" which is not always pursued by the philosopher; yet despite the latter's effort at self-censorship a nuance of that call remains in his work.

Like Stevens, I am tempted to characterize certain philosophical ventures as unacknowledged poetry. This does not alter the fact that literary criticism has benefited in an era of academicism and specialization from thinkers who write vividly about the aesthetic dimension. "The only marvelous bishops of heaven have always been those that made it seem like heaven" (Stevens). Nothing I have said about the specificity of literary criticism should suggest that I am against philosophy in criticism or want to restore the purity of disciplinary genres. My argument is with a certain kind of rhetoric whose idealism is as hollow as it is grand. Culturology has demonstrated for almost a century what Jacques Rivière called its "analytic impotence."[7]

The liaison between literature and philosophical thought intensified after the Second World War. An occupied country like France had learned the value of spiritual resistance in the form of books that seemed to be "philosophy" or "literature," and simply by refusing to be propaganda, or by a subtle change of subject and language, expressed their freedom. The turn to literature was also a return to normalcy, to the sheer relief of mixing at will useful and pleasurable. When Derrida talks of the "errance joyeuse du *graphein*," he points to a liberation from the book that is inspired by books.

Yet in France this recuperative phase went hand in hand with liquidating a discredited political discourse, one that had accepted not only the need to collaborate but also the fascist idea of a revolution in the service of state power rather than democracy. Maurice Blanchot, in a manner that was to prove exemplary, took up pre-Nazi poet-philosophers and philosopher-poets, reclaiming a conjunction between German and French culture jeopardized by the political events. The new French criticism, however, differed from the literary-critical mode that had muted cultural prophecy before the War. What now appeared on the scene, often bristling with exotic word and methodology, was a more complicated reading of cultural events in the light of a burdened language.

The change described in Chapter 3 shows humanistic pedagogy under fire as a philosophy of rhetoric aiming at a modest form of public consensus through the Common Reader ideal.[8] A more radical stance emerges in Continental Europe. Bourgeois humanism, it was claimed, had proved impotent in the face of the catastrophe, and the question was how much of it could be salvaged. What happened, preeminently in France though spreading to America, unfolded as a gradual process, not at all unanimous. At first Sartre's brand of existentialist humanism and his separation of prose from poetry as an honest, communicative medium was much more influential than the dense and difficult ruminations of a Blanchot, or of the Heidegger from whom both authors claimed to draw. Lévi-Strauss too urged a new humanism, founded on the universal mental grammar of structuralism applied to all cultures, not just the West. Yet

181

the rupture did come: a prose with literary density and involution that gave great offense because it challenged the ideal of breaking the code, the ideal of ultimate clarity and language mastery. Metaphors of blindness invade the rhetoric of criticism.

The new discourse, both fictional and expository, substantiated the claim of Emmanuel Levinas, one of the earliest importers of Heidegger, that "The end of philosophy is the beginning of an era where all is philosophy, because philosophy is not revealed through philosophers." To Anglo-American observers it seemed as if the Age of Theory had commenced, but for Levinas the opposite was the case: "Theoretical man has ceased to reign." This meant in effect that the type of consciousness displayed by literature was not denied philosophical status or treated as a lower grade of knowledge to be transcended via the grand historical march of the spirit. The corrosion of theoretical constructs by linguistic process or its literary exploitation (the excess of signifier over signified) entered thought as a challenging condition of thought, not as an unfortunate residue of something yet unmastered. Especially sensitive was the issue of how literature closed off language by the concept of canonical book or how language closed off language by the creation of a consensus-rhetoric. (The false consensus of Nazi nationalism and the forced coordination endemic to totalitarian states are still painful memories at this time.) Blanchot's *récits,* for example, follow a negative course in which certain phrases—powerful clichés, colloquialisms—are questioned as intensely as in philosophical scrutiny, yet the technique for doing so is neither didactic nor explicitly analytic but a decentering narrative. The questionable phrases (and potentially any words) are presented as ghostly lures with a greater immediacy in their proverbial or iterable status than the fictions invented to embody them. Cliché and archetype, their pathos, their banal intimacy, form a Gordian knot that arouses once again the disastrous desire for a decisive purification of language.

Deconstruction goes against that desire, not with it. It reveals in all significant writing a "double inscription" that cannot be reduced to a propagandistic intent—for instance, to an overwriting or canceling of ideological error. Yet is there, as Jeffrey Mehlman has claimed, a tendency in this to amnesty the immediate political past? I personally do not think so, mainly because I see a larger purpose in the scrupulous if generalized analysis of double inscription. Whatever its motive, the new philosophical criticism points to something comfortless in the *entire* Enlightenment project of language reform and embraces such different thinkers as Adorno and Foucault. The book or its author is figured as an archaeological site,[9] a ruin where a certain repetition (beyond the pleasure principle, and certainly beyond a therapeutic humanism) goes from the same to the same, rather than—in any decisive way—from "for" to "against" (or vice versa), or from blindness to insight, or dialectically from disillusion to wisdom and truth. The task of this discourse about error is not made easier by the fact that Heidegger's problematic style of thinking and writing, so crucial to Blanchot, Lacan, Levinas, de Man, and Derrida, had been diverted and tainted by Nazism.

This quick summary means to acknowledge an important critical event described earlier. My focus at this point is not on the difference between the French critical mode and the Anglo-American criticism that strove for integrity between the World Wars, but rather on a continuity that makes their difference more startling. The continuity turns on the attitude of both toward the future, and a correlative attitude toward the past. Neither past nor future should be thought of as fulfillable. Derrida's earliest essays (collected in *Difference and Writing*, 1967) already reject futurity as a present-to-be (*un présent futur*). Commenting on the third volume of Jabès' *Book of Questions,* he conveys the fact that these questions have opened up again, that for the *third* time they are there (*là*) in the form of a book, and already beyond (*au delà*) its closure. The questions seem to phantomize the *Book of Questions,* as the third book becomes a perpetual third. "The future [the beyond] is there like the shadow of a book, the third between the two hands holding the book, the difference [*différance*] in the now [*maintenant* = *main-tenant* = handholding, maintenance] of writing [*écriture*], the gap between the book and the book, the other hand." To pursue Derrida's ghost story, the way he projects otherness, would take us too far, but it is evident from our having to annotate his words that they have a double register that keeps them unsettled on the page though very much in presence. This diction is like the heavy double of an element whose lightness would be more unbearable still. Like irony and ambiguity in prewar criticism, it has the effect of fostering a negative capability, of pulling back from statements about fulfillment or about the future as the horizon of fulfillment.

Literary criticism, appreciated as a style, could be defined as "institutionalized irony." This irony, precisely when institutionalized, may become supercilious and restrictive, limiting originality, intensity, and speculation. Its quality of self-critique can lapse into methodical scientism or an antienthusiastic veneer. Even though today our resistance to a cultural prophecy that masks as history endows the critical essay with an important reason for being, I find myself puzzled. How does one discriminate between a necessary enthusiasm and a dangerous, even reprehensible, delusion? Or how does one distinguish wisdom from wit and sort out experts who have latched onto a theory from critics who cannot cease from mental fight?

Michael Walzer has said that the Hebrew Prophets were our first social critics; and Alfred Kazin, reviewing the *The New Republic*'s career from 1914–1989, regrets the increasing absence of "thinkers with a sense of prophecy." Kazin, starting out in the 1930s, recalls in a book of that title the immense excitement that surrounded every literary job, as history seemed dangerously in the making and some identification with it appeared inevitable. "[T]he issue raised in a book review, a street scene studied for an article, always fitted my sense of the destiny and inclusiveness of history . . . I saw us all moving forward on the sweep of great events. I believed that everyone was engulfed in politics, absorbed in issues that were the noble part of themselves . . . My interest and the genius of history just had to coincide."[10]

What lodestar distinction could there have been, during this time of excitement and turmoil, between Kazin's "genius of history," identified with democratic traditions, and the genius-myth of National Socialism, supported by a condemnation of democratic traditions and by the prophecy of a New Order? War forces a choice between these visions of the leading genius of history. But if the point is to prevent war, or to find a peaceful alternative (Blake's "mental fight"), then one cannot dismiss Lawrence's intemperate attack on Bertrand Russell. "He wants to be ultimately a free agent. That is what they all want, ultimately—that is what is at the back of all international peace-for-ever and democratic control talks: they want an outward system of nullity, which they call peace and goodwill, so that in their own souls they can be independent little gods . . . That is at the back of all Liberalism, Fabianism and democracy. It stinks. It is the will of a louse."[11]

Such a critique of bourgeois individualism is commonplace in this period. It comes from both Right and Left and is based, as in Lawrence, on strong convictions. Lawrence's "independent little gods" suggest his sense of a remedy: a larger and more deliberate enthusiasm, a return to cosmic and sacred feelings beyond the ersatz religion of the modern separatist ego. In France not very much later Bataille, Leiris, Caillois, and Klossovski founded a *Collège de Sociologie* to examine the field of "sacred sociology," that is, the role of religious feelings in the formation of communities, "all manifestations of social existence where the active presence of the sacred is clear."[12] But the influence of the writers associated with the College did not penetrate French and European thought until after the Second World War. "Sacred sociology" is still largely neglected in American circles, despite its prescient understanding of such political religions as fascism and its analysis of secret societies, the army, festivals, public rituals, the relation between sacred and erotic. The College alerts us to residues and derivatives of the sacred in the secular world, and to the danger of neglecting them by underestimating what the Enlightenment dismissed as "enthusiasm."

Even in its rhetorical form, it is not enthusiasm as such, or martial polemics, that can be objected to, but how these stand toward time, toward past and future. We have learned, with Walter Benjamin, that the dead too are not safe from the victors, who slander them or decree their oblivion. This appropriation, in the form of a rewriting of the past or a preemptive identification with the future, aims to coerce history, just as religion did, and to impose an official story. A philosophy of culture dominated by parareligious concepts of decadence and renovation should make us particularly cautious about the intrusion of vitalistic, biological, and millennial metaphors into history-writing. When cultural history becomes therapeutic as well as diagnostic, and writes prescriptions without a license, then it wishes to be art or prophecy, genres both more difficult and sometimes more dangerous to practice.

By contrast, literary criticism is comparative and defamiliarizing, not prescriptive or prophetic. Its style remains in the mode of critique, where the object is not analyzed in order to be appropriated. "Knowing" the work means that we allow it to remain questionable. We disclose obstacles that impede a directer knowledge or thicken its text-milieu and historical layering. Sometimes these obstacles include even the meanings

185

of the work of art: changing modes of intelligibility that produce a bewildering variorum of interpretations and lead us into the skeptical thought that all forceful interpretation is a form of allegory. Recent ethnography too, from Clifford Geertz to James Clifford, has come closer to the spirit of this literary criticism and stressed the partiality of truth, the encoded or nontransparent character of the expressive facts analyzed, and generally the mediated situation of anthropologists who *write* culture.

Some theorists have called the work of art an "answer" to which we must find the question. While this is a good working principle and signals that art can be in advance of thought, it does not cover the fact that art's "answer" questions the questions we put to it without claiming unknowable status. Art, in Stevens' words, *almost* resists the intelligence. Its "liberty interest" can be abridged only by itself rather than by particular applications—really modes of appropriation—however liberal they seem to be.

Yet the "answer" of art, or its proleptic (some would say productive) position vis-à-vis cognitive schemes, has a side that troubles literary theory. I once characterized that "answer" as an antiself-consciousness drawn from consciousness itself—in accordance with a Hegelian model of dialectical mediation. Others have tried a Kantian model, derived from his analytic of the sublime, in which a moment of ideational blockage is described, or a constitutive inadequacy of idea to experience, and where the result of this is not a sacrifice of intellect but rather an elevation of the "defeated" reason. Kant's model captures the threat, even terror, of otherness; Hegel's expresses the burden of historical experience as an internalized consciousness, and Nietzsche will associate that consciousness with the culture-guilt of civilized minds aware of injustices in the struggle for survival.

The theoretical model, in brief, that views art as part of a dialogic exchange, although it does not claim that the "question" is resolved by the "answer" of art, is unsatisfactory insofar as it elides the abrupt, demanding impact of experiences whose character is more an accusation than a question. These experiences contain a seductive or a traumatic element. While they need not be explicitly historical or collective in nature, after historicism it is much harder to step out of history. We identify (through imaginative sympathy) also with the victims, aware of whatever was suffered in the march of time.

Criticism too has to develop an answerable style, one that does not simply intellectualize the *force* of art's answer, its imaginative challenge. Something definitive is needed, as decisive as a moral law, as closural as experience itself in its irreversible aspect. While in the French tradition from Proust to Roland Barthes the emphasis often falls on the relation of art to desire ("We would like," Proust remarked in *On Reading,* "to have the artist give us answers, while all he can do is give us desires"), criticism must come to terms also with the drive for closure, a desire to live beyond desire. Culturology as prophetism, seeking to determine the future and define the destiny of a people, is a powerful intellectual aphrodisiac because it mixes desire and the death of desire. It disciplines the hope it arouses and so becomes a demagogic force. Its success in the interwar period revealed the inadequacy of the role of art in culture or our inability to understand that role. Even today we continue to reduce art to entertainment *or* to a species of high-minded ideology.

From Schiller to Huizinga a broadened theory of play did emerge, to which cultural anthropology is now contributing. The most encouraging recent development in this area has been cultural poetics, which views identity as an invention (close to the fictive) of differential traits. In this "poststructuralist" view of identity-construction, playful and combative are seen as precariously mixed components. The relevance of Huizinga is confirmed, and the mixture can be observed in high-spirited conversation that veers toward challenge, quarrel, and squaring-off as well as in the ritual and flaunting dances of traditional societies. Art too is war by different means or rather, in Kenneth Burke's thinking, a catharsis of its spirit.

But the relation of play to moral or political seriousness remains a problem. The "sacred sociology" I have mentioned began, just before the Second World War, to examine in depth the relations between social existence and the sacred (also the dionysian) in language and public spectacles. However, the parareligious and demagogic nature of cultural prophecy was not fully recognized even by the College of Sociology.[13] In any case, there is no play or irony within the pervasive notions of national or racial character that supported cultural speculation in the period between the World Wars, notions found not only in Spengler, or in Key-

187

serling's and Toynbee's many volumes, but in almost any large-scale history placing Western civilization into the context of world history. They also pervade in muted form a great deal of literary criticism.

I will concentrate here on France and England, with some thoughts on the catastrophe in Germany. My focus is on writers who were not totally seduced by monumental schemes of cultural prophecy and who struggled with the reality of Europe as a multinational entity, more divided than ever after the collapse of the Hapsburg monarchy. This was also, it should be remembered, the period of the great modernist revolution in the pictorial arts; and if many artists, like Picasso, took political sides as fascism and communism grew, their unverbal medium had a resistance to propaganda built into it. For literary criticism (and art criticism too) this resistance would have to be achieved. Stevens remarks in the 1930s:

> The pressure of the contemporaneous from the time of the beginning of the World War to the present time has been constant and extreme . . . We are preoccupied with events, even when we do not observe them closely. We have a sense of upheaval. We feel threatened. We look from an uncertain present toward a more uncertain future . . . The trouble is that the greater the pressure of the contemporaneous, the greater the resistance. Resistance is the opposite of escape. The poet who wishes to contemplate the good in the midst of confusion is like the mystic who wishes to contemplate God in the midst of evil. There can be no thought of escape. Both the poet and the mystic may establish themselves on herrings and apples. The painter may establish himself on a guitar, a copy of *Figaro* and a dish of melons. These are fortifyings, although irrational ones. The only possible resistance to the pressure of the contemporaneous is a matter of herrings and apples, or, to be less definite, the contemporaneous itself.[14]

The mysterious idea that the contemporaneous resists the contemporaneous hints at an equivocal art that acknowledges two kinds of presence: that of actual events, and the way modernists press back by spatial (synchronic) form or its verbal simulacrum. Stevens is aware of Eliot's famous statement in "Tradition and the Individual Talent" (1919) that "the whole of the literature of Europe from the time of Homer, and within it the literature of [the writer's] own country, has a simultaneous existence and composes a simultaneous order." The contemporaneous as

188

collage or montage or a foregrounding of the medium defends against the contemporaneous as contingency—as politics, news, opinion, *fait divers*. The tension between still life and movement in a *Nude Descending a Staircase* or that between history and herrings in a composition that assembles the "news" *(Figaro)* as part of painting's page at once captures and stabilizes the sense of "speed up" so remarked upon at this time. Literary criticism participates in the struggle for form, developing its own reserve, focusing more on technique than idea, and subjecting to stylistic irony ambitious beliefs about the end of an era, or the recovery of an original greatness.[15]

A great diversity of artifacts and cultural contexts can make an observer uncertain of his own value-system. Relativism or skepticism may ensue. This possibility is basic and constitutes what Malraux has called *La Tentation de l'Occident,* where "tentation" means both temptation and trial. Remembering how Napoleon assembled in the Louvre works of art looted from the nations he conquered, and how this influx troubled the identity of the French artist, Malraux writes: "It is not Europe or the past which is invading France as this century begins, it is the world which is invading Europe with all its present and past, its heap of offerings of living and dead forms, its meditations."[16]

Malraux poses the same question as Spengler: can the West deal with these forceful tokens of cultural diversity and otherness? Are they symptoms of its decline or omens of a rebarbarization that will renew it? Malraux's answer, though not a confident one, suggests two directions Europe is taking after World War I. (His book was written between 1921 and 1925.) The first is "the sometimes bitter play of artistic experiments"—where "bitter" points to an uncertainty that begins to invade the concept of monumental art, of the masterpiece. While still striving for classicism or its equivalent, the artist accepts a divided mind and restless experimentation. The second way (that of Valéry, say, rather than Picasso) is to value the contemplation of this highly mobile world of art more than the will to fix it in "bitter experiments."

Related to the second mode of defense—against a foreign heap of forms or the relativism they induce—is what Malraux calls a "revenge of the intellect." The mind that refuses to judge, and makes that refusal a value, "is led on by its own strength to be conscious of its need for a

189

negative classicism"—and so makes a judgment about style after all, by favoring works that embody a "lucid horror of seduction." Contemporary painters turn therefore to the primitive art of Asia, or to a Greece that seems closest to Asia, in order to recapture a lost quality of impersonality antithetical to the violent and changeable character of the modern style. This modern classicism, passionately affirmed as a value despite the mobile intellect that had given up the idea of a more than experimental art, points to Cubism, which conceives of the work (*oeuvre*) as gaining monumentality by "an almost mathematical relationship between its parts."

Malraux, it has been said, chain-smokes ideas. The nervous and mobile character he attributes to art reappears in his own style of writing. Highly elliptical and not shy of paradox, his fictional letters between a young Frenchman in China and a young Chinese in Paris show the pressure exerted by Nietzsche and Spengler on an intellectual whose twenties coincide with the postwar twenties in Europe and who is consciously articulating a new *mal du siècle*. The starting-point of his book is a contrast between East and West, but the young tourists are surprisingly similar. Ling and A.D. are would-be conquerors who find that power escapes them, that the intellect, though it still burns brightly and is as voracious as ever, can no longer transform what it sees. There is too much news, that "heap of . . . living and dead forms"—dead because unmodern, and living though their milieu has passed away.

Such a perspective is not essentially different from Valéry's in "The Spiritual Crisis." That essay, published in the first year after the First World War, envisions a European Hamlet standing on an immense terrace and looking at a million graveyards, a million specters. But, as Valéry continues in a famous passage, "he is an intellectual Hamlet. He meditates on the life and death of truths. His phantoms are all the topics that enter our controversies; his remorse is stirred by all the titles of our glory; he is overwhelmed by the weight of discoveries, of fields of knowledge, incapable of subsuming this unlimited activity." After inspecting, like Hamlet in the play, various skulls (*"Whose was it?* This one was *Leonardo* . . . This other was *Leibnitz"*), Valéry asks the same question Malraux will repeat in his own way. "And as for me, the European intellect, what will become of it?"[17]

Valéry foresees a kind of solution, not Spengler's or Cavafy's rebarbarization, but a dissemination and equalization of talents. He surprises us by claiming that the Europe of 1914 had reached the limit of modernism, defined as the capacity for a synchronic contemporaneity, "the liberal coexistence in every cultivated mind of the most dissimilar ideas, of the most contrary principles of existence and knowledge." Every thinker, he continues memorably, was a "Universal Exposition of thoughts." The caesura of the Great War does not change the prewar situation but tempts the mind to formulate it in crisis terms, to meditate upon its skull. What interests Valéry is not the end of the West but the exact form of its decline. The European genius, whose spoliations were internalized, producing a pure form of contemporaneity, this genius, located once upon a time in a corner of Asia called Europe, exports itself through its own tendency for intellectual, military, and economic exploitation. The inequality that favored Europe will therefore diffuse throughout the world and equalize benefits—until the disorder characterizing genius is replaced by complete order, a "perfect, definitive ant heap." But this means the end of Europe's hegemony, for with such equalization the balance of forces shifts to the side with the most people and land. "We have crazily given back to the masses their proportional forces."

Compared to Valéry, Malraux does not allow himself the irony of a vision proceeding according to a mathematical curve. He describes impasse and refuses to let go of the idea of individual genius. The personality we call a genius represents the essence of man by assuming most fully his condition. This *condition humaine* (a later phrase) highlights the dilemma that tempted so many in this period to talk of the end of the West or of modernity. A major ingredient of this dilemma for both Malraux and Valéry was the individual mind's failure to transform information, as it flooded in through new media and the press. The *individual* feels put in question even as there is an emphasis on the individual talent. "The Great War had made us realize," Valéry wrote, "that the abyss of history is large enough for everyone, for the entire world. We sense that a civilization has the same fragility as a life. The circumstances which will send Keats' works and Baudelaire's to join those of Menander are no longer inconceivable: they are in the daily papers."

Indefatiguably ironic, Valéry points to the leveling effect of newspapers as well as to the surfeit of their *fait divers* and propagation of what Heidegger solemnly analyzed as an inauthentic temporality. Malraux

191

states the phenomenon from the point of view of a young person desiring his own share of immortality (wanting to be part of the canon, we would now say). "The powers capable of changing facts," he writes, "become so rapidly loaded down with them that intelligence realizes it cannot operate at any level of reality, that it cannot create the necessary unity between itself and the conviction which justifies it."[18] As if thinking of Valéry, not only "The Spiritual Crisis" essay but the famous *Monsieur Teste*, Malraux insists that his era's erosion of a psychology of the subject and of a sentimentality that, as in Greece, made human life the measure, is part of the problem and not in any way a solution. "The intensity [of our *vie profonde*] cannot belong to the intellect, which knows this and revolves emptily, a beautiful machine spotted by blood."[19]

I hope I have conveyed something of how it felt to be an intellectual in a *victor* nation after the Great War. In these French writers the emphasis is not on France so much as on Europe; and the curious fact is that France's victory raised the specter of a defeat. What the European Hamlet sees are endless fields of white crosses and red poppies. Valéry turns them into the graveyard of the creators of a civilization that has just emerged from killing over a million of its own, many in the flower of their age, many who would have been creators in the future. Whereas military defeat brings to Germany a recrudescence of cultural prophesy, born of despair yet often triumphalist in spirit, we find a surprising undertone of defeatism in the French Banquet Years. It is based on a perception that the "values of the West" had either inspired or not been able to prevent a massive Civil War among the Western nations. It was after 1918, not after 1945, that Valéry wrote: "The great virtues of the German people have engendered more ills than the vices laziness could ever have created. We have seen, with our own eyes, conscientious work and the most systematic education, discipline, and devotion of the most serious kind, adapted to horrifying schemes . . . It required, without a doubt, a great deal of science to kill so many people, to waste so much property, to devastate so many towns in the shortest time: but it also required *moral qualities*." His conclusion does not refer to Germany alone but to the West as a whole. "Knowledge and Duty, have you become suspect then?"

Cultural relativism is not the ultimate challenge at this time. It is whether one can still believe, after such a war, in the victory of man over fate, evil, or whatever name we give to what opposes human creativeness and happiness. If we call the opposing force nature, then what is doubted is the effectiveness of culture; if we call it culture (including reason and science), then the problem becomes an impasse: as constitutive a crisis as Freud would describe in *Civilization and Its Discontents* (1930). Malraux asserts in the wake of Nietzsche that, having set up and then destroyed God, having discovered and built on man's autonomy, European civilization must now realize that Man too is dead, that the humanistic vision which brought us to this point is confronted by the mortality of all schemes of mastery. Two statements, one by Ling and one by A. D. summarize this position. Ling: "After the death of the Sphinx, Oedipus attacks himself." A. D.: "Europe, great cemetery, where only dead conquerors sleep."

Some tendencies in Malraux and Valéry do drift toward nihilism. Yet in "The Spiritual Crisis," as in his later works, Valéry confines himself to arguing that history-based visions, by which the would-be conquerors inspired themselves, were delusory and without lasting effect. In the modern era, according to him, none of the Great European Powers remained securely in command for more than fifty years. Despite the fact that Europeans are far superior in number and means, the Romans "found in the entrails of their chickens ideas that were more precise and consequential than all our political sciences contain" ("Grandeur et Décadence de l'Europe," 1928). These Valéryan observations, powerfully predictive despite renouncing cultural prophecy, are not nihilistic but in the tradition of Pascal's *roseau pensant,* whose distinction over the brute creation is that it knows what crushes it. What prevented the slide into nihilism, on the one hand, or a reactionary faith, on the other, is difficult to ascertain; Valéry always presents himself as a thinker who disdains the grand gesture (system or cultural prophesy) and positions his observations in the form of critical essay.

While Malraux, whose affect is very different from that of Valéry, adheres to the heroics of cultural self-definition, he too denies progressive or triumphalist perspectives. Residually there *is* the lure of exotic vistas for imagination to adventure in, and so the epistolary *Temptation of the West* is really a first novel. But the lure of the East for the European mind crisscrosses with Chinese Westernization in a way that disenchants the differences between the two cultures—differences that exist in stark contrast yet converge when disenchanted. Their common vanishing point is the impermanence of empire and the eventual impotence of metaphysical ideals that sustain a personal or national will to power.

After the Great War it was even more difficult for a European to see into the future. That disadvantage was turned to an advantage by some of the major writers of France and England. The end that becomes important is the closing down of *endzeit* speculation. In Germany *Geistesgeschichte* and cultural prophecy rebound, but surprisingly little of that becomes popular in English and French circles. (Needless to say, a fringe element of gloom and doom and counterbalancing manias exist in any society.) The project of the intellect in those countries, if I may be permitted so broad a generalization, is precisely a critical discourse that does not depend on speculative cultural history or metaphysical notions of a progressive *légende des siècles* with a clear teleology.[20]

When we do have a forecast, like Valéry's probabilistic diffusion (and defusion) of genius, it suggests a convergence of quantifying method and massification. It is a way of noting, more calmly than Ortega's "revolt of the masses," a sociological development that need not overwhelm rational thought. The main thrust, however, of Valéry's desperate or ironic scientism is to suggest that we modify our mode of time-representation and no longer think in terms of "event," that is, just the kind of thinking we do when we talk about the end of an epoch, and see the Great War as a definitive cesura. (Valéry prefers, it will be recalled, to evoke in 1919 the mind of 1914, and to extrapolate from that.) In his poetry too Valéry retards the proleptic movement of voice and cognition toward an "event," that category including any referential meaning or recognizable idea illustrated by the poem, not just the great event.

The dominance of an ironic style, defined by Paul Fussell in his book on the aftermath of the Great War as a mode of "abbreviated hope," also points to visionary restraint.[21] It is a sign that the very form of forward thinking should change, that large-scale historical and cultural speculation is being disenchanted. The ironic style is often structural as well as tonal, as in Eliot's *Waste Land* technique of montage or the antithetical vacillations of Yeats. The latter's sonnet on Leda ends with a subversive question that restrains what it induces, namely, having to foresee what one is fated to bring forth: "Did she put on [Jove's] knowledge with his power . . . ?"

Here a rhetorical technique substitutes for vision. Technique fosters an edgy and evocative indeterminacy which seems consistent with the older poetics of suggestion inherited from the symbolist movement. This newer indeterminacy, however, is neither primarily self-conscious nor primarily a magical resource recovered from instrumentalized words. It is what it seems to be: a refusal to be drawn into futuristic vision. Even when, as elsewhere in Yeats, a visionary framework is elaborated, that framework remains in the service of poetry (providing, according to Yeats's "instructors," metaphors for poetry). The poet is engaged in saving imagination from abstractness rather than proclaiming what is to come. Yet the balance between irony and prophecy is a precarious one. Technique does not replace vision but intensifies what it restrains. Eliot's brief epic may be a sophisticated machine to lead by indirect means to an overwhelming and not at all rhetorical question.

In *The Waste Land*, as in the Parsifal legend, an intriguing procession of images (but now including fragments of European literature) seems to urge a question on which redemption depends. What question may that be? Is the redeeming potential perhaps in the very asking, the active intervention? Or is it a matter of proper timing? Have we forgotten what the question is, distracted by the strangeness of the spectacle or by too many (literary) spectacles? Is it even possible for poetry to provide the lucky words?

From Eliot's development, and his famous public affirmation in 1929 (equivalent to a conversion) that henceforth he would be an Anglo-Catholic, Royalist and Conservative, it is clear that the question was religious. To what cultural continuity can I give my allegiance? What act of faith will redeem England, if not Western Civilization? Eliot's later career was spent in defining a Christian culture. To do so meant not just redeeming the European past by a poetic and powerful nostalgia, it also meant turning toward a future, on the analogy of a sinner's turn or return to God; and that involved a precarious relationship to time. Eliot is no apocalypticist, not even an ironic one; he tries to stay in the turning movement, which is clock-time itself, or historical time as clock-time writ large, though counterpointed by liturgical rhythms. The "end," the visionary or dogmatic result, is still expressed by Eliot in terms of the emotional and intellectual pressure for a resolution.

At his most successful Eliot can suggest an opening within human

195

time: there seems to be in Christian religion, which is also a culture, an imaginative power that comes from itself and does not require renewal though an imported vitalism or fertility rite. Eliot does not engage in cultural prophecy to inspire himself or his generation; he sticks to criticism, and in poetry to a spectacular "whispering" technique. Yet his picture of the Jew as an alien representing money power (as Hilaire Belloc called it) and embodying a disintegrative rather than classical modernism—the Jew depicted in "Gerontion" and other early poems is a being without land or loyalty, whose freethinking tendencies and cosmopolitan merchandizing unsettle the communitarian order or *Volksgemeinschaft*—this vulgar, scapegoating idea in so sophisticated a thinker suggests that on the two counts of cultural relativism and a discontent coming from acculturation itself, Eliot's Christianity is a more troubled response than the cognitive polytheism of Malraux and Valéry.

In this sketch of cultural developments between the two World Wars, I cannot evade the question: what happened in Germany? No one ventures into that area without anguish. Yet the theme of culture was central to Nazism and hardly distinguishable from its political ambition. During the darkest time of the war Hitler kept dreaming of a postwar period in which he would devote himself entirely to German culture.

National Socialism was a political religion that swept away all relativisms and persuaded a people by terror and propaganda (but also by touching deep desires and relieving deep anxieties) that their true character and *Kultur* could be restored: to found an empire of a thousand years. All restraint of vision disappeared: decadence would be overcome; the West would end, but also culminate in the millennial *Reich*. The criminal actions against the Jews are inconceivable unless we see that a cosmic and Manichaean rhetoric was here inscribed as reality. The slander that the Jews were racially inferior and culturally dangerous was underwritten by an elaborate ideology and then literalized—as in a mentally sick person who cannot distinguish between rhetorical and literal, and is impelled to "realize the metaphor." Anti-Semitic sources joked in the late 1930s about the "Madagascar solution"; and the supposedly Oriental Jews, unassimilable in the West, were "expelled to the East" ("Abschub nach Osten"), a phrase that became a euphemism for extermination in camps east of Germany.

But something further must be said about the impact of cultural relativism and how Nazism turned it into an excuse for its own *Sonderweg,* claiming that Germany had a special identity that needed protection from internal and external enemies. The movement insisted that political coordination was necessary to revive a German *Kultur* of which the State must be the legal guardian. The purification and inward turn of culture, which the Nazi state felt was so imperative that it expelled or killed its Jewish citizens, resembles in a perverted way what Nietzsche attributed to the ancient Greeks, at the time of Bismarck's victorious struggle with France in 1873–74, when Germany first attained its identity as a European power. The Greeks, Nietzsche wrote in "The Use and Abuse of History,"

> were in . . . danger of being overwhelmed by what was past and foreign, and perishing on the "rock" of history. They never lived proud and untouched. Their "culture" was for a long time a chaos of foreign forms and ideas—Semitic, Babylonian, Lydian, and Egyptian—and their religion a battle of all the Gods of the East; just as German culture and religion is at present a death struggle of all foreign nations and bygone times . . . The Greeks gradually learnt to organize the chaos by taking Apollo's advice and thinking back to themselves, to their own true necessities, and letting all the sham necessities go. Thus they again came into possession of themselves [my translation].

Historicism made cultural relativism possible, and though German scholarship had been a leader in this field, it was also the Germans who were panicked into a repressive and self-purifying reaction. A racialist history arose, transforming *Geistesgeschichte* into a nationalistic triumph over historicism.

Germany's dignity was indeed precarious. The country felt exposed to other nations who were maligning it and asking damages for the World War. In that atmosphere anti-internationalism was common. Jews from Eastern Europe were made to appear Bolshevik, while the Western and more assimilated Jews were denounced (in Richard Wagner's phrase) as "plastic demons" who would convert to any belief for financial gain. Relativism, in short, was demonized in the caricature of the international Jew who concealed his nihilism under the mask of a cosmopolitan.

Jews could do almost nothing to counter these charges, for their religious culture was unknown or misrepresented. Unknown, because emancipation (barely a hundred years old) had demanded assimilation, and the scholarly movement called the "secular study of Judaism" (*Wissenschaft des Judentums*) was only starting to penetrate university circles. Misrepresented, because, based on the New Testament, theological anti-Semitism prevented serious consideration of the Talmud and other sources of Jewish Bible commentary. The special way of life, the "culture" that Jews had to renounce in order to become citizens, had no chance to influence the public.

The example of Judaism suggests that cultural relativism was never a real threat in Germany; it was a bogey, and did its damage precisely that way. Only the *perception* of a threat was real, and was kept roiling by cultural prophecy concerned with the future of Germany and the West. Nietzche's critique during the Bismark era of the disillusioning impact of historical knowledge became even more telling after the German humiliation in World War I.

In his Freiburg thesis on *Hegel and the State* (published in 1920 but written some ten years before) Franz Rosenzweig remarked how already in Hegel the idea of the state had been formulated with an eye on "an expanded [*geräumigere*] inner and outer German future." This theme of a viable German future becomes crucial. For Rosenzweig, as for Nietzsche, it fused with the question of the sense of a future itself, given an increasing and cheerless knowledge of history. Rosenzweig eventually turned to religion and declined his teacher Friedrich Meinecke's unusual offer to a Jew of a university position. Rosenzweig had not been able to extract from history any prospect for the future except by a religious meditation which he published as *The Star of Redemption* at the same time as *Hegel and the State*. In *The Star* he separated Jewish from Christian and Pagan history by a remarkable typology that stressed the specificity of each and reunited them only in the future of redemption instead of (like Meinecke) in the future of a cosmopolitan and universalistic ethos. "How is the formal knowledge of history possible? Through redemption."

A concern for the German future, then, often confused with that of civilization itself, stimulated many conflicting diagnoses. They became part of a political turmoil sensitized more than analyzed by them. Even E. R. Curtius felt in 1932 (*Deutscher Geist in Gefahr*) that Germany's identity as a nation-state was endangered by (though not only by) Karl

Mannheim and "skeptical" Jewish intellectuals. I am not claiming that it is only the alarmed reaction to a perceived danger that harms, or that cultural relativism may not become a reality with a demanding and flammable presence. But in Germany there was no truly dangerous cultural fact to back up the persecution of the Jews. If there was danger, it came as always from the *political* sphere, from a clash of Right and Left that roused the fear of Civil War. In the *cultural* sphere it was less a struggle of beliefs or confessions that prepared the ground for the Nazi purges than a fear of losing what belief there was. Nietzche's analysis of the corrosive effect of the historical consciousness on human illusions, and the desperate need for something to restore illusion and *justify* life like a religion, is certainly the best and most bitter guide to what happened. A whole nation, it seemed, went "mad as a refuge from unbelief" (William Blake, on the poet Cowper).

That cultural diversity need not result in a damaging skepticism or (except by reaction) in an overemphasis on the unity of a nation-state is suggested by the authors so far examined. Though we should not neglect the evidence of a reactionary cycle, foreseen by the Saint-Simonians, who predicted an alternation of critical with organic (religious, myth-restoring) epochs, to warn of the danger of such a cycle is at least to be forewarned. Moreover, one of the encouraging signs that the knowledge developed through historicism is more than skeptical or destabilizing is provided by Eric Auerbach.

In the beginning, he reminds us, historicism was an optimistic science, by which Vico apportioned to God a nature God had made, but to mankind a history mankind had made, and could therefore understand even as God understood nature. That thesis, according to Auerbach, provides a foundation for humanistic studies. *Mimesis,* written during the war, stands as a remarkable monument to cultural relativism. It contains no prophecy, except for one comment at the very end. There Auerbach permits himself a glimpse beyond the horizon of "Western history" and speculates that there are signs—not of an end but of an ultimate simplification. But it is *that* he regrets, rather than the complications and conflicts he has told us about. "Beneath the conflicts, and also through them, an economic and cultural leveling process is taking place. It is still a long way to a common life on earth, but the goal begins to be visible

199

. . . The complicated process of dissolution which led to fragmentation of the exterior action, to reflection of consciousness, and to stratification of time seems to be tending to a very simple solution. Perhaps it will be too simple to please those who, despite all its dangers and catastrophes, admire and love our epoch for the sake of its abundant life and the incomparable historical vantage point it affords."[22]

Auerbach, it turns out, is a *post-histoire* historian, but he is also a good antidote to Nietzsche. The historical sense does not have to "uproot the future." Historical justice, a "dreadful virtue" according to Nietzsche, does not have to "undermine and ruin the living thing." Nietzsche is never simple, of course; and although he calls the value we place on the historical a Western prejudice, he won't forgo it. What he wishes to factor in is the vitalism of passion ("for a woman or a theory"), and also the esteem for the moment of living itself rather than for "evolution."

Nietzsche's plea is basically—and ambivalently—for the antiacademic virtues and everyday reality. Does Auerbach's use of history not tend in the same direction? His reality—the object of representation in the literature he analyzes—can be high or low, an adventurer-warrior like Odysseus or a middle-class woman knitting a stocking in a family setting (Virginia Woolf's Mrs. Ramsey in *To the Lighthouse*). Literary history, he shows, has its own dynamic that goes from a system in which the representation of reality is regulated by levels of style (the *genera dicendi*, high, low, middle) to one in which this decorum is overturned, as everyday reality, previously presented only in the lowest (comic) manner, breaks through to claim its own significance and dignity. This summary cannot give any sense of the complexity of the actual historical movement (its *ricorsi*) or of Auerbach's finesse in articulating that. But it makes the point that, in Auerbach's account, literature affirms everyday life, displays it pushing against high-level constraints in every passage analyzed, as well as dissolving these constraints in the broad, ongoing historical picture.

Today this affirmation of everyday life has become something of an ethical principle. It involves an acceptance, even a celebration of the ordinary—this is all around us in contemporary philosophy and social thought.[23] Yet the story of cultural relativism since the eighteenth century, while it has opened our eyes to human possibilities, both those actualized and those presumed to be available for actualization, has also indicated two limits. Actualization leads to endless conflict, to heterogeneous and anomalous claims that are often too strong to be adjusted and so produce a history that may be colorful in retrospect but is as much the story of renewed oppression as of triumphant liberty. Or actualization reaches for a divestment instead of an affirmation of difference, for a nonexotic and even unheroic sort of existence.

My reservations about the new ethic—perhaps a very old ethic, but previously considered either too modest or too unspiritual—are three-fold. A first problem I have hinted at already. The ethic evades the human need for hierarchy, or reduces hierarchy to difference. (Auerbach describes this, on the rhetorical level, as a shift from hypotaxis to parataxis.) Though the author of *Mimesis* looks with equanimity at the prospect of "our common life on earth" *(das Elementare und Gemeinsame der Menschen überhaupt),* the touch of regret I have mentioned honors a multicultural reality with its colorful and ambitious personalities. Low or high in rank, criminals like Vautrin, hypocrites like Tartuffe, arrivistes like Julien Sorel, unfathomable ordinary consciousnesses like Mrs. Ramsay, or the Kings and courtiers of Shakespeare's and Racine's tragedies, they all strive to rise, build, persevere. They belong, magnified by their authors, to times that celebrate genius and power. Even the porters in Shakespeare, Victor Hugo remarked, have genius. In his forecast Auerbach may have been influenced by a residual Hegelianism: the revel of history must end and a prosaic age follows. But nothing is said about where all those expressive energies will go in that prosaic era. Despite its elemental satisfactions, would there not emerge a drive for differentiation or a new principle of high style?[24]

A second objection to affirming everyday life is found in Heidegger's work. His analyses of the inauthenticities of temporal existence (the world of *das man*) give us pause. I take Heidegger to say that the affirmative emphasis on everyday life is a minimalist move toward the refounding of a lost reality. His special theory explains that loss, and is less interesting for our purpose than the great sense of loss itself, and his extension of it to language. We live in a place, a time, and a language that is not our own. To emphasize cultural relativism, which may produce skepticism but more often amplifies the complexity and inventiveness of human life, is to lose sight of a clearer and more immediate source of reality-loss related to technology.

Nothing, as Benjamin also realized, remains in place or unique in an

201

era of mechanical reproducibility. The star-system in film makes it abundantly clear that we become our images, or even the shadow cast by our images, photoids. When Yeats praised Chaucer's poetry for saving his imagination from abstraction, he betrays the fear to which Wordsworth already gave classic expression at the outset of the Industrial Revolution. The world "which is the world of all of us" is being alienated from the human imagination by a technology that was supposed to help us own the earth. But the homeless imagination is an apocalyptic imagination.

This *phantomization* is equally Heidegger's concern, and his language resists it also as language. *Denken* (thought) and *Dichten* (the poetic) combine against it. They counter a rarefaction, a thinning of reality. (*Dichten* is used etymologically to indicate a condensed and concentrated language-sense, cognate with the more phenomenological "thick description" of cultural anthropology.) Yet it remains paradoxical that Heidegger should develop an extraordinary language to redeem ordinary life. By a stubbornness that turned nationalistic in 1933, he envisioned Germany as the *Boden* (the ground or homestead) of thinking that had suffered from *Bodenlosigkeit* (ungroundedness) since the time of the Greeks.

Lastly, the affirmative culture of everyday life, even as a reaction to reality-loss, to "mirror upon mirror mirrored" (Yeats), could blunt the critical faculties at the point they are most needed. "This is the era of bunk and hokum," a famous educational philosopher, an older contemporary of Heidegger's, wrote in 1922. "Its circulation is more rapid and ceaseless; it is swallowed more eagerly and more indiscriminately than ever before. Until the last generation or so, the mass of men have been interested for the most part only in local matters . . . their range might be limited, but within it they employed shrewdness and judgment . . . Rapid transportation and communication have compelled men to live as members of an extensive and mainly unseen society. The self-centered locality has been invaded and largely destroyed . . . Given the new curiosity and the new need of knowing about distant affairs on the one hand and the interest in controlling their exercise on the other, and the era of bunk, of being systematically duped, of undiscriminating sentiment and belief, is ushered in."[25]

A remedy was not easy to discern, and the educational measures inspired by John Dewey increasingly have come under attack. Yet his aim was unexceptionable and represented a sane response to the spread of a propaganda seeking to exploit the reality-effect of the media and to control people whose "self-centered locality" had been destroyed. Dewey's conclusion is that people "will have to cultivate the habit of suspending judgment, of skepticism, of desire for evidence, of appeal to observation rather than sentiment, discussion rather than bias, inquiry rather than conventional idealizations. When this happens schools will be the dangerous outposts of human civilization."

The rise of English and nonclassical literatures as fields of study was meant to reinforce "locality" against more abstract media and canons. The English of English Studies was a form of local knowledge; not the alien, colonialist language provoking Joyce, working against his attempt to create "the uncreated conscience of his race," but the index of an organic community. In this reaction Leavis (see Chapter 5) stands preeminent. At present an attentiveness to *all* vernaculars is being augmented by courses dealing with visual culture, though there is a greater problem with advertisement and film because of their close relation to the magic of realism, to the camera's exploitative glamorization of ordinary life. The more abstract we feel life to be, the more hypnotic our need for the vicarious, pseudohypnotic reality of photography. The form of the detective story is also mainly a device to bag as much "dirty realism" as possible because that alone seems to satisfy reality-hunger.

A question also remains—in the midst of cultural diversity—whether belief in secular education can ever be as intense, as convinced, as religious belief. Religion has an advantage at this moment. Its selective glamorization of everyday life proceeds by way of a ritual and sacramental focus on the great turning points of the life cycle. The open focus is rejected for a spotlight on what is elemental, through a liturgical calendar of feasts and fasts. But the greatest challenge of religion to secular education comes through fundamentalism. It is impoverishment enough that students are not taught the history of interpretation as it developed for centuries in a religious context. For most, interpretation begins with the analysis of works of art, when these works become relatively freestanding. Now fundamentalism, turning against an extraordinary history of exegesis, launches an attack on interpretivism by securing religion's

203

foundation on a Scripture that it claims is inerrant and sufficient for the virtuous life. A more sophisticated attack on interpretivism is also taking place in the field of law.

This is a great challenge to education, and not merely because of the persuasiveness of anti-interpretivism. A greater trouble is that we have been unable to support a freedom of interpretation fundamental to the university by anything stronger than common sense or an ideological shuttling between the affirmative culture of everyday life and the negativity of methodical doubt—an interpretive freedom that includes fiction as well as commentary.

I have not lost track of the role of the literary-critical essay. The explicit concern with rules and institutions of interpretation, or for what endows interpretations with authority, is our own legitimation-crisis. It is part of the larger question of whether interpretation, and specifically a text-dependent though not Scripture-bound interpretation, can be foundational for the humanities. To my mind this question runs parallel with, what is the value of literary criticism?

Let me turn again to Heidegger. He separates interpretation from its regional interest in texts (from sacred, legal, and literary hermeneutics) and makes it more fundamentally a mode of being-in-time, a future-oriented yet nontranscendant activity defining human existence. In the terms of our previous discussion, Heidegger responds to the double problem of skepticism and the pathos of extracting an open future from a corrosive and burdensome historical knowledge. To question is, for Heidegger, not to doubt but to affirm a future in which we can take hold of existence. Interpretive questions orient rather than disorient and are more authentic than prejudicial closures of a prereflective kind that serve the same function.

A disadvantage of this fundamentalized understanding of interpretive thinking is its text-independence. Heidegger complains of the *Bodenlosigkeit* of Western thought, yet he may actually be contributing to that by "forgetting" the Bible and its commentary tradition. (What is also unusual, for Germany, he neglects Goethe.) The exegetical technique he practices in the service of an existential hermeneutics has as its potential focus not an oeuvre but a language, a hypothetical language of Being, displaced along a Greek-German axis. It is not clear why that exegetical technique could not have turned to (or against) the Bible. The occluded language of Being is considered by Heidegger as the only foundation for Western thought, which has been suspended in a void, deprived of its ground since its fatal "translation" into a Latin philosophical vocabulary. Heidegger's notorious exegeses of German poetry and some lines of early Greek philosophy sniff out that language, like a trained dog a powerful drug. He demonstrates the extreme to which a great intellect will go in seeking an end to the drift of the West to the West—a drift that perpetually dissolves and reforms a purer "language of the gods."

If we identify this language, or its trace, with poetry—"It is poverty's speech that seeks us out the most. It is older than the oldest speech of Rome"—we may have to choose between Wallace Stevens and Heidegger, between Stevens' twilight of the gods that prefers their words to them and Heidegger's project to refuse the "Westwardness of Everything" by *reorienting* what words we have and overcoming the westerly drift. "Poverty's speech," for Stevens, is an ideal that poetry challenges itself with, a Roman ascesis within the luxuriance of Romance; it remains, however, an imaginative ideal that may take the color of human life anywhere (Rome, Greece, America) rather than a geopolitical vision demanding fundamental change.[26]

There is a great temptation to say, A plague on fundamentalism, foundationalism, and so on. We get along fine, probably better, without them. One comes to appreciate the conversationalists, from Robert Hutchins to Richard Rorty and Stanley Cavell, who do not seek a dogmatic truth but engage us in critical dialogue. They propose a talking cure and a quest for the ordinary that reconnects us with storytelling and a reluctance to be didactic. Also important is that they take up a tradition of critical prose that, after Montaigne, created a middle style avoiding both carnival and apocalypse, both slanderous rage and idealistic mania, in short, those political and religious enthusiasms which had contributed to civil war in the sixteenth and seventeenth centuries. Such public discourse, starting from private sentiment and informed by moderate epistemological doubt (the latter influenced by the rise of an empirically oriented science), played an increasingly important role in civic thought. It is a prose in which "the relatively conclusive language of proofs struggles with the open-ended discourse which rests on [personal] testimonies."[27] When Saul Bellow deplores the fact that "habits of civi-

205

lized discourse" have lately been scorched, he refers to a tradition closely linked to a literary criticism that moderates both Prophet and Thersites in us.

Despite some danger that the "friendship style" (as Chapter 2 calls it) may degenerate into an anti-intellectual manner, a jargon of civility, it is crucial not to give up that public and conversational mode. Yet the strain felt at present in the Open Society comes from spiritual as well as materialistic demands, from issues of identity, justice, restitution. Simply to call them values is to suggest a trade-off or fungibility that may not exist. Insofar as material redress is involved, such demands are negotiable, and civilized discourse holds up; insofar as they exceed material satisfaction, or its contribution to the good life, civilized discourse is in trouble. No one escapes the rage of righteousness or its invective. The conflict between a religiously based campaign for prolife legislation and a secular campaign against it on the basis of the unenumerated constitutional right of privacy or a general human right that a woman's body is her own, appears more and more as a conflict between imperatives as different as those that separate Antigone and Cleon.

We keep talking, then; but in talking we always come across the question of whether there might not be a firmer grounding for the idea of freedom and also the literary humanities. Here Vattimo's suggestion that postfoundational positions are based on the force of "weak thought" deserves attention. The conversational style and the ethics of ordinariness (a sort of spiritual *prosaics*), though they displace rather than face the "dread voice" of hierarchy and religious passion, are clearly an acknowledgment of the importance of *pensiero debole*.[28] Perhaps there is a link between "weak thought" and the "weak messianic power" (Walter Benjamin's phrase) that attends all interpretive acts. The narrative portion of this essay suggested that historical reflection is affected at every point by hope and fear about the future; and since we cannot predict the future, and do not live in the Biblical era of "open vision," the strong act of looking ahead is basically inspirational rather than inspired—a weak messianism. The crisis comes when we cannot see into the future because we do not see a future. It is eclipsed or occulted, overshadowed by our knowledge of past events or a fatality that, according to Lyotard, increasingly assumes the nonface of systematicity. There seems to be no room for us, for our children, for autonomy. We are excluded, as surely as the damned in an austere Christianity. Or, what is the same, we are overincluded.

The future or its impossibility is the subject of cultural history as it yields to prophecy. Far better to stress the connection between crisis and noncrisis forms of interpretation, so that we do not fall into the trap of seeing an emergency where there is none, or even manufacturing it. Respect for weak messianism does not guarantee of course that the apocalyptic and catastrophic kind will not take over. But it acknowledges the spiritual and religious factor in all thought, as that searches (for) the future. The thinkers previously discussed unblock the sense of a future by removing the sense of an ending.

My final comment returns to literary criticism. It must be clear by now that I have a personal difficulty with assertions that rely on names and summaries rather than on specific source-texts accompanied by close reading—a difficulty even greater when it comes to cultural history and drawing lessons from it. I am ready to concede that my text-dependence is a limitation. Yet I know what troubles me: I do not want to read in order to find illustrations for an argument or thesis, to appropriate texts that way. Reading literature is for me a deliberate *blinding*. I stumble about, sometimes hedonistically, in that word-world; I let myself be ambushed by sense or sensation and forget the drive toward a single, all-conquering truth; and I unravel the text only as it is simultaneously rethreaded on the spool of commentary. Perhaps this snail-horn text-perception is a symptomatic phase within a cultural and intellectual history-writing that too often has been avidly progressive and despairingly clairvoyant. So literary criticism becomes improgressive.

Recently the demand for a didactic, ethical, action-oriented criticism has intensified. Not that we were amoral or apolitical before, but we had seen what demagoguery could do in the name of manifest destiny or nationalism or "spiritual revolution." Also we assumed that moral philosophy had been discredited as no more than an exercise in reasoning, one that could not stand up to the charge of bad faith (covert ideologizing) or the pressure of truly committed persons. Today a "labor of the negative," though respecting dissent and argument and respecting particularly the weak force of Bartleby's "I would prefer not to," does not work in many circles unless, generating a fervor equivalent to religious faith, it prescribes explicitly for social ills.

It may be that the future will not include literary criticism as we have known it from neoclassical beginnings three centuries ago to its multivocal form today. The drive for closer reading seems to have made literary works too open, too porous: a legacy of aporetic structures. Our readings continue to challenge, though less decisively, closures based on the idea of a correct politics. Cultural criticism has become more complex and circumstantial than in the period between the World Wars, yet it still tends to see through texts rather than with them. And there are signs that new days of rage are upon us, on the part of those who are so much in touch with reality that they do not have to be in touch with language.

The best or worst that might be said about critical essays is that they are, despite themselves, minor prophecies that overread the signs of the times. They are also, however, counterprophecies that light up contrary indications and the merely potential relation of the world of discourse to the world. In literary criticism the naming of what may come is not prophecy so much as the branch of a poetics described by Wallace Stevens, one that maintains us "in the difficulty of what it is to be."

Notes · Index

Notes

Introduction: Pastoral Vestiges

1. Knowing and sexual experiences also get mixed up; but that is another basic story.
2. Paul Valéry, *Oeuvres I,* ed. Jean Hytier (Paris: Gallimard, Bibliothèque de la pleiade, 1957), p. 1001.
3. John Ashbery, "Soonest Mended," from *Selected Poems.* Copyright © 1985 by John Ashbery. Reprinted by permission of the publishers, Viking Penguin, a division of Penguin Books USA, Inc., and Carcanet Press, Limited, Manchester.
4. Friedrich Nietzsche, *Philosophy in the Tragic Age of the Greeks* (1873). Nietzsche is thinking about the Heraclitean fire. Contrast Gerard Manley Hopkins, "That Nature is a Heraclitean fire."
5. Heidegger's concluding statement in the *Letter* is still made in the context of a vaticination—the overcoming of metaphysics. The paragraph begins (my translation): "Future thought is no longer philosophy, because it thinks more originally than metaphysics, whose name means the same. Yet future thought also can no longer, as Hegel demanded, lay aside its name of 'Love of Wisdom' and have become wisdom itself in the form of absolute knowledge. Thought is descending into the poverty of its temporary mode of being. Thought gathers language into simple speech."
6. See Alain Finkielkraut, *La Mémoire vaine: Du crime contre l'humanité* (Paris: Gallimard, 1989), chap. 8, "La nuit de l'idylle"; my translation. From a perspective that might be called literary anthropology, Mark Shell has deepened our understanding of the complexities of "Universal Siblinghood." See *The End of Kinship: "Measure for Measure," Incest, and the Ideal of Universal Siblinghood* (Stanford: Stanford University Press, 1988).
7. *On the Constitution of Church and State,* The Collected Works of Samuel Taylor Coleridge, vol. 10, ed. John Colmer (Princeton: Princeton University, 1976), p. 167.
8. From Jacques Derrida, "Psyche: Inventions of the Other," in *Reading de Man Reading,* ed. Lindsay Waters and Wlad Godzich (Minneapolis: University of Minnesota Press, 1989), pp. 29–30.

9. Compare Kenneth Burke, letter to Malcolm Cowley, June 4, 1933, in *The Selected Correspondence of Kenneth Burke and Malcolm Cowley: 1915–1982*, ed. Paul Jay (Berkeley: University of California Press, 1988). p. 205: "[A]ll the resources of prose thought must be developed in order that the poetic can be given its only genuine safeguards. That is: only a thorough body of secular criticism, secular thought 'carried all the way round the circle' can properly equip a society against the misuse of its most *desirable* aspects, the *poetic* or *religious* aspects."

1. The Culture of Criticism

1. Northrop Frye, *Anatomy of Criticism* (Princeton: Princeton University Press, 1957).
2. Northrop Frye, *The Great Code: The Bible in Literature* (New York: Harcourt, 1982).
3. T. S. Eliot, *For Lancelot Andrewes: Essays on Style and Order* (London: Faber & Gwyer, 1928), p. 13.
4. Terry Eagleton, *Walter Benjamin; or, Towards a Revolutionary Criticism* (New York: Schocken, 1981), p. 4.
5. Ibid., p. 94.
6. Wilhelm Dilthey, *Einleitung in die Geisteswissenschaften* (Stuttgart, 1883), p. 15.
7. Ibid., p. xviii.
8. For Dilthey's typology, see "Die Typen der Weltanschauung und ihre Ausbildung in den metaphysischen Systemen," *Gesammelte Schriften* 8 (1911): 75–118; for the construction of historical reality, see esp. "Der Aufbau der geschichtlichen Welt in den Geisteswissenschaften," *Gesammelte Schriften* 7 (1905–1910): 79–188. Karl Mannheim, alluding to the Kantian tradition, remarks: "Epistemology was the first significant philosophical product of the breakdown of the unitary world-view with which the modern era was ushered in. . . . Epistemology sought to eliminate this uncertainty by taking its point of departure not from a dogmatically taught theory of existence . . . but from an analysis of the knowing subject" (*Ideology and Utopia: An Introduction to the Sociology of Knowledge,* trans. Louis Wirth and Edward Shils [New York: Harcourt, 1936], p. 13). We still recognize this phase in Ernst Cassirer's grand synthesis, *The Philosophy of Symbolic Forms,* 3 vols. (New Haven: Yale University Press, 1955–1957). E. D. Hirsch follows Dilthey's method of typological analysis in *Wordsworth and Schelling* (New Haven: Yale University Press, 1960) and initiates his own attempt to make hermeneutics foundational in *Validity in Interpretation* (New Haven: Yale University Press, 1967).
9. Friedrich Nietzsche, *Das Philosophenbuch/Le livre du philosophe,* trans. and ed. A. K. Marietti (Paris: Aubier-Flammarion, 1969), pp. 48–49.
10. Paul de Man, *Allegories of Reading: Figural Language in Rousseau, Nietzsche, Rilke, and Proust* (New Haven: Yale University Press, 1979), p. ix.

11. De Man's understanding of allegory is indebted to Walter Benjamin's *Origin of German Tragic Drama* (1927), trans. John Osborne (London: NLB, 1977), and combats the privileged place of the "incarnationist" symbol in modernist poetics. His "allegory," unlike older allegoresis, does not "fill the figure" except through a mortifying or deconstructive irony. The classic article on Christian typological or figural allegory is Erich Auerbach's "Figura" (1939), in *Gesammelte Aufsätze zur romanischen Philologie* (Bern: Francke, 1967), pp. 55–92. See also "Typological Symbolism in Medieval Literature" in the same collection.

12. Friedrich Schleiermacher, *Hermeneutik*, ed. Heinz Kimmerle (Heidelberg: C. Winter, 1959).

13. The notebooks were excerpted and summarized in the 1960s by Jean Starobinski, who recognized their importance. See his *Words upon Words: The Anagrams of Ferdinand de Saussure* (1971), trans. Olivia Emmet (New Haven: Yale University Press, 1979).

14. The term "grammar," as in Todorov's "Grammar of the Decameron" (*Grammaire du Décaméron* [The Hague: Mouton, 1969]), is a sign that the systemic approach is being applied. The relation of "rhetoric" to "grammar" is often simplified as if the epistemology of the two were continuous. In Anglo-American studies a renewed interest in rhetoric was more easily conciliable with historical considerations. Claudio Guillén in *Literature as System* (Princeton: Princeton University Press, 1971) also attempts to reintroduce a historical dimension. But de Man's first chapter, "Semiology and Rhetoric," in *Allegories of Reading* explores the distinction between grammar and rhetoric. (See also Kenneth Burke's *A Grammar of Motives* [1945] and *A Rhetoric of Motives* [1950], both reprinted [Berkeley: University of California Press, 1969]). For de Man rhetoric, or "the semiological enigma" that results, "radically suspends logic and opens up vertiginous possibilities of referential aberration" (*Allegories*, p. 10).

15. Sigmund Freud, *The Ego and the Id* (1923), trans. James Stratchey, in *The Standard Edition of the Complete Psychological Works of Sigmund Freud* (London: Hogarth, 1953–1974), 19: 3–66.

16. Charles Péguy, *Clio* (Paris: Gallimard, 1932).

17. René Wellek, *A History of Modern Criticism, 1750–1950,* 5 vols. (New Haven: Yale University Press, 1955–   ). Wellek, an émigré scholar who settled in the United States in the late 1930s, became the founder of a type of comparative literature that kept literary studies from the professional deformation of national ideologies. His most influential work remains *Theory of Literature,* written in collaboration with Austin Warren (1949), 3rd ed. (New York: Harcourt, 1963). *Concepts of Criticism* (New Haven: Yale University Press, 1963) contains important essays tracing the change from "philology" to "criticism."

18. Michel Foucault's most concise statement is *L'Ordre du discours* (Paris: Gal-

limard, 1970); Hayden White's first large attempt is found in *Metahistory* (Baltimore: Johns Hopkins University Press, 1973). For an important discussion of Nietzsche's relation to Burckhardt, in the light of his struggle with *Gelehrtenkultur*, see Erich Heller's *The Disinherited Mind: Essays in Modern German Literature and Thought* (1952), expanded ed. (New York: Harcourt, 1975), pp. 67–88. Heller quotes Nietzsche's late, mad letter to Burckhardt: "Dear Herr Professor, when it comes to it I too would very much prefer a professorial chair in Basle to being God; but I did not dare to go as far in my private egoism as to refrain for its sake from the creation of the world" (p.83).

19. George Saintsbury, *A History of Criticism and Literary Taste in Europe from the Earliest Texts to the Present Day,* 3 vols. (London: Blackwood, 1900–1909).
20. Auerbach, *Gesammelte Aufsätze,* pp. 354–363.
21. Ibid., p. 310
22. Ibid., p. 223.
23. E. R. Curtius, *European Literature and the Latin Middle Ages* (1948), trans. Willard R. Trask (Princeton: Princeton University Press, 1953).
24. Leo Spitzer's *Meisterwerke der romanischen Sprachwissenschaft,* 2 vols. (Munich: Hueber, 1929–1930), gives a generous sampling of that research. There was of course required philological activity in the area of English, from the editing and annotating of ballads, to Old English, the history of language, and the study of names. Frank Kermode observes, "At University College in London, the dry philological tradition (lots of Old English, placename study, 'language' in all its aspects) was still strong when I arrived there in the sixties, though major change was wanted by most people. For a long time the *Weltanschauung* was a curious blend of Matthew Arnold and W. W. Skeat" ("The Changing Profession of Letters," *Bulletin of the American Academy of Arts and Sciences* 36.7 [1983]). Cf. the account of "Early English" in John Gross's *The Rise and Fall of the Man of Letters* (London: Weidenfeld & Nicolson, 1969), pp. 167–189. Hans Aarsleff's *The Study of Language in England, 1780–1860* (Princeton: Princeton University Press, 1967) is especially valuable for backgrounding the one acknowledged philological achievement in England—the *New English Dictionary,* the "history of a people in terms of its language"—which was planned in the 1850s and 1860s but which began publishing as the *Oxford English Dictionary* in the 1880s. George Steiner gives a comparatist's view of theories of language and translation from Schleiermacher and Humboldt to the 1970s in *After Babel: Aspects of Language and Translation* (New York: Oxford University Press, 1975).
25. For an amusing and sardonic account of a year spent at Bonn studying for a Ph.D. in German, see E. M. Butler, *Paper Boats* (London: Collins, 1959), chap. 4. The entire book is immensely informative, not only about women and higher education but about *Wissenschaft* in Germany before and after the

Nazi regime. Interesting early observations are found in James Morgan Hart, *German Universities* (New York: Putnam, 1878). The most authoritative modern study of the German learning tradition is Fritz Ringer's *Decline of the German Mandarins* (Cambridge, Mass.: Harvard University Press, 1969).

26. Alexander Meikeljohn's experiments at Wisconsin (also at Amherst) came to the attention of F. R. Leavis, who comments on them in *Education and the University* (Cambridge: Cambridge University Press, 1943 and 1948). At Chicago in the 1930s a core curriculum was developed based on the classical trivium and reinforced by a strong emphasis on great books (see Richard McKeon, "Criticism and the Liberal Arts" in *Profession 82* [New York: MLA, 1983], pp. 1–18). There were also reformist attempts by Norman Foerster, whose *American Scholar* (Chapel Hill; University of North Carolina Press, 1929) gained considerable repute. For two personal accounts of Cambridge, see Muriel Bradbrook, "My Cambridge" in *Women and Literature 1779–1982*, vol. 2 (Totowa, N.J.: Barnes and Noble, 1982), and Raymond Williams, *Politics and Letters* (London: NLB, 1979).

27. Randolph Bourne, "The Undergraduate" (1915), *The World of Randolph Bourne,* ed. Lillian Schlissel (New York: Dutton, 1965), pp. 69, 71. A less concise and interesting version is Bourne's "The College: An Inner View" (1913), *Youth and Life* (New York: Franklin, 1971).

28. Malcolm Cowley, *Exile's Return: A Narrative of Ideas* (1934) (rev. ed. New York: Viking, 1951).

29. Bourne, *World of Randolph Bourne,* pp. 69, 71.

30. Ibid., p. 33.

31. Ibid., pp. 35–36.

32. Ibid., p. 46. Cowley's entire first chapter, "Mansions in the Air," deals with the young intellectual's remorseless "deracination." For an update, see Stephen Spender's *The Year of the Young Rebels* (London: Weidenfeld & Nicolson, 1969), pp. 141–161, which compares the university generation of the fifties and sixties in England with that of the thirties.

33. H. L. Mencken, *The American Language: An Inquiry into the Development of English in the United States* (1919), 4th ed. (New York: Knopf, 1937).

34. *World of Randolph Bourne,* p. 68. The quotation is from Bourne's 1915 essay "Medievalism in the Colleges." Larzer Ziff's *Literary Democracy* (New York: Viking, 1981) partially carries out Bourne's program by examining *literary* developments that oppose social to political democracy—developments that reveal the desperately utopian side of the lack of institutions about which James complains. The call in recent criticism for an analysis that would show how the literary life is determined by institutions like the university has only succeeded in showing their triviality or inauthenticity, as if nothing "real" had been gained since Hawthorne and James. One is left with a sense that "Reality in America" (to use Trilling's rubric) is an endless trashing of virginal possibilities.

35. Randolph Bourne, *The History of a Literary Radical and Other Essays,* ed. Van Wyck Brooks (New York: Huebsch, 1920), p. 26. Brooks's introduction stresses Bourne's fierce, unpartisan intellectuality, but one that strove for a "coalition of the thinkers and workers" or, as AE expresses it, a society "democratic in economics, aristocratic in thought."

36. Edmund Wilson, *Axel's Castle: A Study in the Imaginative Literature of 1870–1930* (New York: Scribners, 1931).

37. Edmund Wilson, *To the Finland Station: A Study in the Writing and Acting of History* (New York: Harcourt, 1940).

38. Granville Hicks, *The Great Tradition* (New York: Macmillan, 1933).

39. For more detail, see Beard's statement in the *New Republic* (29 December 1917), pp 249–251, and Max Lerner on Beard in Malcolm Cowley and Bernard Smith eds., *Books that Changed Our Minds* (New York: Doubleday, 1939).

40. Bourne, *World of Randolph Bourne,* pp. 319–320. Compare, for the 1930s, Max Eastman, *Art and the Life of Action* (New York: Knopf, 1934). It was not until Stanley Cavell's *The Senses of Walden* (New York: Viking, 1972) that philosophy brought "texture" to literary studies and perhaps—if we add Cavell's writings on the movies—to our perception of what the American is in terms of cultural density rather than cultural humility.

41. Bourne, *History of a Literary Radical,* p. 37.

42. The line that leads to a book as substantial as Fredric Jameson's *Political Unconscious* (Ithaca, N.Y.: Cornell University Press, 1981) is European rather than American, and it remains significantly indebted to Mannheim's *Ideology and Utopia* and Max Weber's "sociology of knowledge," which found an early home at the University of Chicago. It also bears the imprint of the Frankfurt School, whose last important figure, Leo Loewenthal, active in the United States for over forty years, is still not adequately translated, though his works are now found in collected form. In England too, as Raymond Williams has observed, there was a failure to produce a significant Marxist literary criticism. The problem in the 1930s was "how to write a different kind of novel or poem. Since literature was class-restrictive, it was the job of a Socialist to break through this restriction, by producing another kind of literature. Questions of literary criticism or literary history thus largely went by the board. . . . In its positive emphasis, the position was not entirely wrong. . . . But the negative refusal to engage with major theoretical and practical questions in the discipline of English studies itself was a crucial failure" (*Politics and Letters: Interviews with New Left Review* [London: NLB, 1979], p. 45). In radical movements today the difference between changing literature through works of fiction and changing it through theory-oriented works of criticism is not insisted on. For Elaine Showalter, "gynocriticism" is any writing that enhances our view of women as producers of textual meaning ("Towards a Feminist Poetics," in Mary Jacobus, ed., *Women's*

Writing and Writing about Women [New York: Barnes & Noble, 1981], pp. 22–41).

43. Matthew Arnold, *Culture and Anarchy*, vol. 5 of *Complete Prose Works of Matthew Arnold*, ed. R. H. Super, 11 vols. (Ann Arbor: University of Michigan Press, 1960–1977), p. 113.

44. See especially Northrop Frye, *Fearful Symmetry: A Study of William Blake* (Princeton: Princeton University Press, 1947).

45. Lionel Trilling, *Beyond Culture: Essays on Literature and Learning* (New York: Viking, 1965), esp. "On the Teaching of Modern Literature."

46. Dick Hebdige's *Subculture* (London: Methuen, 1979) is a sympathetic guide. Two American attempts to recognize democratic or even countercultural trends without yielding too much are W. C. Brownell's *Standards* (New York: Scribners, 1917) and Murray Krieger's *Arts on the Level: The Fall of the Elite Object* (Knoxville: University of Tennessee Press, 1981).

47. Claude Lévi-Strauss, *Tristes Tropiques* (Paris: Plon, 1955).

48. Tzvetan Todorov, *Conquête de l'Amérique: La Question de l'autre* (Paris: Seuil, 1982).

49. Edward Said, *Orientalism* (New York: Pantheon, 1978).

50. Arthur Koestler, *The God that Failed,* ed. Richard Crossman (New York: Harper, 1949), p. 16.

51. See Claus Uhlig, *Theorie der Literaturhistorie* (Heidelberg, 1982), for a fair-minded and comprehensive account. Thomas Greene links Renaissance humanism and the *imitatio* doctrine to modern hermeneutic reflections on otherness in *The Light in Troy* (New Haven: Yale University Press, 1982). F. O. Matthiessen's *American Renaissance* (London: Oxford University Press, 1941) shows how influential the idea can be in consolidating a field ("American studies") by fixing its canon and the reading habits that favor it. Through a revision that now extends beyond the queer case of Poe (once only a French property), the idea of a wholesome native mode of expression in touch with the past has been unsettled by that of a ghostly rhetoric whose sources of life (or life-in-death) are the enigma. This revision was already a vision in D. H. Lawrence's *Studies in Classic American Literature* (New York: Seltzer, 1923), but within the academy it began with Charles Feidelson's *Symbolism and American Literature* (Chicago: University of Chicago Press, 1953) and has reached a point of no return with John Irwin's *American Hieroglyphics* (New Haven: Yale University Press, 1980).

52. F. R. Leavis, *Mass Civilization and Minority Culture* (1930); reprinted in *Education and the University*.

53. Gilles Deleuze and Félix Guattari, *Kafka: Pour une littérature mineure* (Paris: Minuit, 1975), and "What Is a Minor Literature?" trans. Robert Brinkley, *Mississippi Review* 11.3 (1983): 13–33.

54. Herbert Marcuse's *Eros and Civilization: A Philosophical Inquiry into Freud* (Boston: Beacon, 1955) is another important link in the literature that

follows on Freud's *Civilization and its Discontents* (1930), trans. James Stra-chey, *Standard Edition*, vol. 21. In the United States the strong concept of a minor literature has surfaced mainly through a revaluing of neglected writ-ings by women and blacks. So far it has broadened rather than challenged the notion of native classics. But it has also led to an increased awareness of what reading involved as a sponsored activity. See, e.g., Jane P. Tompkins, ed., *Reader-Response Criticism* (Baltimore: Johns Hopkins University Press, 1980).

55. Otto Spengler, *The Decline of the West* (1918–1922), trans. Charles F. At-kinson, 2 vols. (New York: Knopf, 1926–1928).

56. It is to J. G. Fichte's credit that his *Bestimmung des Gelehrten* (1794), ed. Fritz Medicus, *Werke*, vol. 1 (Leipzig: Eckardt, 1908), first raised the ques-tion of the "destiny" or "vocation" of the scholar in relation to other "classes," even though the question shifted immediately into a higher philosophical gear: What is the destiny of man in society, or *as* man? Fichte's first chapter also touches on the theme of culture, understood as the means whereby the unharmonious or falsely imposed empirical influences on personality can be undone so that the pure ego can be in accord with itself once more.

57. Geoffrey H. Hartman, *The Unmediated Vision: An Interpretation of Words-worth, Hopkins, Rilke, and Valéry* (New Haven: Yale University Press, 1954).

58. Ibid., p. 164.

59. Gaston Bachelard's *La Flamme d'une chandelle* (Paris: Presses Univ. de France, 1961) claims to proceed "without the surcharge of any learning, without im-prisoning us within the unity of a method of inquiry." A less happy but still therapeutic and phenomenological emphasis on imaginative embodiment is found in Roger Poole's important study of Virginia Woolf, *The Unknown Vir-ginia Woolf* (New York: Cambridge University Press, 1978).

60. Erich Auerbach, *Mimesis* (1946), trans. Willard R. Trask (Princeton: Prince-ton University Press, 1953).

61. Consult Jung, *The Archetypes and the Collective Unconscious* (*Collected Works*, New York: Pantheon, 1953–1961); Frye's *Anatomy of Criticism*; and also Maud Bodkin's *Archetypal Patterns in Poetry* (London: Oxford University Press, 1934). A related return to elemental forms (A. Jolles, "simple forms") is through "Romance." This route is nourished in England and America by the exploitation of gothic formulas, which goes back to the Romantics. They also gave new life to ballad, folk-, and fairy tales. The brothers Grimm began their work of collecting around 1808, and almost exactly a hundred years later Martin Buber published his first compilation of Hasidic tales (originat-ing only in the late eighteenth century and attributed to known spiritual masters). Much of this activity is recreative as well as philological. The stories of Rabbi Nachmann, for instance, have only recently been translated with care, by Arnold Band; and except for Max Lüthi's interesting genre descrip-

tions of *Volksmärchen und Volkssage* (Bern: Francke, 1961), there is generally much less engagement with the image of human nature in these tales than with their structural constants and principles of combination.

62. Walter Benjamin, *Illuminations,* ed. Hannah Arendt, trans. Harry Zohn (New York: Schocken, 1969), pp. 256–260.

63. Relevant works include H. R. Jauss's *Aesthetic Experience and Literary Hermeneutics,* trans. Michael Shaw (Minneapolis: University of Minnesota Press, 1982), and Wolfgang Iser's *The Act of Reading* (1979; Baltimore: Johns Hopkins University Press, 1979), as well as Stanley Fish, *Is There a Text in This Class?* (Cambridge, Mass.: Harvard University Press, 1980), and Frank Kermode, "The Changing Profession of Letters" (see above, note 24). How to get from reader response to public consensus—how even to form the notion of a "public"—remains perplexing. Auerbach's work in this area is crucially propaedeutic, from his essay on "la cour et la ville" to Dante's "anagogical" addresses to the reader (in *Gesammelte Aufsätze*). If the concept of what art is depends on a so-called community of interpreters (which could be as small as a class under the influence of a teacher), one runs the danger, as Péguy would say, of crowning chaos. In more careful versions of this democratic-pedagogical movement, the dialogue of *lisant* and *lu* is a historical event that allows reader participation (Iser) or something about understanding itself, in its historicity, as it discloses the time- and place-bound nature of interpretation and, by the very act of reading as a "mise en oeuvre" (Péguy), opens or fuses horizons (Gadamer).

64. An alternative understanding revives the concept of authority as it plays itself out not only between author and audience, but between authors and their sense of vocation. How do writers *authorize* themselves? This perspective emphasizes, beyond rhetoric (a relatively public and empirical matter), allusions or inner quotations as they inspire or subvert a writer's words, as they "invoice" them textually. A series of important studies have recently explored the subtle role of allusion in writers wishing to retain religious or visionary authority. See, e.g., Leslie Brisman's *Milton's Poetry of Choice and Its Romantic Heirs* (Ithaca, N.Y.: Cornell University Press, 1973) and John Guillory's *Poetic Authority* (New York: Columbia University Press, 1983). For a view of the "scene of writing" that presupposes an originary force (of desire or sensory hallucination), one which cannot be reduced to intertextual discourse on nontransgressive authority, see Lyotard's *Discours, figure* (Paris: Klincksieck, 1971). The appositional title refers to both language and the force that image or form exerts on it, not belatedly but primordially, resulting in a "scrambled text" that is a composite (not a harmony) of readable and visible. Lyotard deconstructs not only Freud's division of the dream into facade (manifest content) and foundation (dream thoughts) but also the semiological model of articulated language. When he writes that "language,

at least in its poetical use, is inhabited, haunted by the figure," he opens a way back to phenomenological insight.

65. Harold Bloom's *Anxiety of Influence* (New York: Oxford University Press, 1973) is the first of many books mapping this area. Walter Ong (*The Presence of the Word* [New Haven: Yale University Press, 1967]) has placed the agon of artists (or even, as Otto Rank might say, of art and artist) within the frame of "male" initiation rites, where pedagogy joins advanced cultural games (see also Johan Huizinga, *Homo Ludens: A Study of the Play-Element in Culture* (1939; Boston: Beacon, 1955).

66. Compare the ominous remarks on "Gepäckserleichterung" in Ernst Jünger's protofascist *Der Arbeiter: Herrschaft und Gestalt* (Hamburg: Hanseatische Verlagsanstalt, 1932) and Mircea Eliade's use of Nietzsche's "eternal return" in *Cosmos and History* (1949), trans. Willard R. Trask (New York: Pantheon, 1954), originally subtitled *Archétypes et répétition*. The section entitled "The Difficulties of Historicism" interprets the reappearance or archaic cyclical theories in modern times as a defense against the terror of history.

67. Generally it is the grandiose (sublime) or the vulgar (low) that offends a decorum often based on the ancient principle of the *genera dicendi*, or levels of style. Terms of art, however, can be on both sides of the stylistic spectrum. For Keats they were associated with Miltonic sublimity; when derived from art as craft, they become technical and, for some, intrusively erudite or bathetic. The metaphysical poets were admired in modern studies precisely for the way they handled both the New Philosophy and the Old Learning. But the question of art's relation to learning failed to transfer itself to critical style, which remained (in Eliot, in Cleanth Brooks) devotedly neoclassical in its avoidance of technical terms.

68. Raymond Williams, *The Long Revolution* (London: Chatto & Windus, 1961), p. 251.

69. Theodor Adorno, *Negative Dialectics* (1966), trans. E. B. Ashton (New York: Seabury, 1973).

70. Leavis, *Education and the University*, p. 16.

71. I. A. Richards, *The Philosophy of Rhetoric* (New York: Oxford University Press, 1936).

72. To typify the situation that prevailed from the founding of the MLA to the recent shift, I quote from the MLA presidential address of 1897, by Albert S. Cook of Yale. "The function of the philologist . . . is the endeavor to relive the life of the past; to enter by the imagination into the spiritual experiences of all the historic protagonists of civilization in a given period and area of culture; to think the thoughts, to feel the emotions, to partake the aspirations, recorded in literature; to become one with humanity in the struggles of a given nation or race to perceive and attain the ideal of existence," *The Higher Study of English* (Boston: Houghton Mifflin, 1906), pp. 19–20. Since the first publication of this chapter (1984) the New Historicism has

become prominent, associated with such names as Stephen Greenblatt, Jerome McGann, and Majorie Levinson. In the latter two, especially, historical reconstruction is admonished not to accept the language of the works under discussion. This reverses the older historicist imperative, which did not on the whole demystify the "pieties" of canonical authors but sought to give a comparative and questioning frame to modern or contemporary values.

73. Paul Zumthor, *Langue, texte, enigme* (Paris: Seuil, 1975). Zumthor's work is pathbreaking in this area. The intertextual consciousness was also helped by works such as Beryl Smalley's on Bible study (*The Study of the Bible in the Middle Ages* [Oxford: Blackwell, 1941]), which shows how not only the Bible but patristic and scholastic commentary formed the literary text in medieval Latin. A similar, more modern relation between commentaries and text is demonstrated by J. L. Lowe's famous "source study" of Coleridge, *The Road to Xanadu* (Boston: Houghton, 1927) (intertextual *avant la lettre*), and E. S. Shaffer's understanding of genre development, *"Kubla Khan" and the Fall of Jerusalem* (Cambridge: Cambridge University Press, 1975). All these raise vividly the question of the relation between art and learning, or art and commentary. The joining of medieval to modern perspectives has been equally important to inaugurating what Wlad Godzich and Jeffrey Kittay call *prosaics*. See their *The Emergence of Prose: An Essay in Prosaics* (Minneapolis: University of Minnesota Press, 1987). Their work is essential background to my own interest in the development of critical prose.

74. Deleuze and Guattari, *Kafka*, pp. 32–33. See also "What is a Minor Literature?" pp. 13–33.

75. Francis Gummere, *Old English Ballads* (Boston: Ginn, 1903), introduction.

76. In his introduction to Vladimir Propp's *Morphology of the Folk Tale*, ed. Louis Wagner, trans. Lawrence Scott, 2nd ed. (Austin: University of Texas Press, 1968), Alan Dundes distinguishes between the syntagmatic (sequential) structuralism of Propp and the paradigmatic structuralism of Claude Lévi-Strauss, in which elements are taken out of the "given" order and regrouped to reveal a latent pattern or content. Both types, however, break down a value distinction between modern and primitive literature. Propp concludes by quoting from Veselóvskij on contemporary narrative literature and its complicated thematic (also psychological) structure and photographic realism. When "this literature will appear to future generations as distant as antiquity . . . when the synthesis of time, that great simplifier, in passing over the complexity of phenomena, reduces them to the magnitude of points receding into the distance, then their lines will merge with those which we are now uncovering when we look back at the poetic traditions of the distant past—and the phenomena of schematism and repetition will then be established across the total expanse," p. 166.

77. William Wimsatt, *Day of the Leopards: Essays in Defense of Poems* (New Haven: Yale University Press, 1976).

78. Paul de Man, *Blindness and Insight: Essays in the Rhetoric of Contemporary Criticism*, 2nd rev. ed. (Minneapolis: University of Minnesota Press, 1983), pp. 3–19.

79. Leo Spitzer, *Linguistics and Literary History: Essays in Stylistics* (Princeton: Princeton University Press, 1948).

80. Georges Poulet, *Studies in Human Time* (1949), trans. Elliot Coleman (Baltimore: Johns Hopkins University Press, 1956). Poulet's work was especially liberating in the 1950s and 1960s because its reconstructions expanded into the domain of life and letters, which had been the province of humane biography. It followed yet transformed the Taine tradition of "scientific criticism," which was materialist in orientation. (For an excellent summary of that tradition, see Audiat, who prepared Poulet's way.) Unlike many New Critics, Poulet did not ration an author to his or her fictional work. Yet like the New Critics, he purified an empathetic or divinatory technique (the *critique d'identité*) by a structural method that eliminated marginal or gossipy fact unless it had a bearing on the shaping subjectivity of the writer under consideration. His method betrays the same kind of "participation mystique" (exposited with Cartesian rational fervor) that Marcel Raymond explores.

81. The best brief survey of deconstruction is Christopher Norris' *Deconstruction* (London: Methuen, 1982).

82. George Lukács, *Theory of the Novel* (1920), trans. Anna Bostock (Cambridge, Mass.: MIT Press, 1971), and *History and Class Consciousness* (1923), trans. Rodney Livingstone (Cambridge, Mass.: MIT Press, 1971).

83. Auerbach, *Mimesis,* pp. 3–23.

84. See Jacques Derrida's essay on Levinas in *Writing and Difference* (1967), trans. Alan Bass (Chicago: University of Chicago Press, 1978); de Man on Lukács in *Blindness and Insight,* pp. 51–59; but also work in English Studies that begins in the 1950s, and is described by G. Douglas Atkins and Susan Handelman. By Hellenism I mean the Winckelmann-Schiller-Hegel tradition, which reaches into Pater. E. M. Butler's *Tyranny of Greece over Germany* (Cambridge: Cambridge University Press, 1935) follows the story in one national culture. Heidegger's Greek grapple goes beyond Hellenism but not beyond an ideal historical vanishing point he recuperates from (basically) the philological efforts of Diels, published as *Die Fragmente der Vorsokratiker* (Berlin: Weidmannsche Buchhandlung, 1903). Auerbach's chapter in *Mimesis* reacts to its own Hellenism by a significant antithetical analysis of the story of Isaac's sacrifice.

85. Jacques Ehrmann, ed., *Structuralism. Yale French Studies* (1966; Garden City, N.Y.: Anchor-Doubleday, 1970); and Richard Macksey and Eugenio Donato, eds., *The Structuralist Controversy: The Languages of Criticism and the Sciences of Man* (Baltimore: Johns Hopkins University Press, 1972).

86. Frederick Pottle, *The Idiom of Poetry* (Ithaca, N.Y.: Cornell University Press, 1941).

87. Frye, *Anatomy of Criticism*, p. 18, and ibid., pp. 10, 20.
88. See Victor Erlich, *Russian Formalism: History, Doctrine,* 2nd ed. (The Hague: Mouton, 1965), and Juri Striedter, *Literary Structure, Evolution and Value: Russian Formalism and Czech Structuralism Reconsidered* (Cambridge, Mass.: Harvard University Press, 1989).
89. Frye, *Anatomy of Criticism*, p. 11.
90. Feminist criticism, like all vernacularist movements, has both earthy and utopian elements. Relics of womanly writing do exist—novels, poems, diaries—that need historical recovery and attention. Sandra Gilbert and Susan Gubar go in that direction in *The Madwoman in the Attic* (New Haven: Yale University Press, 1979) and its sequels. Gilbert and Gubar also question a theory (Bloom's) based exclusively on male culture. In such a context, women speak with "veiled lips" (Luce Irigaray, *Amante Marine: De Friedrich Nietzsche* [Paris: Minuit, 1980]), so that more radical projects, perhaps utopian, are evoked to innovate a freer, more specifically womanly, speech.
91. See Peter Szondi, *Hölderlin-Studien* (Frankfurt: Insel, 1967), the first chapter of which is a critique of hermeneutic theories so involved with themselves that they fail to recognize the literary specificity of the object to be known.
92. Roland Barthes, *Critical Essays* (1964), trans. Richard Howard (Evanston, Ill.: Northwestern University Press, 1972), p. 260.
93. Jean-Paul Sartre, *What Is Literature?* (1948), trans. Bernard Frechtman (New York: Philosophical Library, 1949).
94. M. M. Bakhtin, *La Poétique de Dostoïevski,* trans. Isabelle Kolitcheff (Paris: Seuil, 1970); and *Problems of Dostoevsky's Poetics,* trans. R. W. Rotsel (Ann Arbor, Mich.: Ardis, 1973).
95. Wayne Booth, *The Rhetoric of Fiction* (Chicago: University of Chicago Press, 1961).
96. Kenneth Burke, *The Philosophy of Literary Form* (1941), 3rd ed. (Berkeley: University of California Press, 1973).
97. Ferdinand de Saussure, *Course in General Linguistics* (1916), ed. Charles Bally, Albert Sechehaye, and Albert Riedlinger, trans. Wade Baskin (New York: McGraw-Hill, 1959).
98. Jacques Lacan, *Écrits: A Selection* (1966), trans. Alan Sheridan (New York: Norton, 1977).
99. Roland Barthes, *A Lover's Discourse* (1977), trans. Richard Howard (New York: Hill & Wang, 1978).
100. The work of Norman O. Brown anticipates Barthes. In a prose as learned, aphoristic, and plaited as Nietzsche's, Brown carries on the earlier classicist's revolt against *Gelehrtenkultur*. In *Love's Body* (New York: Vintage-Random, 1966) he refutes all superficial oppositions of embodiment and intertextuality.
101. T. S. Eliot, *The Sacred Wood* (London: Methuen, 1920), p. 154.

102. Ibid., pp. 154–155.
103. Ibid., pp. 156.
104. Ibid., p. 157.

2. Tea and Totality

1. George Steiner, *In Bluebeard's Castle: Some Notes Towards the Redefinition of Culture* (New Haven: Yale University Press, 1971), p. 30
2. Stuart P. Sherman, *Americans* (Port Washington, N.Y.: Kennikut, 1922), pp. 4–5.
3. " 'Where shall *we fressen?*' says Mr. Mencken. 'At the Loyal Independent Order of the United Hiberno-German-Anti-English-Americans,' says Mr. Hackett. 'All the New Critics will be there.' "
4. Yet C. J. Rawson shows how precarious the "friendship style" was. Swift, he says, "repudiates that intimacy between author and reader which Sterne and Richardson celebrate," even as he calls for "a Parity and strict correspondence of Idea's between Reader and the Author." He fears that familiarity may breed contempt or lead to garrulous self-revelations. "Swift, as much as Sterne, is reaching out to the reader, and the alienation I spoke of does not in fact eliminate intimacy, though it destroys 'friendship.' There is something in Swift's relation with his reader that can be described approximately in terms of the edgy intimacy of a personal quarrel that does not quite come out in the open . . . It is attacking play." See *Gulliver and the Gentle Reader: Studies in Swift and Our Time* (London: Routledge & Kegan Paul, 1973), chap. 1. For a recent effort to depict the relation between reader and writer as—potentially, and not always easily—a friendship, see Wayne Booth, *The Company We Keep: An Ethics of Fiction* (Los Angeles: University of California Press, 1988). Also, for an important analysis of the primacy of conversation as a hermeneutic *and* religious model ("There is no intellectual, cultural, political, or religious tradition of interpretation that does not ultimately live by the quality of its conversation"), see David Tracy, *Plurality and Ambiguity: Hermeneutics, Religion, Hope* (San Francisco: Harper and Row, 1989). Tracy's book also considers modern and postmodern theories and forces that *interrupt* conversation.
5. I am told by Wallace Martin, who has excerpted Orage's remarks on style in *Orage as Critic* (London: Routledge & Kegan Paul, 1974), that when this comment was made *The New Age* was in financial trouble and Orage needed chatty reportage from Read to increase the popular appeal of a weekly devoted to serious literary and political discussion. Orage's remarks, therefore, are more symptomatic of English taste than of Orage. Yet though Orage dreamed of a "fearless English prose," "written in the vernacular with all its strength and directness," he always qualified that, "but with grace added unto it." His statement, similarly, that in a "pure style," the writer's "idiosyncracies, his class, his education, his reading should all be kept out of

sight" also betrays the decorum of the *honnête homme*. Yet compared to what was going on in the *Times Literary Supplement*—"the deadliest mouse in the world of journalism," according to Orage—he was indeed a lively presence. When the *TLS* opined, "The English Plato is still to be," Orage countered with: "I shall withdraw Plato from the position of model, in which I put him. Plato, it is evident, is likely to be abused; without intending it, his mood, translated into English, appears to be compatible only with luxurious ease; he is read by modern Epicureans. And I shall put in Plato's place Demosthenes, the model of Swift, the greatest English writer the world has yet seen" (*Orage as Critic,* pp. 194–196).

6. In a Victorian reaction against the German study of language, which had placed Sanskrit alongside Greek and Latin, and suggested their Indo-European origin, one English scholar declared: "Englishmen are too practical to study a language very philosophically." Quoted by Linda Dowling, "Victorian Oxford and the Science of Language," *PMLA* 97 (1982): 165.

7. If Ricoeur is right, we would have to rethink the emancipation of the university from seminary and divinity school. "To preach," he has written, "is not to capitulate before the believable and the unbelievable of modern man, but to struggle with the presuppositions of his culture, in order to restore this *interval of interrogation* in which the question can have meaning." And, "All that reestablishes the question of humanity taken as a whole, as a totality, has a value of preunderstanding for preaching." Marxism and religion (and, to a degree, psychoanalysis) are for Ricoeur, as they were for Benjamin, the giant forms to be confronted; not in order to be reconciled but to discover "a reading of the great forces which regulate our economic life, our political life, and our cultural life" ("The Language of Faith" (1973), in *The Philosophy of Paul Ricoeur,* ed. Charles E. Reagan and David Stewart [Boston: Beacon, 1978]). On the issue of totality see also Geoffrey H. Hartman, "The New Wilderness: Critics as Connoisseurs of Chaos" in *Innovation/Renovation,* ed. Ihab Hassan and Sally Hassan (Madison: University of Wisconsin Press, 1983), now in *Easy Pieces* (New York: Columbia University Press, 1985).

8. "It is two thousand and hundreds of years since, that the theory was proposed that thought is conversation with oneself," Eliot writes similarly in his essay of 1931 on Charles Whibley, which contains important reflections on the conversational style (and of Eliot himself, Blackmur remarked that "his method has been conversational, for he begs off both the talent and the bent for abstract thought"). Henry Fielding's "Essay on Conversation," like Swift's "Hints towards an Essay on Conversation," summarizes toward the midpoint of the eighteenth century the blend of moral, social, and aesthetic motives that go into this ideal. Fielding writes that "the pleasure of conversation must arise from the discourse being on subjects levelled to the capacity of the whole company; from being on such in which every person is equally interested; from everyone's being admitted to his share in the discourse; and

lastly, from carefully avoiding all noise, violence, and impetuosity." Erich Auerbach illustrates vividly the rise of this ideal in seventeenth-century France (though there are of course adumbrations in Italian circles of the sixteenth century) through an examination of the phrases "le public" and "la cour et la ville" (see Chapter 10, note 1). Hume remarks in "Of Civil Liberty" that "in common life, [the French] have, in a great measure, perfected that art, the most useful and agreeable of any, *l'Art de Vivre,* the art of society and conversation." In the same essay Swift is identified as the first British writer of "polite prose."

9. George Snell is quoted in R. F. Jones, *The Triumph of the English Language* (Stanford: Stanford University Press, 1953), p. 229. The conversational style never took in the United States, at least not as fixed by eighteenth-century English usage (epistolary rather than spoken and barely concealing its artfulness). There is most of the time a deliberate swerving from elegance, producing the effect of an undertow of colloquialism, or of some kind of slang (real or imaginary). See the form of Blackmur's comment on Eliot, note 8, or the assimilative and proverbial style of Kenneth Burke.

10. De Man is thinking of Hellenism as interpreted by the Winckelmann-Schiller-Hegel tradition, which still reaches into Pater's thought (see the essay on Winckelmann in *Studies in the Renaissance*). He does not oppose Hebraism to Hellenism but suggests, with Hölderlin and Heidegger, a more radical "Greek" attitude, which he refused to confine within a historicist or periodizing frame. Yet the religious shadows cast by this sort of inquiry cannot be avoided. American criticism, on the whole, is "incarnationist," as de Man recognizes; and it often associates this bias with Christian doctrine. Similarly, then, contemporary anti- or nonincarnationist views would move toward the pole of Hebraism, whether or not influenced by canonical texts from that sphere. Consult, e.g., Maurice Blanchot's "Etre Juif" in *L'Entretien infini* (Paris: Gallimard, 1969) or "L'Interruption" in *L'Amitié* (Paris: Gallimard, 1971); and generally Edmond Jabès, who can aver: "Writing is a revolutionary act, a scrupulously Jewish act, for it consists in taking up the pen in that place where God withdrew Himself from his words; it consists indefinitely in pursuing a utopian work in the manner of God who was the Totality of the Text of which nothing subsists." The withdrawal alluded to is a kabbalistic notion also important for Harold Bloom. Traherne, the English poet, opposes "An easy Stile drawn from a native vein" to "*Zamzummin* words."

11. The etymology is well known. See F. L. Lucas' fine book, *Style* (London: Cassell, 1955), pp. 15–16, which quotes the OED.

3. From Common to Uncommon Reader

1. See *Spectator* 565, Friday, July 9, 1714.
2. F. R. Leavis, *Education and the University: A Sketch for an 'English School'*

(London: Chatto and Windus, 1943), p. 107. For a sober review of the inactual Common Reader, see Frank Kermode, *An Appetite for Poetry* (Cambridge, Mass.: Harvard University Press, 1989). Common Reader in the sense of "ordinary public reader" emerges late: see, e.g., Virginia Woolf, *The Moment and Other Essays* (London: The Hogarth Press, 1947), p. 124.

3. F. R. Leavis, *Revaluation: Tradition and Development in English Poetry* (London: Chatto and Windus, 1959), p. 19.

4. Leavis, *Education and the University*, p. 19. For Wyndham Lewis, writing under the impression of the *first* World War, English and American democracy was equally vulnerable to the propaganda of an "Educationalist State." See his devastating vision of the "gentlemanly Robot" in Part IV, chap. 2, of *The Art of Being Ruled* (1926; Santa Rosa: Black Sparrow Press, 1989).

5. F. R. Leavis, *The Common Pursuit* (London: Chatto and Windus, 1958), pp. 185–186.

6. From Stephen Spender's "Rhineland Journal," reprinted in *The Golden Horizon*, ed. Cyril Connolly (New York: University Books, 1955), pp. 126–127.

7. Hannah Arendt, *Lectures on Kant's Political Philosophy*, ed. Ronald Breiner (Chicago: University of Chicago Press, 1982), pp. 28, 43.

8. In the reviving field of political philosophy, Habermas' development of critical theory into an effort to assure the possibility of consensus through "communicative reason" is both crucial and controversial. He advocates a "model of unconstrained consensus formation in a communication community standing under cooperative constraints . . . communicatively structured life worlds that reproduce themselves via the palpable medium of action oriented to mutual agreement." (See *The Philosophical Discourse of Modernity* [Cambridge, Mass.: MIT Press, 1987], chap. 11.) But if we shift from the issue of consensus to questions of the quality of consent—as we do when we respect the private space of the act of reading—then we reintroduce the individual and his or her "unreason." (In the United States the most influential discussions of such issues have come from jurisprudence as it develops a philosophy of law, the best-known contributors being John Rawls and Ronald Dworkin.) At present that "unreason," it must be emphasized, is not necessarily any more irrational than Antigone's resistance to Cleon and her refusal to omit memorial rites—which would have contributed to the forgetting, as well as dishonoring, of the dead. Having passed through totalitarian terror, what should not be forgotten in the name of political accommodation, or even the future, is how the state apparatus can turn politics into a means whereby dissent is suppressed and consent is coerced. Jean-François Lyotard in *The Differend: Phrases in Dispute* (1983; Minneapolis: University of Minnesota Press, 1989) examines the difficulty of a consensus, and the possibility of just argument, witness, and litigation after Auschwitz.

9. Bonamy Dobrée, "Some Aspects of Defoe's Prose," in *Pope and His Contemporaries: Essays Presented to George Sherburn,* ed. James L. Clifford and Louis A. Landa (Oxford: Clarendon Press, 1949), p. 170.

10. When this essay was first given as a lecture on the Beckmann professorship at the University of California at Berkeley, I added the following. "Lecturing is an impolite form. It is a monologue timed to test the patience of its audience, and it allows no conversation. In case I have sinned against Good Form by the picaresque density of my presentation, let me, penitentially, offer this passage from Thoreau's *Walden,* which explains why, as an Old World immigrant rather than an American Adam, I seem to pursue a different 'economy' of discourse. If I have burdened you, here is Thoreau protesting the luxury of culture in the Old World as well as the wasteful materialism of the New. 'When I have met an immigrant tottering under a bundle which contained his all,—looking like an enormous wen which had grown out of the nape of his neck—I have pitied him, not because that was his all, but because he had all *that* to carry.' "

4. The State of the Art

1. This essay was written in May 1986 for a collective volume called *The Future of Literary Theory,* ed. Ralph Cohen (London: Routledge, 1989). One thinks one is writing for the future and that four or five years should not matter. But I already see, from this point in time, that the essay reflects too exclusive a concern with fundamentalism and its challenge to freedom of interpretation. Had I been asked to write this essay now, the emphasis would have included other than religious kinds of positivity. The quest to make theory politically accountable—always a difficult, sometimes a repressive factor in the intellectual life— is approaching the 1930s in intensity. In that era Left and Right, and other warring dichotomies, fortified a dangerous habit of stereotyping, which I. A. Richards focused on, long before deconstruction. During the last three years an extremely hostile questioning of deconstruction (after the disclosure of Paul de Man's articles of 1940–1942 in the collaborationist Belgian newspaper *Le Soir,* see Chapter 6) have troubled us with a sense that in the literary humanities too, not just religion or the political religions, the quest for moral and intellectual fundamentals reinstates itself with a surprising righteousness. At this point, then, while I stand behind my essay, I am less certain that literary theory has a future. We may have to produce not only (as I indicate) a better sociology of literature; we may also have to overcome the suspicion that theory is but an exercise in ideology, or the opium of intellectuals who wish to evade political commitments and harsh judgments.

2. I. A. Richards, *The Philosophy of Rhetoric* (New York: Oxford University Press, 1936), p. 40.

3. For some reflections on the rise and impact of propaganda, see Chapter 3, "From Common to Uncommon Reader."

4. The paragraph from I. A. Richards' *Coleridge on Imagination* (New York: Harcourt, Brace, 1935) continues as follows: "It guides us in our metaphorical, allegorical, symbolical modes of interpretation. The hierarchy of these modes is elaborate and variable; and to read aright we need to shift with an at present indescribable adroitness and celerity from one mode to another. Our sixteenth- and seventeenth-century literature, supported by practice in listening to sermons and by conventions in speech and letter-writing which made 'direct' statement rare to a point which seems to us unnatural, gave an extraordinary training in this skill. But it was skill merely; it was not followed up by theory" (p. 193, n. 1).

5. Lines from "From an Ordinary Evening in New Haven," *The Collected Poems of Wallace Stevens* (New York: Alfred A. Knopf, and London: Faber and Faber, 1985); used with permission.

6. Richards quotes Coleridge's description of "Shakespeare's time, when the English Court was still foster-mother of the Stage and the Muses; and when, in consequence, the courtiers and men of rank and fashion affected a display of wit, point and sententious observation, that would be deemed intolerable at present—but which a hundred years of controversy, involving every great political, and every dear domestic interest had trained all but the lowest classes to participate. Add to this the very style of the sermons of the time, and the eagerness of the Protestants to distinguish themselves by long and frequent preaching, and it will be found that, from the reign of Henry VIII to the abdication of James II, no country ever received such a national education as England." See *Coleridge on Imagination*.

7. See Chapter 2, "Tea and Totality," for a fuller account. Stanley Cavell prefaces his *Themes out of School: Effects and Causes* (San Francisco: North Point, 1984) with a defense of the causerie that modifies "causes" by the idea of the casual (topical) conversation and even the ungenteel shmooz. He reinstitutes a tension between origin and occasion, between the formal or scientific discourse on origins (causes) and the idling power of the occasional essay. Richard Rorty, in a similar revolt against the truth claims of his profession, also prefers the idea of philosophy as a conversation. The rediscovery that there is a question of style in philosophy brings about a conversational antistyle (with a Jamesian formality in Cavell), and shows that philosophy and literary studies as professions are running parallel yet out of synch with each other.

8. See Chapter 10, note 3.

9. Virginia Woolf, "A Summing Up," reprinted in *The Complete Shorter Fiction of Virginia Woolf,* ed. Susan Dick (New York: Harcourt Brace Jovanovich, 1985), pp. 202, 204–205. "Sexless" is puzzling. It describes more, surely, than the cry's indeterminate gender. Does the indeterminacy suggest a dehu-

manizing erosion of gender difference? Or does "sexless" imply (despite Woolf's dislike of D. H. Lawrence) a Lawrentian critique? Lawrence's until recently unpublished *Mr. Noon*, written in the 1920s, uses authorial intrusions to mock the "Gentle reader, gentle lecteuse" tradition and its desexualized "dummy" values. Indeed, Lawrence prefers to address the woman reader as more capable of removing false sublimations. "The sterner sex either sucks away at its dummy with such perfect innocent complacency, or else howls with such perfectly pitiful abandon after the lost dummy, that I won't really address the darling any more." Woolf's "usual terrible sexless . . . cry" may evoke the world of the prostitute, powerfully intruding on virginal and majestic Sasha. One is made to feel that both worlds are sexless, but that, if anything, the dutiful chatter that Sasha tolerates and even abets is more sadly empty. The branch that "dripped gold; or stood sentinel" also evokes a more savage or primal world through the sentimental haze of words and the—perhaps complicit—irony of the author, conscious, like many writers of that time, of Frazer's *The Golden Bough* and an emerging theory of archetypes.

10. W. Somerset Maugham, *The Summing Up* (Garden City, N.Y.: Doubleday, Doran, 1938), pp. 35, 37–38.
11. See "What is Orthodox Marxism" and "Reification and the Consciousness of the Proletariat" in Georg Lukács, *History and Class Consciousness: Studies in Marxist Dialectics,* trans. Rodney Livingstone (Cambridge, Mass.: MIT Press, 1971).

5. Placing F. R. Leavis

1. *The Leavises: Recollections and Impressions*, ed. Denys Thompson (Cambridge: Cambridge University Press, 1984).
2. Chris Baldick, *The Social Mission of English Criticism: 1848–1932* (Oxford: Clarendon Press, 1983).
3. Fred Inglis, *Radical Earnestness: English Social Theory 1880–1980* (Oxford: M. Robertson, 1982).
4. *The Critic as Anti-Philosopher: Essays and Papers by F. R. Leavis,* ed. G. Singh (London: Chatto & Windus, 1982).

6. Judging Paul de Man

1. *Wartime Journalism, 1940–1942, Paul de Man,* ed. Werner Hamacher, Neil Hertz, and Thomas Keenan (Lincoln: University of Nebraska Press, 1988).
2. See *The New Republic* (March 7, 1988). Now expanded, in *Reading de Man Reading,* ed. Lindsay Waters (Minneapolis: University of Minnesota Press, 1989).
3. For a concise account of the purge as it affected men of letters in France, see Pierre Assouline, *L'Epuration des intellectuels* (Brussels: Editions Complexe,

1985). Interesting details are also given in Herbert Lottman, *The Left Bank* (Boston: Houghton Mifflin, 1982). I have not found any account of the purge in Belgium, which seems to have been at least as severe. The French scene moved with surprising speed to restore purged writers. In 1947 Jean Paulhan declared that it was time to "give back to France all her voices." Jeffrey Mehlman has represented Derrida's work as "the textual instantiation of the amnesty or radical forgetting that seemed to constitute the horizon of Paulhan's writings on postwar politics in France." See *Representations* 15 (1986): 1–14.

4. There is a considerable amount of literature on the circle that was assembled by Otto Abetz and the Propaganda Abteilung. For a good bibliography, see Karl Lohut, ed., *Literatur der Resistance und Kollaboration in Frankreich* (Tübingen: Narr, 1984), p. 245.

5. John Brenkman, "Fascist Commitments," in *Responses: On Paul de Man's Wartime Journalism*, ed. Werner Hamacher, Neil Hertz, and Thomas Keenan (Lincoln: University of Nebraska Press 1989).

6. See Henri de Man's *Zur Psychologie des Sozialismus* (Jena: Diederichs, 1927), translated into English and French shortly after. Henri gives his own account of the events of March 1942 in *Gegen den Strom: Memoiren eines Europäischen Sozialisten* (Stuttgart, 1953), p. 255. The Nazi policy toward the labor force in the occupied countries (and possibly its exploitation of Henri de Man's "aestheticizing") needs more research.

7. For the pattern of collaboration in France, its ambiguities, and the involvement of journalists and intellectuals, see Zeev Sternhell, *Neither Right nor Left: Fascist Ideology in France* (1983), trans. David Maisel (Berkeley and Los Angeles: University of California Press, 1986), and Pascal Ory, *Les Collaborateurs* 1940–1945 (Paris: Seuil, 1976). Quite a number of writers did not dissociate themselves from collaboration until the end of 1942. Abetz, moreover, had shown an interest in Belgium as early as 1936 and entertained connections with both Becker (not a Rexist, as Brenkman claims, although aided at *Le Soir* by a Rexist, Pierre Daye) and Henri de Man. See John Hellman, *Emmanuel Mounier and the New Catholic Left, 1930–1950* (Toronto and London: University of Toronto Press, 1981).

8. One reason for the persecution of many journalists is given by Lottman. He remarks in *The Left Bank* (chap. 4) that while the *rhetoric* of the extreme Right did not change substantially under Vichy and the Occupation from what it had been in the 1930s, the *consequence* of that rhetoric could be crucially different in wartime circumstances. It could signal "the death-sentence of adversaries. What had been insolence, outrageous dissidence, became denunciation, treason. One can note numerous cases of arrest, deportation and execution following attacks in the collaborationist press." (Lottman, however, does not give details).

9. The best account of Volkish ideology, which preceded National Socialism

and glorified instinct, is in George L. Mosse, *The Crisis of German Ideology: Intellectual Origins of the Third Reich* (New York: Grosset & Dunlop, 1964). On the psychosocial importance of claiming a specifically *German* identity, see Saul Friedländer, *L'Antisémitisme nazi, Histoire d'une psychose collective* (Paris: Seuil, 1971), pp. 68–74.

10. The most convincing critical analysis of this matter I know is by Saul Friedländer in "Some Aspects of the Historical Significance of the Holocaust," *The Jerusalem Quarterly* No. 1 (1976). He discloses a deadly convergence between the ideological complex I have described, which saw the Jew as an outsider, and a counterrevolutionary political philosophy, which made the Nazi an insider. In his words: "anti-liberal feelings vastly contributed to the total isolation of the Jew, to the elimination of whatever protection he had within Western society, to his becoming a total 'outsider' at the very moment when these same anti-liberal feelings, as well as the anti-Marxist aspirations of the middle-classes helped to advance the view of the Nazi as 'insider.' The convergence of these ideological trends contributed to the passivity of the onlooker at least during the decisive period in which help could still have had a major effect."

11. So, explicitly, van Huffel (who organized the anti-Semitic page for which de Man wrote) in a piece of his own, *Le Soir*, February 11, 1941: "The nature [*génie propre*] of Judaism is totally inassimilable and fundamentally opposed to our western conceptions." (Quoted by Alice V. Kaplan in *Responses*, p. 273.)

12. In addition to the *Psychology of Socialism*, see two important pamphlets: *Die Intellektuellen und der Sozialismus* (Jena, 1926) and *Sozialismus und National-Faschismus* (Potsdam, 1931). The second of these declares that its theme is seen "from the position of the intellectual," and it contains a cannily precise account of the role of the white-collar worker (*Stehkragenproletarier*) in the rise of Nazism.

13. See "Paul de Man's War," first published in the Spring 1988 issue of *Critical Inquiry*, now in *Responses*.

14. E. R. Curtius, *Deutscher Geist in Gefahr* (Stuttgart and Berlin, 1932), p. 85.

15. Ibid., pp. 94–95; for Mannheim, see *Ideology and Utopia* (1929), and for the general problem, Edward Shils, *The Intellectuals and the Powers* (Chicago and London: University of Chicago Press, 1972).

16. Henri de Man, *Gegen den Strom*, p. 249; my translation.

17. I have not been able to comment on (1) a style of oblique reference, which glances at political matters without concrete specification, and in the earlier prose gives the impression of reserve and prudence or (2) an ambivalence toward interiority (e.g., novelistic "recherches jusque dans les recoins les plus secrets de l'âme") heightened in 1940–1942 by the gospel of energy, action, and vital force characterizing Rightist political philosophies. Such "excess of interiority" is later analyzed in de Man's studies of Wordsworth,

who had passed through a revolution fascism was countering with its own. Ortwin de Graef and Lindsay Waters have published perceptive comments on this matter.

18. While Drieu and Brasillach are especially susceptible to this heroic vitalism, there was a sense in many French circles that the "forces vitales" had fatally declined during the era of bourgeois democracy. This charge is found even in Jacques Maritain's *A travers le désastre*, written in 1940 after the defeat, and published by the clandestine Editions de Minuit in 1942.

19. Martin Jay, "The Descent of de Man" in *Salmagundi* (Spring 1988).

20. Hints of an ethics, based on a critique of both conventional and Kantian views, do occur in *Allegories of Reading* (New Haven: Yale University Press, 1979): "The passage to an ethical tonality does not result from a transcendental imperative but is the referential (and therefore unreliable) version of a linguistic confusion." They have been extended by J. Hillis Miller in *The Ethics of Reading* (New York: Columbia University Press, 1987), chap. 3. But given the referential vice in which de Man's reputation is caught, such highly elliptical statements provide little help. It seems that we are always moralizing a "linguistic predicament," that our intentions try to catch up with the "performative" action of a language that disfigures or deconstructs them, as it does all identity-claims whereby we strengthen self-presence. The idea of presence is subjected by de Man to an analysis similar to Heidegger's of *Dasein*.

21. See Jürgen Habermas, "Heidegger—Werk und Weltanschauung" in Victor Farías, *Heidegger und der Nationalsozialismus* (Frankfurt am Main: S. Fischer, 1989), pp. 11–37. Habermas carefully documents the stages of retroactive falsification. On the issue of Heidegger's silence, Jacques Derrida offers the thought that explicit judgment (not only "I was stupid in 1933" but also "Auschwitz is absolute terror, and I condemn it absolutely") would have led to "absolution" and prevented precisely what we are now engaged in: a difficult inquiry into the relation of his philosophy to National Socialism and related ideologies. (Derrida in *Antwort: Martin Heidegger im Gespräch*, ed. G. Neske and E. Kettering [Pfullingen: Neske, 1988], pp. 157–161.) What is being asked for, however, is not simply a "sentence" but a self-reflection at the same level as the rest of Heidegger's or de Man's work. The de Man puzzle, by the way, is not made easier by the fact that his one direct comment on 1940–1942 which has just come to light (see the last document in *Responses*) claims that Henri de Man was his father.

22. Jacob Taubes, *Ad Carl Schmitt: Gegenstrebige Fügung* (Berlin, 1987), p. 70.

7. Meaning, Error, Text

1. See, however, Susan Handelman's *The Slayers of Moses: The Emergence of Rabbinic Interpretation in Modern Literary Theory* (Albany: State University of New York Press, 1982).

2. So the *Boston Transcript,* in the same article (March 14, 1924), reports that Hitler grew "purple with rage in an interchange with Kahr regarding the meaning of 'Word of honor.' "

8. Advanced Literary Studies

1. Virginia Woolf, *Moments of Being* (Brighton: Sussex University Press, 1976), p. 70. Other references to this work appear in the text.
2. S. D. Goitein, *A Mediterranean Society: The Jewish Communities of the Arab World as Portrayed in the Documents of the Cairo Geniza,* 5 vols. (Berkeley: University of California Press, 1967–1988).
3. Immanuel Wolf, "On the Concept of the Science of Judaism" (1822), *Year Book II* (London: East and West Library, 1957), pp. 194–204; and Leo Zunz, *Gesammelte Schriften,* 3 vols. (Berlin: L. Gerschel, 1875–1876).
4. Leo Spitzer, *Linguistics and Literary Theory: Essays in Stylistics* (Princeton: Princeton University Press, 1948), pp. 2, 4.
5. Louis Althusser and Etienne Balibar, *Reading Capital,* trans. Ben Brewster, 2nd ed. (London: NLB, 1977), p. 3.
6. G. W. F. Hegel, *Phenomenology of the Spirit,* trans. A. V. Miller (New York: Oxford University Press, 1977), paras. 90–110.
7. Compare the following quotation with what will be said later about words: "Mother's death and Stella's death kept us, I suppose, together. We never spoke of either of them; I can remember the awkwardness with which Thoby avoided saying 'Stella' when a ship called 'Stella' sank." Wolfe, *Moments of Being,* p. 107.

9. The Philomela Project

1. Geoffrey H. Hartman, *Beyond Formalism* (New Haven: Yale University Press, 1970), p. xiii.
2. William Blake, *Jerusalem,* last plate.
3. We do have considerable information about the political and intellectual influence of women when they belong to or rise into *le grand monde,* as in eighteenth-century France. Their conversation is recorded by the men who passed through their salons or observed them at court or in the *coulisses,* yet their own correspondence too is significant. "The relique of woman's grace, the letter, is her conversation itself," Edmond and Jules de Goncourt comment in *La femme au dix-huitième siècle,* 3rd ed. (Paris: Firmin Didot frères, 1887), chap. 11. Sometimes even an extraordinary poetic achievement, like that of Mexico's Sor Juana, may need rescue because of our parochialism, not only sexism. Octavio Paz calls his book on her a "restitution": the historian combines in Paz with the imaginative writer to remove a falsification of her life's work, to restore her to herself and our century. See Octavio Paz, *Sor Juana:*

or, The Traps of Faith, trans. Margaret Seyers Peden (Cambridge, Mass.: Harvard University Press, 1988). An unusual effort to reach into the life of women who belong to the illiterate or lower classes is that of Natalie Zemon Davis, *Fiction in the Archives: Pardon Tales and their Tellers in Sixteenth Century France* (Stanford: Stanford University Press, 1987), esp. chap. 3: "Bloodshed and the Woman's Voice."

4. Charles Taylor, *Sources of the Self: The Making of the Modern Identity* (Cambridge, Mass.: Harvard University Press, 1989). In France, Emmanuel Levinas' ethical philosophy—on a phenomenological base—has gradually been recognized.

10. Literary Criticism and the Future

1. The most incisive treatment of the *honnête homme* is by Erich Auerbach in *Scenes from the Drama of European Literature* (Minneapolis: University of Minnesota Press, 1984), pp. 164ff.; the original German essay was published in 1933, and supplementary remarks appeared in *Literatursprache und Publikum* (Bern: Francke, 1958), p. 255). Auerbach describes both the universality and the lack of content in this courtesy ideal. He relates it to the growth of a homogeneous group, composed of the *noblesse d'épée*, who had lost much of their function and were economically dependent on the court, and of the *noblesse de robe*, who were hereditary officeholders, equally unproductive as the highest social class of a declining *grande bourgeoisie*. The socioeconomic context in which the ideal originally flourished is a complex one both in France and in England. For France, Thomas E. Crow's *Painters and Public Life in Eighteenth Century Paris* (New Haven: Yale University Press, 1985) shows vividly the intense cultural politics during an age in which patronage was essential. It confirms indirectly that ideals like that of *honnêteté* were meant to reduce the dangerous energies of slander and ridicule *(libelle)* as painting began to go public—to find a salon and museum space. On England, Terry Eagleton has fleeting remarks in both *Literary Theory: An Introduction* and *The Function of Criticism* (see note 5). Auerbach, in a separate essay—*Gesammelte Aufsätze zur Romanischen Philologie* (Bern: Francke, 1967)—sees Montaigne creating the *honnête homme* as a new human type, whatever its social or material determinants. Although the ideal is primarily a conversational one (see also Baltasar Gracián's *El Discreto*), in Montaigne the mentality of being a *writer* is basic. *Honnêteté* had staying power as a personal style extending to written expression.

For Auerbach the *honnête-homme* concept is linked to the development of an educated public, made up in the seventeenth century by "la cour et la ville" but in the eighteenth century essentially urban and bourgeois (compare the English Common Reader ideal). He did not live to complete his study of the relation between literary language and the public; *Literatur-*

sprache und Publikum traces it from the Augustan period in Rome to late medieval and early modern. Recently, however, there has been excellent work on "the terms of value of the discourse we now describe as civic humanism," as John Barrel (after J. G. A. Pocock) phrases an ideal developed by a self-consolidating bourgeoisie, and in which "the republic of fine arts was understood to be structured as a political republic," with the aim of promoting public virtues rather than specific party politics. This surely connects with a visionary rather than classical concept of a Common Reader. It pits Blake against Reynolds, though they are fighting the same battle. See Northrop Frye, *Fearful Symmetry: A Study of William Blake* (Princeton: Princeton University Press, 1947), chap. 12, secs: 1 and 2, and John Barrel, *The Political Theory of Painting from Reynolds to Hazlitt: The Body of the Public* (New Haven and London: Yale University Press, 1986). Critical style as a mode (not just a medium) of thought, its relation to the above ideal, and whether its ideal tendency remains too abstract, a "sphere of purely formal equality and identity for all mankind, irrespective of cultural or economic distinctions" (David Lloyd, "Kant's Examples," *Representations* 28 [Fall 1989]) are issues that this chapter carries into the contemporary period.

I am aware, however, that the emphasis on urbanity ("Court and Town," the symptomatic phrase singled out by Auerbach, already points to it) omits a conflict that can be characterized by another symptomatic phrase, "Town and Country." The appeal to a *peasant culture*, or a consciousness of its suppression by modern developments, helps to motivate a great deal of literature from the late eighteenth century on; it has an explosive impact on intellectual life in the 1930s, reflected (urbanely) in Leavis and Thompson's "organic community" (*Culture and Environment,* 1932) and (not so urbanely) in fascist ideology. An "organic community," though not necessarily rural, integrates the rural on the basis of its supposedly deeper sense of place, of a passionate, inalienable connection with the land (soil, earth, nation). Is there a "rurality" of style, as there is an urbanity? This aspect is broached with great tact and an English focus in Raymond Williams' *The Country and the City* (New York: Oxford University Press, 1973).

William Empson devotes no less than three chapters of *The Structure of Complex Words* (1st ed., 1951) to "honest"; chap. 9 is specifically on "Honest Man." The English development too shows a richness of associations drawn from class conflict and the social milieu. Honesty, for the rising class, meant a robust simplicity, or shedding hypocrisy—no longer hiding what its members are. But for the upper class it often meant unassuming behavior: a simplicity that was the opposite of a bluff ostentatiousness. The word never quite reduces, as in France, to the label for an amalgamated social type but remains an index of antithetical meanings. Yet it does flatten out somewhat, perhaps under French influence, through "Addison's tricks with the word . . . The speaker pretends to be simple and humble but is in fact comparing or combining different ideals. What the decent *bourgoisie,* who were rising in the world and buying country homes, would call honest, is played off against what some at least of the court aristocracy would call honest. But to say this is to describe an actual play; it is the whole conception of the *Beggars' Opera.*" To read Empson is to realize that the "profound meanings in these common words" cannot be purified or straightened, and that the Common Reader, like Empson himself, must be uncommonly sensitive to contextual depths in such overdetermined words.

2. "You do not assume indeed the solemnity of the pulpit, or the tone of stage-declamation: neither are you at liberty to gabble on at a venture, without emphasis or discretion, or to resort to vulgar dialect or clownish pronunciation." William Hazlitt, "On Familiar Style," *Table Talk* (London: John Warren, 1822). The long development that led to honest prose is traced by Morris Croll in terms of the emergence of "*standard* prose" in a Europe where Latin, the language for intellectual and scholarly work, was being affected by anti-Ciceronian currents of style and passing into a "state of equilibrium" with the vernaculars. In the period of Montaigne and Bacon, according to Croll, a "writer in Latin would show the colloquial and concrete qualities of his speech in his own language; a writer in French or English would derive from his Latin the rhetorical firmness, the exact use of abstraction, the logical process which the learned language imposes." The standard form of literary prose is determined "by the *general* thought of the age which it expresses, its collective wisdom and experience; it is neither remotely and professionally intellectual, on the one hand, nor a simple record of facts and sensations, on the other." See Morris W. Croll, *"Attic" and Baroque Prose Style: The Anti-Ciceronian Movement,* ed. J. M. Patrick et al. (Princeton: Princeton University Press, 1966), pp. 181–184.

3. In England one does not perceive the direct influence of the French salons, which from the time of Mme de Lambert to that of Mme de Stael maintained what can almost be called an ideology, that of conversation, the "social genius of France . . . the true genius of the women of that time" (Edmond and Jules de Goncourt, *La femme au dix-huitième siècle,* 3rd ed. [Paris: Firmin Didot frères, 1887], chap. 9). On the salons, see especially chap. 11 in the same work, and cf. Roger Picard, *Les Salons littéraires et la société francaise, 1610–1789* (New York: Brentano, 1943), pp. 86ff., and 157ff. No such institution as the salon existed in England, though some of of its writers—Matthew Prior, Lord Bolingbroke, Horace Walpole (and of course Benjamin Franklin from America)—frequented French salons. While the salons differed greatly in character, and belonged to *le grand monde* and its intrigue, collectively they fostered the ideal of the *honnête homme,* and a shift from birth to intellect. As the Goncourts wrote: "The book of the hour, the new play, the pamphlet or philosophic treatise were judged during the current of sociable talk [*causerie*], their leaves lightly

turned over, so to say, by the fingertips of eighteenth century high society, which knew how to pronounce on every matter" (*La femme*, chap. 11). Though more bourgeois in orientation, the ambition of eighteenth-century English journals was not unlike this. Behind the "honest man" in France were women like Mme de Tencin, of whose salon the Goncourts write that it was "the first in France where a person was received for his intellectual merit [*parce qu'il valait spirituellement*]" and that in it "the man of letters began the great role which became his in the society of that era." Mme de Lambert, the Goncourts note, held up to her son the ideal of *honnête homme* as the ultimate ambition. The conversational ideal continues into the *Causeries* of Sainte-Beuve; his *Lundis* reflect in their title each salon's regular habit of receiving Mondays, Wednesdays, and so on, once each week.

Needless to say, there was a reaction to the negative side of that stylized conversation, to its cerebralness and polite hypocrisy. Rousseau denounces in his *First Discourse* (1750) the "deceptive veil of politeness" and the "vaunted urbanity," which hide sincere emotion and thought. For German, a language still striving for malleability, stability, and status, see E. A. Blackall, *The Emergence of German as a Literary Language, 1700–1775* (Cambridge: Cambridge University Press, 1959), chap. 12, "The Culture of Wit and Feeling." In England too the enforced sociability and benevolence of the friendship style provoked vital correctives. For a thorough and stimulating discussion of the issues involved, see Karlheinz Stierle and Rainer Warning, eds., *Das Gespräch* (Munich: Wilhelm Fink, 1984). Lionel Trilling's *Sincerity and Authenticity* (Cambridge, Mass.: Harvard University Press, 1971) is a short history of the "honest soul" caught between society and solitude, seeking to maintain its "authenticity" or unity of being despite having to become known on the social stage, having to play out, quite visibly, its being there. Though Trilling speaks of "something like a mutation in human nature" that occurred around 1600, it seems to me that his book emphasizes a slowly moving process in which "the consent of private men" (as Locke will call it) is jeopardized by the very forces—socializing and democratic—that affirms it.

4. I should emphasize that literary criticism, viewed not essentialistically but as a lively and developing genre, is freeing itself from cultural propaganda (*Kulturpolitik*) rather than cultural history. I generally agree with Ernst Gombrich that, while *Geistesgeschichte* inspired the holistic approach that gave cultural history its confidence, the dependence on a Hegelian "metaphysics" of supraindividual collective spirits (*Zeitgeist, Volksgeist,* etc.) also impeded it. Even comparative literature worked for some time with the notion of "national genius" or regional spirit of place. This notion continues to have an empirical value, but during the era I am exploring (roughly the twentieth century) testimonies are found that the rate of change and alienation increases. Modernization not only weakens the sense

of identity based on place but leads to a reenforced ideal of place with nostalgic and political appeal. Alain Fournier's *Le Grand Meaulnes* (1913), and Proust in a very different way, evoke a lost purity attached to a vanished "domain" and are already within a nostalgic *imaginaire* anticipated by Nerval. The sinister side of that pastoral domain can be illustrated by quoting from the rabidly anti-Semitic Edouard Drumont's *Les Tréteaux du succès* (1900), with its notion of "la France d'alors": "nous ne pouvons nous empêcher de penser que la France d'alors, où de si éclatantes clartés illuminaient les sommets, était un peu différente de la France que nous ont faite les Juifs" (pp. ii–iii). For a brief synopsis of the glorification of "l'Ancienne France" in French fascist or protofascist literature, see Paul Sérant, *Le Romantisme fasciste* (Paris: Fasquelle, 1959), chap. 1, "La Décadence française."

5. Fredric Jameson, *Fables of Aggression: Wyndham Lewis; the Modernist as Fascist* (Berkeley: University of California Press, 1979), pp. 128–129. Terry Eagleton, *The Function of Criticism: From the Spectator to Post-Structuralism* (London: Verso, 1984), chap. 1.

6. Terry Eagleton's ironic view of this development, however, continues to haunt us. "The whole *Scrutiny* project was at once hair-raisingly radical and really rather absurd. As one commentator has shrewdly put it, the Decline of the West was felt to be avertable by close reading." *Literary Theory: An Introduction* (Minneapolis: University of Minnesota Press, 1983), p. 34.

7. Jacques Rivière, *L'Allemand: Souvenirs et réflexions d'un prisonnier du guerre* (Paris: Gallimard, 1918).

8. I. A. Richards' protocols in *Practical Criticism* (London: K. Paul, Trench, Trubner, 1929) already had brought evidence that the British system of higher education was failing to teach reading: when faced by fairly complicated language, students remained susceptible to stereotype and cliché. Finding meaning in poetic texts was an exercise in premature assent to the notion of meaning itself.

9. "A book," Marcel Proust had written, "is a vast grave-yard where on most of the tombs one cannot read any longer the effaced names."

10. Alfred Kazin, in *The 75th Anniversary Issue of the New Republic*, November 6, 1989.

11. Cited with relish by F. R. Leavis, and quoted in John Gross, *The Rise and Fall of the Man and Letters* (London: Weidenfeld and Nicolson, 1969), chap. 10, "Cross-Currents of the Thirties."

12. See Denis Hollier, ed., *The College of Sociology, 1937–39* (Minneapolis: University of Minnesota Press, 1988).

13. Mircea Eliade's understanding of sacred time, however, presently so influential in and beyond American religious studies, may be indebted to the 1930s turmoil in which he participated as an active sympathizer with the enthusiastic religious politics of the Romanian Iron Guard.

14. Wallace Stevens, *Opus Posthumous* (New York: Alfred A. Knopf, 1975), pp. 224–225.

15. The philosophy of history too begins to tackle nondialectical, non-totalizing—even equivocal—models of temporality that focus on the future as unpredictable, on the present as indeterminate yet hermeneutically exigent, and on the past as an unfinished, explosive force in human thought. The best-known example is Benjamin's "Theses on the Philosophy of History" (1939).

16. André Malraux, *The Temptation of the West,* trans. Robert Hollander (New York: Random House, Vintage Books, 1961), pp. 77–78.

17. Paul Valéry, *Oeuvres I,* ed. Jean Hytier (Paris: Gallimard, 1957), pp. 988–1000; first published in *The Atheneum* in 1919. Cf. "L'Européen," I, 1000–1014. The translations are my own.

18. Malraux, *Temptation of the West,* p. 117.

19. Ibid., p. 120. Robert Hollander's translation is modified here.

20. Frank Kermode's by now classic *The Sense of an Ending* (New York: Oxford University Press, 1967) both charts and participates in that discourse.

21. See Paul Fussell, *The Great War and Modern Memory* (New York: Oxford University Press, 1975), esp. chap. 1, "A Satire of Circumstances."

22. Erich Auerbach, *Mimesis: Representation of Reality in Western Literature,* trans. Willard R. Trask (Princeton: Princeton University Press, 1953), pp. 552–553.

23. See, for example, the writings of Richard Rorty (following up Pragmatism and William James in particular), Stanley Cavell, and Charles Taylor.

24. As early as Tocqueville a tension in democracies between the right to liberty and the right to equality had been pointed out. The liberty of each person might not lead to the equality of all, but rather to the tyranny of some, and the equality of each might jeopardize the free and potentially unequal development of the individual.

25. John Dewey, *The New Republic,* October 4, 1922.

26. The Stevens poems cited and reprinted by permission (copyright Alfred A. Knopf and Faber & Faber Ltd., 1985) are "To an Old Philosopher at Rome" and "Our Stars Come from Ireland," *The Collected Poems of Wallace Stevens.* The issue of what, according to Heidegger, has happened to language needs fuller treatment than I can give it here. I do not emphasize that sense of the cheapening of words, their "modern" degradation into chatter, blamed variously on the misuse of print-technology (journalism) and democratic trends (especially parliamentary—i.e., talkative—democracy). See my *Criticism in the Wilderness* (New Haven: Yale University Press, 1980), pp. 153–154, and "Culture's Aftermath" in *The Holocaust and Its Effects on the Humanities,* ed. Kitty Millett (Minneapolis: University of Minnesota Press, 1991).

27. Yaron Ezrahi, "Science and the Civic Spirit of Liberal Democracy," *The*

Descent of Icarus: Science and the Transformation of Contemporary Democracy (Cambridge, Mass.: Harvard University Press, 1990).

28. Gianni Vattimo, *La Fine della modernità* (Milan: Garzanti, 1985). See also the suggestive finale, "The Prosaic World," to Wlad Godzich and Jeffrey Kittay, *The Emergence of Prose* (Minneapolis: University of Minnesota Press, 1987). After a careful historical scrutiny of prose in relation to verse, they ask directly: "What is the promise of prose?"

A Note on Sources

Earlier versions of some chapters, often revised and expanded for this book, appeared elsewhere as noted.

1. "The Culture of Criticism": *PMLA* (May 1984): 371–397.
2. "Tea and Totality": "Tea and Totality: The Demand of Theory on Critical Style," in Gregory S. Jay and David L. Miller, eds., *After Strange Texts* (University: University of Alabama Press, 1985), pp. 29–45.
3. "From Common to Uncommon Reader": "Theory and Critical Style: From Common to Uncommon Reader," *Revue Internationale de Philosophie* 41 (1987), nos. 162–163, 398–413.
4. "The State of the Art": "The State of the Art of Criticism" in Ralph Cohen, ed., *The Future of Literary Theory* (New York: Routledge, Chapman, and Hall, 1989), pp. 86–101.
5. "Placing F. R. Leavis": "Placing Leavis," *London Review of Books,* 24 January 1985, pp. 10–12.
6. "Judging Paul de Man": "History and Judgment: The Case of Paul de Man," *History and Memory* 1 (1988): 55–84.
7. "Meaning, Error, Text": *Yale French Studies* 69 (1986): 145–149.
8. "Advanced Literary Studies": "The Advanced Study of Literature," *ADE Bulletin* 80 (Spring 1985): 11–14.
9. "The Philomela Project": "Criticism and Restitution," *Tikkun* 4 (January–February 1989): 29–34.

Index

Index

Book of Questions (Jabès), 183
Boswell, James, 97
Bourne, Randolph, 30, 31, 33, 215n27, 34, 216n35
Bradbrook, Muriel, 117
Brenkman, John, 128–129, 135, 136–137, 147
Brooks, Van Wyck, 30, 31, 216n35
Brown, Norman O., 83, 223n100
Brunot, Ferdinand, 29
Buber, Martin, 97, 218n61
Burckhardt, Jacob, 26
Burke, Kenneth, 10, 32, 47, 51, 56, 67, 122, 212n9, 226n9; on propaganda, 54; and theory, 80–81; and art, 187

Call Me Ishmael (Olsen), 81
Cambridge "School of English," 29, 110
Canon, 22, 109, 154, 157, 167, 170, 182, 192, 217n51; and "minor" literature, 36, 48, 171, 218n54
Carnap, Rudolf, 144
Causeries (Sainte-Beuve), 62
Cavell, Stanley, 71, 205, 216n40, 229n7, 240n23
Celan, Paul, 84
Civilization and Its Discontents (Freud), 193
Clifford, James, 186
Clio (Péguy), 26, 27
Coleridge, Samuel Taylor, 13, 44, 46, 107, 120
College of Sociology, 185, 187
Columbia University, 30, 32
Commentary, 124
Common Reader, 15–16, 43, 79, 87, 176, 227n2, 235n1
Communication, dream of, 68
Community of interpreters, 219n63
Conquête de l'Amérique (Todorov), 35
Consensus, 88, 182, 219n63, 227n8
Constructive philosophy, 107
Contemplative life, 5, 39
Continental tradition (of criticism), 42–43, 61
Conversational style, 46, 62, 65–67, 69, 81, 89, 205, 225n8, 226n9, 235n1,

237–238; and causerie, 62, 65–66, 229n7, 237n3. See also Friendship style
Cowley, Malcolm, 30
Crane, Hart, 121
Critic as Anti-Philosopher (F. R. Leavis), 113, 118, 121
Critical prose, 55–56, 160, 212n9; terms of art in, 13–14, 47, 56, 71, 80, 82, 83, 220n67; development in England, 29, 75, 99–100, 176–177; and middle style, 65, 176; Burke on, 81; Sartre on, 181; prosaics, 206, 221n73, 241n28. See also Conversational style
Criticism: communicative aspect of, 2; historical context of, 2; and ethics, 11, 144, 146–147, 173f, 207, 233n20; independence of, 13; language of, 13–14; and prophetic speech, 15; culture of, 17–56, 166; and style, 18, 96 (see also Style); history-writing as, 26; phenomenological, 39; shift from philosophical, 46–48, 49; Englishness in, 56, 60–61; and rhetoric, 58–59; Germanizing in, 59–60; as extended conversation, 65–66; basic features of, 66; avant-garde, 74; without theory, 75 (see also Theory); and public, 88; as strange conversation, 89; beginnings of, 92–93; defined, 165; as creative, 166; as genre, 176; and the future, 176–208, 228n1; new French, 181; and irony, 184, 194; comparative and defamiliarizing, 185–186; answerable style of, 187; improgressive, 207. See also Anglo-American tradition; Anglo-French tradition; Continental tradition; Critical prose; Literary Studies
Criticism in the Wilderness (Hartman), 15
Croce, Benedetto, 29, 47
Cubism, 190
Cuddihy, J. M., 97
Cultural anthropology, 186, 187; and cultural poetics, 187
Cultural criticism, 16, 208
Cultural history, 185, 207, 238n4
Cultural prophecy, 15, 181, 184, 187, 192, 193–196 passim, 207–208

Index

Index